PORTFOLIO

FOR GOD'S SAKE

Ambi Parameswaran has spent a large part of his thirty-five-year working career in advertising at DraftFCB Ulka where he rose to be Executive Director and CEO.

An engineer from IIT Madras and MBA from IIM Calcutta, he also completed his PhD from Mumbai University in 2012. Ambi has authored/co-authored six books on topics ranging from brand building and advertising to consumer behaviour.

When he is not busy at work, reading, writing or teaching, you can find him at a music concert. His wife, Nithya, is an ex-marketer turned stock market investor. His son, Aditya, is an alumnus of IIT Bombay and Stanford.

PRAISE FOR THE BOOK

'The way he stirs the pot with a dash of humour, some very apt quotes and some good old-fashioned research is what makes the book a winner all the way'—*Business World*

'Using anecdotes and research from thirty years in advertising, this is a fascinating book on the business of Indian religion'—*Free Press Journal*

'This is an easy-to-read, jargon-free book that keeps you intellectually engaged till the end'—*Business Today*

'All told, this is a book that is worth reading and is a must in every B-school library'—*Business India*

'What a magical conundrum for marketers! The facts in this book are thought-provoking and beg and prod you to debate. It's a brilliant 4D documentary, so For God's Sake, just go, get it'—*Financial Express*

'*For God's Sake* has a simple agenda: to understand the ways in which religiosity interacts with the manner in which we are marketed to, the way we shop and the way we express our desires'—*Business Standard*

FOR GOD'S SAKE

An Adman on the Business of Religion

AMBI PARAMESWARAN
Foreword by AMISH TRIPATHI

PORTFOLIO
PENGUIN

An imprint of Penguin Random House

PORTFOLIO

USA | Canada | UK | Ireland | Australia
New Zealand | India | South Africa | China | Singapore

Portfolio is part of the Penguin Random House group of companies
whose addresses can be found at global.penguinrandomhouse.com

Published by Penguin Random House India Pvt. Ltd
4th Floor, Capital Tower 1, MG Road,
Gurugram 122 002, Haryana, India

Penguin
Random House
India

First published in Portfolio by Penguin Books India 2014
Published in paperback 2015

ISBN 9780143424871

Typeset in Minion by R. Ajith Kumar, New Delhi
Printed at Repro India Limited

www.penguin.co.in

MIX
Paper from
responsible sources
FSC® C047271

This is a legitimate digitally printed version of the book and therefore might not
have certain extra finishing on the cover.

Contents

Foreword   vii
Preface to the Paperback Edition   xi

1. Introduction   1
2. The Mystery of the Missing Bindi   9
3. A Great Year for Weddings   19
4. From 'Off Season' to 'On Season'   30
5. An Old Festival Gets a New Look   39
6. Inaugurate with a Puja—Enjoy Perpetual   48
   Prosperity
7. Planning a Home Gets the Divine Touch   55
8. Will Travel for God   61
9. Why Do Women Pray More?   74
10. So Long and Thanks for All the Fish   82
11. TeleRama to TeleDrama   90
12. Riding the Puja Boom   99

13. God Okay, Gandhi Not Okay   105

14. Every Fifth Indian Will Be Muslim   111

15. Thank God, He Created 'Nothing'   123

16. Burqa Ke Peechhe Kya Hai?   129

17. Pray for Better Health   136

18. Religious Music Can Rescue Ads   146

19. Parsi-owned Car Sells in a Jiffy   157

20. Timeless Religious Art   164

21. Religion Goes Hi-Tech   171

22. Honesty, Charity, Religiosity   176

23. Can Spirituality Lift Business Education?   184

24. The Last Word   191

Acknowledgements   197
Religion: An Essential Vocabulary   200
Selected Further Reading   245
Index   249

Foreword

I spent many years in the wilderness of atheism till I discovered God and He empowered me to write the Shiva Trilogy, and it was His blessing that they went on to become big sellers, prompting me to resign from my job and pursue writing as a full-time career.

God inspires what I do and I am grateful to Him for His blessings.

So when Ambi called me to request that I write a Foreword for his book *For God's Sake*, I did not hesitate for a minute. The book, which is an anecdotal take on how God and religion influence our day-to-day life, is indeed timely and relevant. On the one hand we as consumers are drifting in many different directions. Our love for God is what is keeping us moored and anchored, in spite of the winds of change buffeting our lives.

In this book, Ambi is slicing and dicing the many ways religion is impacting our everyday life, from the way we design our houses, to the way we plan our holidays, to the way we celebrate our festivals and so on. While the experts had predicted the slow decline of religion, I don't see that happening for a long, long time—if anything, the force of devotion is becoming stronger. As we live in a VUCA world (the term coined by the US Army War College to indicate the volatile, uncertain, complex and ambiguous world we live in), the one thing that we can be certain about is God and our own faith and beliefs.

It is no wonder that in this VUCA world we are seeing consumers and citizens of India going back to their roots to look for greater meaning, or a simple ritual, that helps them feel more grounded. The manifestations are all around us, in the books we read, the music we listen to, the programmes we watch on television. But is there a method to this and is there a way we can understand how it will impact our own lives and businesses?

Ambi has used his own three-decade experience in marketing, advertising and communication to address each dimension. The stories he will tell you are all drawn from his own experience and, therefore, they are on one level personal and at another level very real. Each topic is presented through a combination of personal stories which are then linked to a religious anchor, be it the Vedas or the *Manusmriti* or the Koran, and then each chapter presents a way you too can benefit or not get hurt by the trend.

There is something that you can take out of this book and put to use in your day-to-day life, unlike many other non-fiction books you may read.

I would like to imagine that India will rise as a superpower in the coming few decades, if not earlier. Our own religious beliefs will continue to anchor us as we grow more wealthy.

I am also hopeful that as we become more and more literate, we will start seeing the commonality of all religions, and we will find His grace in every belief system, as Shiva or Vishnu or Shakti Maa or Allah or Jesus Christ or Buddha or any other of His myriad forms. A day will come when we will start appreciating our great nation with its inherently liberal culture which melds beautifully with our traditional views on religion, rather than hold in esteem the fraud-liberalism we practice today where those who are religious are looked down upon.

We will once again become a 'Cradle of Civilization'.

May God bless us all! May God bless our great nation, India!

AMISH TRIPATHI

Preface to the Paperback Edition

It was a cold winter morning in Ranchi. I was in the city to speak at the TEDx event hosted by IIM Ranchi. The student volunteer who picked me up from my hotel asked me if it would be okay if we stopped to pick up another speaker. 'Of course,' I said.

So we went to the Ramakrishna Mission where I met Swami Sarvapriyananda[1]. On our way to the venue of the talk the Swamiji and I got talking about his interests, and about my new book *For God's Sake* that was just about to reach the bookstores. Swamiji, who had embraced spiritual quest after completing his MBA from XIM Bhubaneswar, was intrigued by the area of my research and my book's approach to religion and marketing. We spoke about how the Protestant work ethic treatise by Max Weber was the

---

[1] Swami Sarvapriyananda joined the Ramakrishna Order at Ramakrishna Mission Vidyapith in Jharkhand in 1994 and has since served at various educational institutions run by the Mission.

first exploration of religion and commerce. And how it was in the late nineteenth century Germany that it was proposed by Karl Marx and Friedrich Nietzsche that religion as we know it would not live for very long. Swamiji then told me a joke of how some supporter of Nietzsche had written on a wall, in large and bold letters: 'God is Dead—Nietzsche'. Soon after Nietzsche's death in 1900 someone apparently wrote below that, in even larger letters: 'Nietzsche is Dead—God'.

I thought this anecdote would make a very interesting opener to my TEDx talk and used it to get the audience into a good mood. Little did I realize that the speaker to follow me was Brinda Karat, the Rajya Sabha member from the Communist Party of India (Marxist). In her talk she decided to clarify that communists are not necessarily all supporters of Nietzsche's view of God.

When my book came out in early 2014 the country was in the grip of despondency and frustration. God seemed to be the only possible saviour. It is difficult to imagine how within twelve months the mood has changed to one of optimism and energy, interestingly spurred by a political leader, though from the religious right wing, who is speaking the development mantra.

My book did not address the aspects of Hindutva and how religion plays a role in Indian politics. I felt that these areas have been very well covered by books written by learned media experts and psephologists. Interestingly the rise of the BJP and Narendra Modi over the last one year has not been driven so much by hard-core Hindutva philosophy as by a strong, economically driven developmental mantra. It would be interesting to see how the political and religious right wing play out their agendas over the next five years, but if I were to extrapolate some of the hypotheses in the book, there is a sweet spot where religion, at least the way it is practised in India, can be happy bedfellows with a developmental, capitalist agenda.

For God's Sake is my first book that is aimed at the lay reader. Advised by my editor Anish Chandy, I reduced the marketing theories to the bare minimum and packed the book with interesting anecdotes. I was happy to note that reviewers found this approach very refreshing. No wonder many of my friends and well-wishers, mostly from the corporate world, found the book to be a great read; gratifyingly, their spouses too found the book refreshing.

When I started writing the book chapter by chapter in 2012–13, I was a little concerned about the terrain I was covering. Given the fact that I am not a theology expert or an anthropologist, I was concerned that I may tread into dangerous territories. Fortunately I have been proven wrong. It was heartening to get letters from elderly leaders who were all very complimentary of the way I had handled some complex topics like vaastu shastra, auspicious dates, religious festivals, religious tourism, women's empowerment, the significance of pujas, or even the 'vegetarian vs non-vegetarian' debate.

My publishers assure me that the book has done well but what has been of great amusement to me has been the fact that the book had featured in the top ten bestseller list in airport bookstores for months together. I wonder if air travellers feel they need a dose of God when they are flying.

Hopefully the paperback edition will help the book continue to fly high, both literally and figuratively.

Let me close with another interesting anecdote. I was meeting this person for a chat regarding an opening in our organization. She was amused to find that her son was reading *For God's Sake* just as she was leaving her home for the meeting. When queried on this serendipitous incident, her son told her that he has been given the book as 'recommended reading' in his class at BMM in St. Xavier's College, Mumbai. She congratulated me on the fact that my book was in the suggested reading list at St. Xavier's within a few years of its launch! I had to correct her and say that my book was yet to celebrate its first birthday.

So maybe it is the title, or maybe it is the new mood sweeping the country –whatever it may be, enjoy the book, and I hope you find it of some value to you in your life as a corporate executive, a student, a businessman, a consumer, a homemaker or a retiree. May God be with you always!

1. Introduction

Agara mudala ezhuthellam adi
Bagawan mudarre ulagu

> *(The alphabet begins with A; so does the Universe with God)*
> Thiruvalluvar (second century BCE)

'What do you mean by the word religiosity?' was the question raised by the Research and Review Committee of Mumbai University while considering my thesis topic 'Religiosity and Consumer Behaviour'. I had already spent a year working on the subject and their question came as a bolt from the blue. Did this mean they had serious objections to the topic since they considered it to be incendiary? Or was it that they found it impossible to figure out the connection between religion and consumer behaviour? Or was it just a simple question that arose from their unfamiliarity with the term religiosity?

If you have attempted a PhD, or know anyone working on one, you will be aware that the biggest challenge in doing original research is finding a topic that is unique and yet relevant. I realized that either I had stumbled upon a topic that the Mumbai University's R&R committee had not seen before or I was back to square one.

Fortunately, it turned out to be a simple issue of explaining the origin of the word religiosity and being a bit more specific about the topic. I ended up focusing my thesis on a specific type of consumer product, instead of making it a general purpose consumer behaviour exploration.

As I completed my PhD, I realized that the topic of religiosity and consumer behaviour is quite interesting but very little has been written about it. This led to the idea of writing a book that looked at the myriad ways in which consumer behaviour in India is influenced and guided by religious beliefs and practices.

'In God We Trust. Rest Strictly Cash' read the sticker near the cashier's counter in a fancy goods shop in Mylapore, Chennai, not too far from the famous Kapaleeswarar temple and the birthplace of Thiruvalluvar, the most famous Tamil philosopher-poet, now revered as a saint. In a sense the shopkeeper had unwittingly endorsed the view of modern-day Indians. Yes, they are embracing a new, intense form of religiosity, but they also want to have the cash to enjoy a richer, fuller life. In fact, religion, gods and rituals have become new avenues for seeking and spending cash.

Is this trend new and unique to India?

In the early twentieth century, Max Weber, the father of the science of sociology, conducted a breakthrough study in the relationship between religion and economic growth. He coined the term Protestant Work Ethic. Weber propounded a theory on the relationship between the rise of the Christian Protestant faith and the growth of capitalism in Europe in the eighteenth and nineteenth centuries. Weber's near contemporaries like Karl Marx, Sigmund Freud and Friedrich Nietzsche were quite sure that with the growth of science and scientific thinking the twentieth century would see the demise of religion and god worship.

We are now more than a century or two from when those

wise men made this wise prediction. Interestingly, PEW Global Surveys indicate that except for some north European countries where these thinkers lived religion has seen a revival all over the world. In *Shopping for God*, the author James B. Twitchell traces the growth of the megachurch phenomenon in the United States.

While our founding fathers saw us as a secular state and government-owned media channels abhorred airing explicit religious content for many decades after Independence, the course was altered in 1987. Starting 25 January, for seventy-eight weeks, every television-owning home in India was given a strong dose of religion every Sunday with the airing of *Ramayana*. This was followed by *Mahabharat*, which ran from 2 October 1988 for ninety-four weeks on Doordarshan. The growth of religiosity in India cannot possibly be linked solely to these television serials, but these telecasts and the phenomenal viewership they garnered probably set the agenda for a hyper-religious India.

As Indians became more and more prosperous with the liberalization of the Indian economy in the early 1990s, they also became more and more religious in many subtle and not so subtle ways. Increasing religious fervour is not restricted to the old women of India. Several studies have shown that high religiosity cuts across income, sex, age and religious barriers. They also reveal that the more religious consumer is often the more demanding consumer, wanting more and more, often for less and less.

When a new car is bought, the car dealer usually gives the proud new owner a box of Indian sweets and a small Ganesha figurine for the dashboard. Chances are the first trip the family takes in the brand-new car is to the neighbourhood temple; astute pujaris in every temple that qualifies as 'new car worthy' have even worked out a super special 'new car' puja. Most smartphones in India sport at least some religious apps, Ganesha

CHRISTIAN

JUDAIC

ZOROASTRIANISM

JAIN

ISLAMIC

SIKH

HINDU

Some Religious Symbols

screen savers and Hanuman Chalisa being big favourites. New houses are not bought without the vastu consultant giving his nod, often also prescribing the right location for the puja room or the puja cabinet.

Tourism industry data indicates that religious tourism is the single biggest growth segment as Indians, rich and poor, want a special dose of salvation. The Tirupati and Vaishno Devi temples have had their coffers filling up to the brim. People walking up to the Sabarimala temple today include autorickshaw drivers from Madurai, Hyderabad and Bangalore as well as liquor barons from Andhra Pradesh, Karnataka and Tamil Nadu. Traditionally, the temple was only opened for a few months in a year, but it is now kept open a few hours every morning.

Unheard of religious practices have grown new wings. Akshaya Trithiya was probably found only in religious texts until a few decades ago. Now every jeweller will reel out his special 'sales' plans for the next Akshaya Trithiya. Another example is the phenomenon of Karva Chauth, which has started seeing a following not just in North India but across the country, with habitually late-working management consultants and financial analysts rushing home so that their loving wives can have a meal after seeing their face and the moon.

This has unleashed innovative modes of celebration. Spanking new malls are now also places of worship with special decorations for Onam, Pongal, Durga Puja, Baisakhi, Ugadi, Valentine's Day, Akshaya Trithiya, Diwali, Ganesh Puja, Eid and Christmas.

This book is an exploration of the ways religiosity interacts with the way we are marketed to, the way we shop and the way we express our desires. The book's focus is very much on the changing Indian consumer. We explore numerous areas where religion and religiosity play a role, sometimes in the open but often on the sly. We also delve into the religious dogmas, myths and beliefs that still tend to influence us in our consumption behaviour.

Each chapter attempts to present a picture of the new religious Indian consumer and will hopefully raise valid questions on what these could imply for businesses. What could the business opportunity be? What could the threats be? What may the lessons be? What could the long-term impact be?

We will examine several aspects of religious belief and practices, and look at how they play a role in our lives as consumers of products and services. We will also do a bit of crystal-gazing about how religion will affect our lives in the future. Some of these predictions may come true, but the attempt is not to predict the future; it is to look at what the future may bring, and what we can do to be prepared.

India is a multi-religious, secular country. While Hindus form the majority at 80.5 per cent (2001 Census), we also have a sizeable Muslim population (13.4 per cent, the third largest Muslim population in the world, after Indonesia and Pakistan). Christians account for 2.3 per cent, Sikhs for 1.9 per cent, Buddhists for 0.8 per cent, Jains for 0.4 per cent and other religious groups for 0.6 per cent.

Origins of Religion in India

What are the origins of what we call religions in India, how did they spread and how have they changed over the years? Such topics are meant for a textbook on religions of India and I cannot even attempt to scratch the surface. But to understand the chapters that follow, it would make sense to take a short detour. I promise we will return to the main road soon. Right through the book we will refer to eras as BCE (before the Common Era, which used to be referred to as BC) and CE (Common Era, which used to be referred to as AD).

Hinduism is arguably seen as the oldest living religion in the world and can be traced back to 3000 BCE. The oldest surviving text of Hinduism, the Rig Veda, was produced during the period 1700–1100 BCE. The Upanishads, Puranas and epics such as the Ramayana and Mahabharata were composed roughly during the period 600–100 BCE. Several schools of thought such as Samkhya, Yoga, Nyaya and Vedanta were all codified after 200 BCE. The Code of Manu or Manu Smriti was written around 300 BCE.

Gautama Buddha was born in 563 BCE, attained enlightenment at the age of thirty and travelled around north-eastern India, teaching his path of awakening. He passed away at the age of eighty in 483 BCE in Kushinagar, located near modern-day Gorakhpur in Uttar Pradesh.

Mahavira, the twenty-fourth Tirthankara who founded Jainism, was born in 599 BCE and lived till 527 BCE. The other important Jain guru was Parsvanath (812–772 BCE), the twenty-third Tirthankara. Literature says that Jainism could be as old as Hinduism, and was in its formative years a form of protest against Brahminical Hinduism, and may even have been influenced by Zoroastrianism.

Buddhism was built up as a pan-Asian religion during Emperor Ashoka's reign of thirty-eight years, which ended in 232 BCE.

In the following chapters we will refer to the Vedic era and the Puranic era as two distinct eras. We will also examine how Hinduism was totally transformed, thanks to the influence of Buddhism and Jainism that stressed ahimsa or non-violence.

By absorbing some of the fundamental tenets of Buddhism, Hinduism grew during the period 400 to 1000 CE.

Jews arrived in Kochi, Kerala in 562 BCE and more Jews came as exiles from Israel in the year 70 CE after the destruction of the Second Temple, but their numbers did not grow substantively.

Thomas the Apostle visited Kerala in the year 52 CE and baptized Jewish settlers. Christianity took root around the third century CE and got a leg-up during the British rule.

Islam too arrived first on the shores of Kerala via Arab traders in the seventh century CE soon after the passing away of Prophet Muhammad (in 632 CE). India was under Mughal rule from the sixteenth to eighteenth centuries, and it was then that Islam spread across India, especially North India.

Following the overthrow of the Zoroastrian Sassanid empire in 651 CE by the Arabs, many Zoroastrians migrated, and some ventured into Gujarat in western India. Their descendants, now known as Parsis, form a small, vibrant community that has played a pivotal role in the development of modern India.

In fact, as a counter to the spread of Islam in India, a more pious and populist form of Hinduism, the Bhakti movement, swept across central and northern India during the sixteenth and seventeenth centuries.

Sikhism was founded in the fifteenth century CE by Guru Nanak in the Punjab region and continued to grow under nine successive gurus to become one of the largest and youngest religions in the world.

As these religions spread across India, they influenced each other. Practices of one religion got modified by the birth of another. The growth of a new religion changed the character of an older religion. Many of these changed the way Indians celebrated festivals, their dietary habits, the way they conducted worship and more.

While the book will look at a range of topics including home design, festivals, auspicious periods, Muslim consumers, marriages, tourism, food, music and more, we will start our journey from an interesting starting point. A point in fact.

The bindi.

2. The Mystery of the Missing Bindi

The modern arrangement of the 'sari', cunningly draped to reveal the outline of hips and to emphasize the narrowed waist and the swell of the breasts was, like the choli, for long a device of the nautch-girls and is only a comparatively recent fashion among respectable Indian women.

Benjamin Walker, *Hindu World:*
An Encyclopedic Survey of Hinduism (2005)

It was September 1994. Our agency DraftFCB Ulka (then Ulka Advertising) had just completed a new advertising film for the soap brand Santoor. The new creative was set in an aerobics studio and featured the Santoor woman exercising to some lively music. The ad, which was being shot by the veteran ad film director Prahlad Kakkar, was going to be a breakthrough. All of us in the agency believed that it would work in the marketplace to resurrect the brand that had hit a plateau after seeing great growth for a few years. We had in fact bet the agency's reputation on this ad with our long-term client Wipro. But I was very worried.

I suddenly remembered that right through the film the Santoor woman was not shown sporting a bindi. In the story, she was a mother and her kid enters the scene with a loud 'mummy' squeal much to the surprise of onlookers. How could we have missed out on the bindi, I wondered.

First thing next morning I called our film manager Monia Pinto and asked her if we could 'rotoscope' a bindi on the model Priya Kakkar's forehead (rotoscopy is a technique whereby you insert a digital image into a real-life moving picture; it was relatively new and very expensive in the mid 1990s; the Hollywood film *Who Framed Roger Rabbit* had used this to great effect). Monia, the liberal that she is, pooh-poohed my worry. As did many of my other colleagues.

The film was presented to the client, aired on television and became a landmark film in the history of brand Santoor. The Santoor woman, sans bindi, went on to play cricket, teach hula hoop to her kid and even made film stars dance to her tune over the next decade, helping make Santoor the third largest soap brand in the country.

But the bindi thought stayed with me.

The bindi is a part of Hindu culture and even has a strong tantric underpinning. Both men and women wear the bindi or bindu, which means drop or globule. It is supposed to be the sacred symbol of the universe, depicted as a dot or the zero. Applied between the eyebrows, it is purported to be the position of the sixth chakra, a place which is also the exit point of kundalini energy. Tantric literature abounds with explanations on the red bindu (symbolizing fire/blood) and white bindu (symbolizing semen). Married women also wear red vermilion or sindoor in the parting of their hair, which is first applied there by their husband on their wedding day, during the sindoordana ceremony. Only married women are allowed to wear the sindoor, according to Hindu custom. Interestingly, though Islam does not have a bindi or sindoor custom, most Muslim women in Bangladesh sport a bindi. Even in Pakistan, Muslim women at times wear designer bindis, quite ignoring the Hindu symbolism of the bindi. So while Muslim women from our neighbouring countries are quite at ease sporting a bindi (never the sindoor), it is extremely rare to see an Indian Muslim woman wear a bindi. I wonder if their avoidance of the bindi is also their signal to the external world that they acknowledge the religious angle and can't conceive of it being a fashion accessory.

Not too many people know all this sociocultural background to the humble bindi. And the Indian advertising industry is populated by young men and women from upper-middle-class families. Most of them are what are called EMTs (or English Medium Types). The scenario is changing rapidly now with an increasing number of HMTs (Hindi Medium Types) joining the tribe, but the EMT orientation remains. These EMTs were told, in the early days of their training, to ensure that advertising did not hurt anyone's sentiment, least of all the Indian woman's. So all ads that showed married women had to show them with a mangalsutra and a bindi! (Professor Julien Cayla of the University of New South Wales discovered that Indian Muslim women, whom she has studied extensively, were almost immune to this religious symbolism in most Indian television advertising.)

My curiosity was piqued and I wanted to see if Indian advertising had evolved from the 'bindi–mangalsutra' trap. Accessing advertising archive services, my colleagues and I managed to extract around a hundred television commercials for packaged consumer goods (soaps, toothpastes, shampoos, tea, etc.) from 1987, 1997 and 2007. We wanted to see whether the portrayal of Indian women had changed in the three decades under study.

Using content analysis techniques, we analysed the ads across several dimensions such as role portrayed by women (spouse, mother, working woman, celebrity) and occupation and setting (home, workplace, shopping, etc.). In addition to these specific well-documented international metrics, we also added a few of our own Indian metrics. These were the dress worn by the woman (sari, other Indian apparel, western apparel) and the presence or absence of the bindi and other religious symbols (mangalsutra).

We discovered the portrayal of women had not changed very much over the thirty years. By and large, women were shown as homemakers, at home caring for their family.

However, something else we discovered came across as a big surprise. We found that advertisers were moving away from showing Indian women draped in a sari. In fact, there was a rapid fall in women shown in a sari across product categories. One hypothesis was that brands were trying to portray women in a more modern avatar and so the first relic to be axed was the beautiful but cumbersome sari.

There were two other discoveries of interest to us in our understanding of rising religiosity. The television advertising study revealed that there was a dramatic drop in women shown sporting the mangalsutra. As against almost 75 per cent of the 1997 ads showing women with a mangalsutra, the number had dropped to less than 35 per cent in 2007—a very significant drop.

Finally the bindi. We discovered that the bindi was vanishing at a more rapid pace than the sari. From almost 75 per cent of women in ads in 1997 sporting a bindi, it was down to less than 30 per cent in 2007. (The next time you watch television, do check if you can spot an ad that shows a woman sporting a sari, a mangalsutra and a bindi. And reflect if these symbols trigger something in your mind. What do you think is the woman's education level? What social class do you think she belongs to? What is her age? What would her outlook to innovative products and services be? What kind of mother would she be? As a wife, what would her big worries be?)

We then turned our gaze towards print advertising.

When *Femina* celebrated its fiftieth birthday a few years ago, we took the opportunity to revisit our hypothesis of the missing bindi. Our researchers spent several days at the *Femina* archives pulling out ads that portrayed women. We pulled out ten ads per year in a random but systematic process and in the end got to look at almost 500 ads that featured a picture of a woman over the five-decade period.

These 500 ads were subjected to the same analysis as the television ads. We found that as against 3 per cent of ads portraying working women in the 1960s, the number had increased to 16 per cent in the new millennium. Once again, the sari and bindi stood out in our analysis. While 55 per cent of women shown in the ads from the 1960s were draped in a sari, the number was down to 9 per cent five decades later. What about the bindi? The dot had almost vanished—from 45 per cent to 5 per cent in the same period.

Devdutt Pattanaik, who has studied Indian mythologies and epics in depth and published several bestselling books reinterpreting the ancient stories, drew attention to an interesting bindi-related contrast. He called these bindi-less women in Indian ads 'Advertising Widows'. He pointed out that while women in ads were abandoning their bindis, women in television serials seemed to have a continuing love affair with more and more exotic forms of bindis.

In his breakthrough book *Gender Advertisements* (1979), Erving Goffman presented a visual analysis of the portrayal of women and men in American advertisements and concluded that advertisers tend to use the 'hype of hyper-ritualization' to communicate their message. So what is supposed to be feminine is made even more feminine and what is supposed to be masculine is made more masculine. Gender stereotyping was the telegraphic tool in the trade of advertisers to communicate their product message.

By rapidly doing away with the sari, mangalsutra and bindi, Indian advertisers are trying to portray the modern Indian woman, even if she is performing the gender-defined role of a homemaker. This does not mean that women have become less religious, less god-fearing or even less faithful to their husbands, as we will see in the chapters that follow. The marketers of modern Indian products are resorting to the 'hype of hyper-ritualization'.

In contrast to Indian advertising, the sari and bindi are predominant in Indian television programming. How does one explain that? Can we surmise that Indian general entertainment television is still pitching its story at lower-middle-class women, where the numbers lie? Or is, as a colleague suggested, advertising all about 'aspiration', while television entertainment is all about 'identification' bordering on voyeurism?

Surprisingly, movies across India have started jumping on the 'sari-less/bindi-less' bandwagon. The heroine is shown sporting modern clothes as she cavorts around trees. However, the sari and bindi make a token appearance when she gets married to her lover; even in a hurried wedding performed in a village temple, the sindoor makes an appearance.

The bindi–sari story may be a lot more complicated than we have assumed. And how is one to decode this mess?

One simple, short code is that when you portray a woman in your ad with a sari and a bindi you are going to trigger the 'conservative' button in your consumer's memory. So if you are trying to market a modern gadget like a washing machine or a microwave, you are well advised to show your protagonist in modern attire. The famous Whirlpool Mom, who debuted on television a decade ago, appeared just once in a sari; thereafter, she was always shown in western clothes, often trousers and shirt. And never with a bindi.

However, if you want to channel traditionalism in your communication, it would make sense to show the consumer in a sari with a bindi. So the daughter who got a new tattoo is in a pair of jeans and her mother is in a sari in the Tata Docomo ad. Or the mother who is preparing a special Ayurvedic remedy for her daughter's acne problem, as in the Chandrika ad, could be in a sari.

Now, on to the big question: Will wearing a sari and bindi slowly vanish, only to be resurrected during special festive occasions, like the kimono in Japan? The middle-class Indian consumer is still very much wedded to the sari–bindi routine as would be evident if we were to enter any suburban train in Mumbai or any sarkari office. However, in private sector offices, we are seeing the slow disappearance of the sari and bindi.

There is an interesting sideshow with the sari and bindi. In several Indian banks, where women occupy senior positions, there is an unstated policy that the official dress is a sari, with a bindi being optional. The very same women executives wear western formals when they board an aircraft leaving Indian shores. Why do they doggedly come to work in a sari when in India? I was told by some women that they felt their typical customer, often a male, is a lot more comfortable speaking with a bank manager dressed in a sari rather than one in trousers or a skirt. The general feeling is that a woman in trousers comes across as a little more 'aggressive' to the typical Indian customer. Advertisers who relish showing an Indian woman consumer in trousers obviously don't agree with this view.

Similarly, you can expect to be greeted by a hostess in a sari when you enter a Taj hotel or a Tanishq showroom. This again is an attempt at symbolizing an Indian tradition of hospitality and courtesy, not to mention Indian silks. Often these women even sport a bindi. Not too long ago, we were used to Air India hostesses dressed in saris, sporting a nice large bindi. Then came the private airlines and they all decided to have their air hostesses in skirts and blouses. Why? Because they felt that modern western attire would communicate to the air traveller a new ethos of professionalism and efficiency. Given the way they have grown, maybe they were right.

I would like to speculate that in the next few decades we will see more and more women joining the labour force in a mind-boggling variety of jobs. The sari is not going to continue occupying its place of dominance in its current form. The bindi too may not be prominently displayed, once the woman is wearing trousers (though I have noticed women cops wearing trousers and sporting a bindi). In that sense, advertisers are trying to portray what the woman of the future will look like.

You might be surprised to know that the sari, which is a great symbol of India, isn't very Indian after all. As Benjamin Walker observes, a lot of the clothes we wear in India are of foreign descent, especially the sari. It seems the six-yard sari, the perfect masterpiece of unstitched clothing, became popular only during the Mughal era. The origin of the word sari could be from the Sanskrit 'sati' or the Persian word 'sar' meaning head. During the Vedic age and many centuries that followed, it was the unstitched two-piece clothing that was common. Where a one-piece garment was worn, it was placed over the head or around the shoulders and allowed to fall about like a blanket, as ancient Indian paintings and sculptures show. In fact, most paintings from ancient India do not portray women in saris at all.

Sri Saraswathi Devi

Sri Chamundi Devi

Sri Raja Rajeswari Devi

Most ancient illustrations/statues of Indian goddesses do not feature a sari. The Vedic diary produced by Srinivasa Print Works, Sivakasi contains over 200 illustrations of gods and godesses, but very few show them in a sari. *Reproduced with permission*

The sari itself has undergone several transformations over the centuries. The sari as we see it today, a five-and-a-half-metre drape, which goes across the bosom and falls over the left shoulder, at least in urban India, became the standard only around the time India attained independence. The late Indian prime minister Indira Gandhi was possibly the biggest symbol of elegant sari wear, as was Rajmata Gayatri Devi of Jaipur. The sari also underwent a transformation in the kind of material used to manufacture it. From cotton and silk, we saw saris coming out in polyester and polyester blends.

I remember working on Khatau Sarees in the early part of my career and the line that went with the print campaign said: 'Some of the most beautiful moments in a woman's life are shared by Khatau'. While the sari design has remained virtually unchanged except in terms of the material used as well as the prints, the blouse has been more versatile. Ably helped by Bollywood, blouses became small, and big. We saw full-sleeved blouses as well as sleeveless blouses. Sometimes heroines even appeared blouseless. Indian dress designers are as yet taking baby steps in sari redesign.

Going forward, I see great opportunity for ready-to-wear saris. Fabindia already sells ready-to-wear dhotis for men. There is a big potential for innovative saris too. Just look at the way women have taken to innovative blouses. In the coming decade, I feel the sari will undergo several transformations. Here are a few ideas, some of which are already available though not as widely as they could be. Imagine a ready-to-wear sari, pre-stitched to your size. Now add to that an upper part, the pallu that could be switched. So just like a modern wear blouse and skirt or a shirt and trousers, we could have a pallu that is attached to the bottom half with a set of buttons or a zipper. Add to that the blouse, and you have a three-part sari that can be mixed and matched to suit the occasion. Just remember, about ten years ago the humble kurta worn with a churidar was reinvented as the kurti which is today worn with jeans, leggings, pyjamas—and churidar. In a similar vein, there is vast potential for reinventing the sari in myriad shapes, sizes and textures.

3. A Great Year for Weddings

By all means marry; if you get a good wife, you'll become happy;
if you get a bad one, you'll become a philosopher.

Socrates (469–399 BCE)

'The coming year [2009] is a good year for weddings, we expect sentiment to improve and sales to pick up,' said Aniruddha Deshmukh, president of Raymond, India's largest brand of men's formal clothing. I was a little surprised, and asked him to explain. He elaborated, 'A significant part of our sales comes from weddings, not just for the bridegroom, but we have also seen at least another ten men get new suits made for each wedding. Last year was a little dull by both the Hindu and Christian calendars. It was a leap year.'

What have weddings got to do with a leap year?

Leap years were the creation of Julius Caesar in the first century BCE to synchronize the calendar with the seasons. It was left to Pope Gregory XII to perfect the system in 1582, and hence the name Gregorian calendar that continues to be used till date. Unfortunately, the new changes were accompanied by a set of superstitions. Romans and Greeks were superstitious about starting any new personal or professional relationship in a leap year.

Even in Ukraine, where every day has been assigned to a saint, a leap year is seen as unlucky for marriages. Myth has it that Cassian, who is assigned 29 February, refused to help a peasant whose cart was stuck in the mud. St Nicholas came to the poor farmer's aid, giving god sufficient reason to grant St Nicholas two days a year and banishing Cassian to just one day every four years. This aggravated Cassian, who vengefully brings sickness and ill health every time he appears, every leap year.

As per the Hindu calendar too, there are 'good years' with a large number of muhurats and some not so good years with fewer muhurats. The Chennai jeweller GRT Thanga Maligai distributes calendars earmarking good wedding dates. According to the calendar, there are only ninety-one auspicious wedding dates in 2013. Hindu wedding dates are spread almost evenly through the year except for a month or two, depending on the region you are coming from. For instance, in Tamil Nadu marriages don't take place in Aadi (15 June to 15 July) and Margazi (15 December to 15 January).

Muslim weddings occur throughout the year, the only probable exception being Muharram, in the first month of the Muslim year, as it was the day Prophet Muhammad's grandson Hussein and others were killed. During Ramadan, the month of fasting, giving and abstinence, weddings are allowed but the celebrations are expected to be muted. For Christians, Lent is not considered a good period to get married. The six weeks or forty days leading up to Easter Sunday are earmarked for prayer, penance, repentance, charity and self-denial.

In addition, there are real dampeners like the monsoon. Ashada, one of the two inauspicious months in the Hindu calendar, conveniently falls during the monsoon, though it is difficult to say if this was wisely planned or accidental good fortune.

All said and done, The Big Fat Indian Wedding is our biggest celebration and indulgence and no wedding is complete without a strong dose of religiosity. As Jawaharlal Nehru observed while presenting the Hindu Code Bill in Parliament in 1955, 'Hindu marriage is a religious ceremony undoubtedly.' Nobody doubts that. It has religious significance.

A report in the *Hindustan Times* (1 April 2013) pegs the size of the wedding industry at Rs 1.5 lakh crore. Given the size of India's grey economy, the real figure could far exceed any official estimate. Expenditure on weddings encompasses attire, jewellery, wedding events (puja, cuisine, decoration, entertainment, etc.) as well as travel/hotels/transport and other associated costs (not to mention the products bought as wedding gifts which could include cars, homes and consumer durables). The report indicates that 10 per cent of Indian weddings are planned to accommodate over a thousand guests! South Indians are notorious for hosting a large number of guests while North Indians prefer to stage special events. Several kalyana mandapams dot Chennai, many of them set up by industrial and filmi families, each with a capacity to accommodate thousands of guests. The phenomenon of venues identified solely for weddings is perhaps unique to South India. In the rest of India, community halls, school playgrounds or even farmhouses double up as wedding venues. The concept of boutique designer weddings hosted for just a few hundred select families has not yet found many takers in South India, given the proclivity for large-scale weddings in the region.

The Event and Experience Marketing Association of India (EEMA) has recognized marriages as a legitimate event category in their annual awards, along with other categories like product launch, exhibition and rural activation. I had the opportunity of serving as the chairman of the EEMA awards jury a few years ago and was rather surprised at the 'subcategories' in the wedding category: below Rs 1 crore; Rs 1 to 5 crore; and above Rs 5 crore. Each award entry was accompanied by a large photo album and DVDs as proof of their efforts. There are event management companies that specialize only in wedding planning. And if you look around your own colony you will find a few young wedding planners, the type presented in the Bollywood hit *Band Baaja Baaraat*.

Brands have tried to use weddings to stimulate sales, bond with their customers and build empathy. Godrej Storwel has made some memorable ads—in one, the entry of the bride into her new home (*Saajan ke aangan mein pehla kadam*, the bride's first step in her in-laws' place is auspicious) is portrayed in the context of the new Godrej Storwel joining her new family. Bajaj has shown a newly married couple driving off on a scooter and so has Tata Indica.

Now we are seeing companies riding the wedding bandwagon in many new ways. For instance, Malabar Jewellers has come out with a coffee table book called *Brides of India*. These books present in great detail the jewellery needed to bedeck a bride. There are sections for every conceivable community across religions. Malabar Jewellers has brought out two calendars and two volumes of *Brides of India* so far and my guess is that there are enough religious communities in India for them to continue with these books for the next ten years or more.

Let's swing to another industry that has received a wedding boost: the beauty industry. No wedding was or is complete without a trip or several trips to the beauty parlour. The growing affluence of Indians has opened up many new dimensions to this beauty craze. The dermatologist has entered the arena with special packages for treatments like facial peels, something we saw only beauticians offering a few years ago. I will not speak here about other surgical enhancements that are gaining ground. Often the beauticians will come to the bride's and groom's houses. Of course, the beauty treatments are not just for the bride and the young but also other relatives, cutting across gender and ages, all of whom get facials, manicures, hair colouring and what have you.

Yet another area that has developed in the recent past is the concept of a destination wedding. Places like Neemrana Fort in Rajasthan offer full packages for hosting weddings. These events, all of which could fit into the top segment of the Wedding Category of the EEMA awards, target not only affluent Indians but also super-rich NRIs as well as Indophiles from Europe and the United States, including the glitterati. Each of these weddings could cost a million dollars or more. They are offered as a total package of three or four days of fun and frolic, each day with a different theme and entertainment programme.

Bollywood stars have woken up to this new market. Several are known to dance at weddings for obscene amounts of money, while others charge an 'appearance fee' just to walk in, get a few photographs clicked and walk out.

In this hyper-material world we live in, what have weddings got to do with religion? We can see that religion determines the good and bad period for weddings. According to the *Hindustan Times* report, 74 per cent of the young prefer an arranged marriage and over 90 per cent would seek parental consent. We will see later how one key dimension of Indian religiosity is the need to stay connected to one's own community/religious group. So the marriage arranging market continues to be vibrant, dominated by 'kundali comparing' astrologers. Classified sections of newspapers now face competition from websites that offer specific matrimonial services. In addition to these, there are matrimonial sites that cater to specific linguistic groups (gujaratimatrimony.com) and even divorcees (secondmarriage. com).

Besides, there are online wedding planning software and online end-to-end wedding organizing services that provide a complete suite of services, from booking the venue and helping in the shopping to making arrangements for the honeymoon. Then, there are e-commerce sites for wedding invitation cards and sites that link couples with the various service providers. This is becoming all the more important as many couples may be working in remote locations and want to be fully in control of the event and not leave it to their ageing parents.

Horoscope matching continues to be a thriving business all over India, though the tenor may have changed over the last few decades. From being a ritual that was the preserve of the upper castes, all classes of consumers seem to have adopted it with semi-trained roadside temple priests matching horoscopes as a lucrative side business.

According to ancient Hindu custom there are several types of weddings:

- Brahma wedding, where the daughter is given as a gift to a worthy scholar of the Vedas and of good character
- Daiva wedding, which is like the Brahma wedding, but here the father of the bride is a priest
- Arsa wedding, where the father of the bride receives a bull and a cow
- Prajapatya wedding, where the proposal of marriage comes from the bridegroom
- Asura wedding, where a wife is purchased
- Gandharva wedding, where the couple marry for love, without parental consent
- Rakasa wedding, where a man carries off his wife weeping from her home
- Paisaca wedding, where a man has 'secret sex' with a woman when she is sleeping or is inebriated.

To these eight types of weddings, we can now add three more—the sub-Rs 1 crore wedding, the Rs 1 to 5 crore wedding and the above Rs 5 crore wedding.

Hindu weddings are elaborate affairs consisting of several steps, all of which have been passed on for generations—arghya, respectfulness, or showing hospitality (from the bride's father to the bridegroom); kanyadana, giving away the virgin, or the formal gift of the daughter to the groom; manalashta, eight blessings, offered by priests with a sheet suspended between the bride and groom (interestingly, the mangalsutra originated as a tali, a devadasi custom in South India); kanthibandana, necklace-exchange; panigrahana, hand-grasping; asmarohana, stone-mounting; homa, or the ceremonial fire; Agni-pradikshina, fire circumambulation; and finally, saptabadi, seven steps, where the bride and groom take seven steps before the fire. Each step here symbolizes a particular blessing—food, strength, wealth, happiness, progeny, cattle and devotion.

Ethnographers are of the opinion that till *Laws of Manu* was written around 300 BCE (it is a matter of debate whether there was one Manu or a group of writers who gave the finishing touches to this magnum opus), marriages between castes and classes were quite common and there was no law prohibiting such relationships. In fact, Aryan tribes thought nothing of marrying native Dravidian tribes—this may explain why there are dark-skinned North Indians and fair-skinned South Indians. But with Manu's laws becoming established practice by the advent of the Common Era, cross-marriages became extremely rare.

With the rapidly declining sex ratio in modern-day India, we see girls in big demand in states like Punjab, which have a very poor sex ratio. In such states, there is no taboo on getting a bride from a lower caste or class, as long as she is from a distant state. This trend may continue to grow in the coming decades because weddings are obviously critical for the long-term growth of a community and, in a perverse way, women will gain some respect in these male-dominated societies.

So, to start with, a traditional Hindu wedding is meant to be an elaborate affair, a trend that is regaining popularity with increasing affluence. Weddings are growing in size and scale, across the country. Customs like the sangeet are now common even in South India, where it was practically unknown. I am sure practices such as the oonnjaal or the swing, where the bride and groom sit on a swing, will soon become part of the North Indian wedding.

These days, many weddings have a simultaneous translation service for the benefit of foreign guests and the younger generation who may not be familiar with the rituals. In some cases, you even get a little booklet detailing the significance of each ritual.

I have noticed that younger Indians are not averse to these ritualistic practices, unlike a generation or two before them. While the grandfather may have had objections to taking off his shirt and displaying his chest hair, the grandson today may be quite happy to show off his shaved chest and his five pectoral muscles. That aside, there seems to be a latent admiration of these ancient customs, some that go back to Vedic times. I suspect this is because Indians are now a lot more comfortable with their own religiosity and are not trying to hide it in the closet. The western world too has woken up to the fact that Hindu customs may not be 'pagan' after all.

In many ways, weddings are a key driver of demand, in several categories of products. Smart companies have understood this and factored it into their marketing plans. As we saw, they have made it an integral part of their consumer connect programmes.

The implications for you, whichever business you are in, are not difficult to conjure. First of all, you need to see what weddings have to do with your business. Do you know and do you track wedding seasons actively? If not, does it make sense to track these dates? And is it worth your while to plan special activities around weddings? Chances are you understand the importance of weddings and are doing something about it. If not, it's time you started looking at the charts and planning your next move. Name the industry and chances are the wedding market will impact your business. I am not talking of just the jewellery or apparel or hotel and tourism businesses. Even consumer goods companies can exploit the market potential.

Food product companies can offer special packages to wedding caterers. Amul can offer giant-sized condensed milk and butter packs that cater to the wedding market. Soft drinks manufacturers too can offer special deals to ensure their product is distributed at the wedding. If they pay to be the brand of choice at a movie chain—Pepsi, for instance, is the beverage of choice at PVR Cinemas and has to pay what is known as 'pouring rights' fees—I am sure they are also working on tying up with the biggest caterers in each big city. How about a durables retailer? Or a departmental store?

In the US, there is the brilliant concept of a wedding registry. I have seen it only in one of the many wedding cards I have got in India. This is how it works. A newly married couple readies to set up home. Given the cost of the many things needed and the fact that they are young and starting out in their careers, they look forward to receiving all the help they can get. So, before the wedding they visit a few key departmental stores. The store management offers to keep a 'register' for their wedding. The couple indicates the products they would like from the store: it could be anything from linen to cutlery, furniture to appliances. The invitation card mentions the store which has the wedding registry. Invitees can go to the store and decide on the products they want to gift. The store takes care of all the shipping and handling hassles and even provides a customized card with the gift. Some stores also offer 'part gifting' where two invitees can contribute to the gift. This way, friends and relatives buy a gift the couple can use and there is no danger of unwanted, duplicate gifts.

Wedding registry is a concept waiting to happen in India. I wonder why it is taking so long. It is possible that affluent Indians have figured out an elegant way of handling unwanted gifts, by insisting on 'no gifts'. But this is killing a good selling opportunity.

At a meeting with a director of a business school, I discussed the issues facing second-rung and third-rung business schools. I told him that there are over 3000 business schools producing some four to six lakh MBA graduates a year. Industry cannot absorb so many MBAs, even if the economy grows at a fast clip of 9 per cent a year. And not all MBAs go on to start their own business. We agreed that but for the top 50–100 business schools, the other 2900 do not impart any real management education. If at all, MBA graduates from these business schools can only get jobs that can also go to an undergraduate with a bachelor's degree. If this is the case, why spend lakhs to send your son or daughter to a business school, I wondered. He explained that I had missed the point. Getting your son or daughter through a business school improves their rate in the marriage market. The boy can command a better dowry; and the girl can get a simple job, maybe find a boy and bring down the dowry rate. I am sure most of these business schools are aware of this and may even be encouraging this trend. So are business schools in the process of becoming matchmaking centres?

Many years ago, we worked on an IT training school based out of Singapore that was setting up shop in India. We discovered that the attraction of an IT training centre depended more on which training school the best-looking girls went to and not so much on the quality of teaching. Maybe, business schools have become an expensive replacement for the good old IT training centre.

Let me give you an even better example of an Indian businessman who has exploited the opportunity offered by weddings. A wedding used to mean men in suits and women in saris. Not any more. Each wedding has several events, and each event has its own dress code. So if the wedding and the reception calls for suits and saris, what about the sangeet ceremony? Women wear designer ghagra-cholis and the men need to wear something equally appropriate. Enter the men's designer kurta-churidar. Every Indian town has seen the mushrooming of male ethnic wear shops, just as we have seen the growth of traditional sari shops. Amid all this, a brand called Manyawar seems to have managed to build tremendous traction, selling over Rs 500 crore worth of goods in 2012. Only a handful of men's ready-made garment brands have sales of this magnitude. The surprising part is that Manyawar has managed to build such a huge base in just a few years.

Chances are that the wedding market will continue to boom in India with growing affluence. There is already an acute scarcity of wedding venues in bigger cities and this will only get worse, opening up new opportunities for innovative venue options—temples, school grounds, clubs, hotels . . . What next?

We had a British-born creative director some years ago. He and his parents are confirmed Indophiles. He married his Kiwi sweetheart at a theme wedding in Rajasthan, under the most auspicious circumstances. 'It was a wonderful wedding, but it turned out to be a lousy marriage,' he says now.

Amen to that.

4. From 'Off Season' to 'On Season'

Sometimes I arrive just when God's ready to have someone click the shutter.

Ansel Adams (1902–84)

Pradipta Mohapatra was perplexed: 'What is this Chennai New Year Sale all about? It does not exist anywhere else in the country, but in Chennai it seems to be a craze. At our Spencer's store we have expanded our offering recently. We would definitely like to know how we can capitalize on this New Year Sale phenomenon. Can you find out more?'

Our Chennai office was working with Spencer's in the early 1990s and this question was posed to me. I could understand Pradipta's confusion. He had moved to Chennai after a successful stint in the tyre industry, spent largely in Kolkata. He was very erudite and in his own manner wanted to engage me in a debate on the topic.

When we work on brands, we often try to dig into the past to see what lessons it holds for us. We call this 'brand archaeology'. This helps us find what drove the brand's success in the past and if some fragment of that DNA can be revived and made relevant to the modern consumer.

So I decided to do some brand archaeology on the New Year Sale phenomenon of Chennai. I was no stranger to this. I was born and brought up in Chennai and knew that my dad used to go and buy something interesting every New Year.

Tamils have strong beliefs about the importance of timing in everything in life. They have a good time of the day and a bad time of the day, rahu kalam, and will avoid embarking on any new thing during the latter. Similarly, there are good months and bad months. Margazhi, roughly 15 December to 15 January, is seen as a month of penance and so no new ventures are initiated then—no weddings, no purchases, etc.

Sales of durables would plummet during Margazhi. An astute retailer in Chennai, Vivek & Co, decided to turn the logic on its head. They approached leading manufacturers, all resigned to poor sales during Margazhi, and got them to agree to huge discounts based on volume commitments. They also got them to fund the advertising. After the back-end was tied up came the challenge of attracting consumers. On 1 January 1985, Vivek & Co unleashed a never-before discount festival. The Chennai consumer had not seen such a blitzkrieg of advertising with tempting discounts on the best of brands. Vivek & Co even created loss leader products to pull customers into their showroom (on loss leader products the retailer makes a notional loss). The New Year Sale phenomenon was born. It was a hit beyond every marketing expert's wildest imagination. Here was a conservative town that had decided to throw off the Margazhi month blues to buy new refrigerators, television sets, mixers, washing machines and more.

The New Year Sale wave caught on, and many other retailers joined the bandwagon. The movement subsequently spread to other parts of Tamil Nadu and to Karnataka.

My brand archaeology expedition helped us answer Pradipta's question to his satisfaction. We could even work out a special New Year Sale where we offered, for the first time in Chennai, a 'cost price guarantee' that worked like magic. That year, Spencer's sales on New Year's Day exceeded their sales for the whole of December. Not just that, the store which until then had suffered from a premium price British hangover was seen as a real Chennai player in the hyper-competitive durables market.

So what had Vivek & Co managed to do? Did they really get Chennai residents to give up their beliefs on what was a good time or a bad time to make purchases? I don't think so. What they did manage was to get the consumer to park their religious shibboleths aside for a few days, even if the period was not auspicious. The real lesson from this story is that while Indian consumers may be hidebound in their religious views, they are willing to suspend these beliefs when it comes to getting a good bargain.

The Hindu calendar or almanac that most traditional homes use is called a panchanga, or five limbs since it covers five subjects. These are solar days, lunar days, nakshatras or lunar asterisms, yoga or lucky conjugation of planets, and karana, a special division of the day, of which there are eleven in all. According to the Hindu calendar, there are lucky (shubh) and unlucky (ashubh) periods in addition to these general divisions. Then there are good and bad days based on one's personal horoscope. Like in the Graeco-Roman calendar, in the Hindu calendar too each day of the week is named after a planet. Tuesday is supposed to be inauspicious, but to ward off the ill effects it was named Mangalvar, a derivative of mangala meaning fortunate. Again, Saturday or Shanivar, the day named after Saturn, is considered unlucky and a month that has five Saturdays is especially inauspicious.

The Hindu calendar too has twelve months, but they are aligned differently from the Gregorian calendar and some months are considered unlucky. The twelve Hindu calendar months have a solar month name and a lunar month name—Mesha or Chaitra (March–April), Vrishabha or Vaisaka (April–May), Mithuna or Jayeshtha (May–June), Karka or Ashada (June–July), Simha or Sravapa (July–August), Kanya or Bhadrapada (August–September), Tula or Ashvina (September–October), Vrishika or Kartika (October–November), Dhanu or Margasirsha (November–December), Makara or Pausa (December–January), Kumbha or Magha (January–February), Mina or Phalguna (February–March).

There are six ritus or seasons in the Hindu calendar and each ritu has two months—Vasanta/spring (March and April), Grishma/summer (May and June), Varsha/rains (July and August), Sarad/autumn (September and October), Hemanta/winter (November and December) and Sisira/cool (January and February). In some regions, the rainy season covers the four months from Ashada-sukla to Kartika-sukla (June–September).

In the Hindu calendar, the dark half of the year (Dakshinayana), between summer and winter solstices, is less auspicious and seen as the 'night' of the gods. The light half (Uttarayana), when the sun's warmth and length of days are increasing, represents the 'day' of the gods. The bitter months of Dhanu (15 December to 14 January) and Mina (13 March to 13 April) are also ashubh. Similarly, Adik mas (leap year month in the Hindu calendar) is inauspicious since it is believed to have pollution accumulated over a three-year period. The month of Ashada (June–July) is also considered inauspicious.

As we know, Hindus look for a 'good date' for all activities, including marriage, consummation, thread ceremony and cutting a child's hair for the first time, all of which are considered life cycle events. Auspicious dates must be selected for moving into a house and opening a store. Agricultural commencements like first ploughing and first planting too need a good date. Maybe, they even had a good day to buy a horse or a buffalo—and now a car.

In the automotive industry as well, attempts have been made to break the year-end taboo (it is also not a good period as the model year changes in January; so a car bought in January 2013 will fetch a better resale price than one bought a month earlier as it would be known as a 2013 model).

Larger retailers like Big Bazaar are trying to understand the impact of religions and festivals on their business. They have even hired Devdutt Pattanaik as their 'chief belief officer'. There are two ways in which they are using these insights. Each state and each community has its own set of festivals and celebrations. Onam, for instance, may be a big festival in Kerala but a non-event across the border in Coimbatore. Cuttack and Vizag may also have such differences. Similarly the festivals to be played up may be different in Grant Road, Mumbai, versus Andheri, Mumbai. So the first exercise is to dig deep at the state and district levels for festivals. Each of these festivals is then mapped to each store, and each store is encouraged to tailor special offers to match the festive sprit. This is indeed a very exciting project given the multi-religious nature of the Indian people. So one may need to map religious communities, festivals and stores in an interesting array of dates and offers. Stores that cater to a bigger Jain population may have a different offer during the same period from a store with a negligible Jain population in its catchment area. At a national level Big Bazaar has pioneered the concept of 'Public Holiday Sale', the 'Sab Se Sasta Din'; days like Independence Day and Republic Day have become big shopping days in addition to days devoted to remembering our founding fathers.

The Vivek & Co story points us towards a different dimension. As marketers we can convert what has traditionally been seen as a 'poor' season into a hot-selling season if we can understand the archaeology behind the belief and give consumers enough reasons to cross the bridge. Taking a leaf from Vivek & Co, retailers are trying to convert the unlucky month of Ashada, the Aadi month in the Tamil calendar, into a sale month. It has now become common to see ads from retailers, jewellery outlets and sari shops in Tamil newspapers and television channels broadcasting the super-duper 'Aadi Discount'. In August 2013, I even noticed ads that combined Eid and Aadi discounts, a unique combination, I would imagine. Since Ashada comes before the peak selling season of Diwali, retailers tend to use this sale to get rid of old stocks. However, you don't see these discount ads in Kerala since the Malayalee shopping festival Onam falls in August–September. In Mumbai and other metropolitan cities, we don't see Ashada discounts but the 'end of season sale'.

One marketing success is undoubtedly the Kalnirnay phenomenon. Conceptualized by Jayant Salgaonkar, Kalnirnay is nothing but a calendar, or a calmanac, a calendar plus almanac, or panchanga. Starting as a hand-printed almanac for 10,000 Marathi subscribers in 1973, Kalnirnay became a 19 million copy phenomenon providing information on all Indian festivals, auspicious dates and times as well as cultural titbits. Though the bulk of the sales is from the Marathi version, Kalnirnay is also published in English, Hindi, Gujarati, Tamil, Telugu and Kannada. Over the years, it has evolved into thirty-five variants of the traditional wall calendar, including a pocket diary, car calendar, year planner, desk almanac and even a mobile app. Salgaonkar's genius was also evident in the way he used the back page of the calendar to provide cooking tips, short stories, railway timetables, exotic recipes, short stories, health tips and even money-saving ideas. The product was marketed as an advertising medium and large advertisers have happily advertised in it. When he passed away on 20 August 2013, the who's who of Maharashtra politics was there to pay their respects.

On the other hand, we are often confronted with a disclaimer from our team about a season not being 'good'. Instead of taking this at face value, it may make sense to dig a little deeper to see what is so 'bad' about the season or month. If it is an economic reason, then it is a little difficult to fix, though discounts work at all times. But if it is nothing more than the Hindu panchanga, we can surely find interesting solutions. Let me present an example from a very different standpoint.

Chennai hosts an annual Carnatic music season during December–January, where top-rated musicians perform at all the sabhas. I have attended a few concerts at the Music Academy and Narada Gana Sabha. I remember around ten such sabhas hosting concerts. In 2012, I decided to spend a week in Chennai, ably pushed by my dear friend Ravi of Chennaionline.com, who has been a regular at the Chennai concerts for many years. On the first day, I picked up *The Hindu* and counted more than fifty venues across the city that were hosting some ten concerts every day (there are so many concerts by so many great artists at so many venues that Chennaionline.com even offers a Concert Finder Service on its website). I also realized that in addition to food for the ears, many concert venues were also offering real good food for the tummy too.

Upon investigating, I found that since Marghazi was inauspicious for weddings, most wedding caterers were idle during this period and they used this opportunity to set up shamianas at leading music venues and sell food items usually served at weddings. They also distribute their visiting cards at these venues, thus increasing their visibility. December–January also ties in well with the migratory season of NRIs, who fly home in large numbers to avoid the bitter winter of the West and spend time with their parents and relatives in the South during the Christmas season. So, in a sense, a very inauspicious period becomes the best period to listen to the most divine music and have sumptuous food every day. How is that for a marketing miracle!

I think such a concept is waiting to happen in other parts of India. Why can't Mumbai have a music season in the same period when wedding halls are all empty and caterers are idle? You may well argue that Mumbaikars will not be interested in attending Hindustani or Carnatic music concerts. I think there will be a big market for all kinds of music, from the divine to the mundane. Someone has to pick up the gauntlet and then convert a dull season into a peak season, like what Vivek & Co did with the New Year Sale.

I would like to submit that the phenomenon of the New Year Sale will become a big national movement in the next decade. Retailers across the country face a lull in their businesses after Diwali, which usually falls around end October or early November. If they can create a collective movement to drive consumers to visit the store on New Year's Day, they will create a new selling opportunity.

I have observed that the increased religiosity across the country has also manifested itself in new practices. For instance, four decades ago, 1 January was seen as the Christian New Year. It was not the Hindu New Year, which falls on different dates in different parts of the country (yet another opportunity to segment and sell). So it is logical that Hindus should go to their temples on the Hindu New Year's Day. But try going to a temple on 1 January anywhere in India. You will be in the queue for at least an hour.

It is interesting to draw a parallel between our own New Year Sale story and the phenomenon of Black Friday in the US where stores offer incredible discounts. In the US, Thanksgiving is celebrated on the fourth Thursday of every November. The date was mandated by the US government and is a big holiday. The origins of Thanksgiving can be traced to the Protestant Reformation in the UK and was to be a day of thanking the Lord for a bountiful harvest (look at how thanking the Lord for a great harvest transcends continents and religions—Baisakhi in North India and Pongal in Tamil Nadu being just two examples). However, in modern-day US, Thanksgiving Day is celebrated across all religious denominations. Even our own NRI community celebrates it with gusto, perhaps with a special puja at their local Hare Krishna temple. The day following Thanksgiving is the official start of the Christmas shopping season. The season should actually start slow, but retailers have figured out a way of pumping steroids into the first day of sale and also getting rid of the autumn collection, with super discounts. The Black Friday phenomenon is so big that stores open as early as 4 a.m. and consumers line up outside from midnight to grab a good deal.

Inventing new shopping occasions is a part of ritualistic behaviour across the world. So we don't need to feel bad about our own new rituals and celebrations. What did not exist a few decades ago is now seen as common practice. In a similar vein, chances are you will be driven to buy something new every 1 January, like my dad, leaving my mom to figure out what to do with the third toaster to enter the house.

This logically leads us to the next area of our investigation, the hyper-growth of festivals across India.

5. An Old Festival Gets a New Look

India has two million gods and worships them all. In religion all other countries are paupers, India is the only millionaire.

Mark Twain (1835–1920)

We were sitting in the swanky conference room of an apparel marketing company waiting to meet their new CEO, an apparel expert of repute in European markets. He walked in, greeted his team and the team from our agency and posed a question: 'I noticed today that a number of our staff are dressed in traditional saris, all of them green. What is happening?'

One of the younger women executives volunteered an explanation. 'Sir, this is the week of the Hindu festival Navratri. For nine days, traditional Hindus worship the goddess Durga. It has now become a fashion for women to wear saris to office on these nine days, a different colour every day!'

The next question from the CEO was interesting: 'How did this start? Has it been a tradition for the last thousand years as you guys tell me about everything or is this a clever marketing ploy of a sari company?'

No one in the room had a ready answer. The pleasantries done with, the meeting got under way, but some of us from the agency couldn't let go of this vexing issue. I started my career in Mumbai in 1979 and have worked for well over twenty-five years since in the city. This 'Navratri colour-coordinated sari phenomenon' had caught my attention only in the past decade.

The team entrusted with the task of finding out the origin of the phenomenon came back with a rather simple explanation. I still doubt its veracity but here it is: around ten years ago an astute editor of the Marathi daily *Maharashtra Times* decided to announce the 'colour of the day' during Navratri. The campaign exhorted women readers to wear a sari of a specified colour on each day. These were the days before Facebook, Twitter, Instagram and Pinterest. But if you have travelled in Mumbai suburban trains, you know it is all these and more rolled into one, along with bhajan music, so it is also iTunes.

The trend started with the women who were observing the traditional nine-day puja for the goddess Durga, but soon spread to other communities as well. My assistant Jensy Praveen and our colleague Mincy Fernandes, both Malayalee Christians, have been sporting colourful saris during Navratri.

In North India, Navratri is celebrated as the victory of Rama over Ravana, culminating with the burning of the straw-filled figure of Ravana. In many other parts of the country, the festival commemorates the victory of Durga over Mahishasura, the buffalo demon. Bengalis set up wonderfully decorated pandals, or marquees, to mark the festival. It is ironical that the Communist Party of India-Marxist (CPI-M) even sells Marxist literature in Kolkata's puja pandals. I wonder what Karl Marx would say about that! In Tamil Nadu, Navratri sees a display of dolls known as kolu in homes, with women visiting each other, singing and celebrating the victory of Durga. In Gujarat, every neighbourhood hosts garbhas, where social rules are relaxed and boys and girls, men and women sing and dance the night away. Garbha nights are seized by teenagers as official 'mixing' nights and they attract few disapproving frowns.

In Mumbai one can see all these manifestations of Navratri. In Bengali neighbourhoods like Chembur, you have the Durga pandal; the Shipping Corporation of India has one of the best pandals in Mumbai. In localities such as Sion and Matunga, dominated by South Indians, you can see the display of dolls and celebration with music and sweets. And you can also see Ravana being burnt at Cross Maidan, Churchgate. The biggest of them all are the grand garbha nights. Gujarati singers like Falguni Pathak are in huge demand and it not unusual to see 5000 people packing into a huge ground dancing to the pulsating beat.

I would like to submit that this trend of wearing colour-coordinated saris will spread to other cities in the near future, just as hitherto unknown festivals have gained currency in many parts of the country. The spread of new festivals and the varied ways of celebrating them will be aided by social media such as Facebook, Pinterest and Twitter.

Take, for instance, the Ganesha festival or Ganesh Chaturti. We know that in 1893 Lokmanya Bal Gangadhar Tilak conceptualized the transformation of the domestic celebration of Ganesh Chaturti into a community celebration as a means of bringing different castes and classes together. The idea of a community Ganesha pandal was born in Pune and spread all over Maharashtra in the days before Independence. Over the last three decades, we have been seeing community pandals spring up in many parts of India, including Bangalore and Hyderabad.

This new-found desire to celebrate at the drop of a hat has no better example than Akshaya Trithiya. Virtually unheard of until a few decades ago, Akshaya Trithiya, also known as Akha Teej,

is an auspicious day for both Hindus and Jains. What it stands
for is anybody's guess. It is variously believed to be the birthday
of Parashurama, one of Lord Vishnu's incarnations, and also
the day Ganesh started writing the Mahabharata, as dictated to
him by Ved Vyas. My mother's explanation is that it is the day
Lord Krishna came to the help of Draupadi when she was being
disrobed by the Kauravas with a sari that unravelled without
end. Akshaya to her means 'never-ending' and she believes that
Akshaya Trithiya is a day of giving, not of buying.

In *Indianomix*, the authors Vivek Dehejia and Rupa
Subramanya say that Akshaya Trithiya is the most auspicious day
for buying gold after Dhanteras, the first day of Diwali. According
to them Akshaya Trithiya is associated with the god of wealth,
Kubera, and it is therefore considered auspicious to buy jewellery
in his honour. Since the date often falls before the big wedding
season, it makes additional sense for some to stock up on gold.

Buying gold during the holy period of Akshaya Trithiya may
have some mythological justification, but what about the host
of other products that are pushed during the time. A real estate
developer's ad says, 'This Akshaya Trithiya invest in an address
that comes with a landscaped garden, gymnasium and rare peace
and quiet.' Not to be left out of this buying frenzy, a Czech car
company, now owned by Volkswagen, enticed customers to
'welcome prosperity with a Skoda Fabia' on Akshaya Trithiya.
Add to these ads the usual ones from jewellery brands like
Tanishq and Gitanjali and you are almost led to believe that you
are not a devout Hindu if you don't buy gold, a car, a flat screen
television or even a flat.

Let us consider another festival, Karva Chauth. It's India's
answer to Valentine's Day, where the wife fasts from sunrise
to moonrise for the health and prosperity of her husband.
Karva Chauth got a big fillip from Bollywood with movies like

Dilwale Dulhania Le Jayenge and *Baghban* and is now a raging phenomenon across India, with many husbands and boyfriends maintaining a sympathetic fast with their loved ones.

Raksha Bandhan or Rakhi is also gaining popularity. Hindu mythology ascribes several stories to the festival extolling the brother–sister bond: one has Draupadi tearing a part of her sari to tie on Krishna's wrist to stop it from bleeding and another has Sachi tying a rakhi on her husband Indra's hands to empower him to defeat the asuras. But the most enduring story behind the festival is that of the widowed queen of Chittor, Rani Karnavati, sending a rakhi to the Mughal king Humayun. A couple of decades ago, Rakhi was celebrated only in western and northern India. It was therefore amusing to see in the papers in August 2013 a photograph of the diehard Dravidian leader and Dravida Munnettra Kazhagam (DMK) chief M. Karunanidhi getting a rakhi tied to his wrist by a North Indian lady. Chances are Rakhi is on its way to becoming a huge pan-Indian festival in the coming years.

So what is really happening and how did Rakhi grow to such proportions? I think mass media, savvy retailers and a growing spending class has triggered this phenomenon, which is now national and becoming as big as Diwali in some sense.

No country has a longer calendar of holidays than ours. Festivals come in all shapes and sizes, some are seasonal, some celebrate harvest, some commemorate the birth or victory of a god. We also have other festivals commemorating significant events in mythology or phases of the moon, eclipses, solstices or equinoxes. We have festivals celebrating Krishna, Vishnu, Shiva, Parvathi, Kartikeya, Kama, Dattatreya, Ganesha, Rama, Gauri, Gayatri, Lakshmi, Saraswati, Chitragupta and other deities. We even have festivals dedicated to 'lesser gods' such as Naga Panchami and Hanuman Jayanti. Hindus celebrate festivals through several rituals, including worship (puja), fasting, vigil (jagarana), bathing (snana), fairs (mela), singing, taking vows, lighting lamps, gambling, games, drinking, feeding mendicants and, of course, offering gifts to Brahmins. In addition to festivals celebrated nationally there are regional festivals that are specific to local customs and deities like the festival of Jagannatha at Puri.

Many Hindu festivals are named after a god, like Shivratri (Night of Shiva); or the month, like Sravani Purnima (the full moon of the month of Sravana); or after the day of the fortnight in which they occur, like dvitya (second day of the fortnight), tritya (third day), chaturti (fourth), panchami (fifth), shashti (sixth), saptami (seventh), ashtami (eighth), navami (ninth), dashami (tenth) and ekadashi (eleventh).

The key festivals celebrated across the country include Diwali; Ganesh Chaturti (celebrated on the fourth day of the bright fortnight of Bhadrapada, between August and September, commemorating the birthday of the elephant god); Holi, which is supposed to be a fertility festival; Janmashtami (eighth day of the second month of Bhadrapada, commemorating the birth of Lord Krishna); Maha Shivratri; Makara Sankranti; Navratri and Ramnavami (again celebrating the birth of Rama). In addition, there are a whole lot of interesting festivals like Ganga Dasahara (the day River Ganga descended on earth), Sravani Purnima (which marks the middle of the monsoon season), Sri Panchami (fifth day of the light half of Magha, January–February, which is the spring festival) and Tripuri Purnima (the full moon of Kartika, October–November, an important date for Saivites). All of this does not even cover one-tenth of the festivals celebrated around the country.

We will see a further growth in festivals in the coming years. This is just a signal that Indians are willing to embrace new ways of consumption and are looking for reasons to do so. And what better reason than their own mythologies! Marketing companies, the media and retailers have realized that Indian consumers, though growing in affluence, are always looking for a bargain. Combining a festival with a deal is a way of breaking out of the consumer inertia. If in the past there was just one big buying season in each part of India, we can now think of many more. These will continue to grow and get absorbed by all sections of society across religious groups.

While retailers and marketers are waking up to the extra opportunities available to market their wares, I think they grossly underestimate the cultural and religious diversity of the country. For instance, Eid-ul-Fitr is the biggest Muslim festival. Like every other festival, this too is celebrated by big-time shopping and merrymaking. So a lot more Muslims are flocking shopping centres and may be indulging in window shopping, nothing more. Several upmarket malls in Ahmedabad decided in 2013 to charge a shocking entry fee of Rs 20 per person—this amount was redeemable when the customer bought something in the mall. Apparently, this charge was levied only on those identifiable as Muslims. In a parallel story some shopping centres in the US did not permit Muslims to park their cars in the designated parking slots. While some malls are shooing away Muslim festive shoppers, some are capitalizing on the opportunity by offering qawwali nights and Sufi evenings. According to Harish Bijoor, a leading marketing consultant, 'Marketers go by numbers [Muslim numbers may be small in many areas], and not by sentiments. However, with the new generation, this opportunity [Eid] can be tapped into. For example, in the US, market retailers are shifting strategy from celebrating religious occasions to celebrating holidays [and the festive spirit].'

What can a marketer take away from all this? I think we need to see religious festivals as not just days with religious significance but as opportunities to engage with our customers better. We need to understand that India is a multi-religious country and religious festivals are not just for those who belong to that religion, they are for all of us. And if they fall on a holiday, all the better. The first question therefore is: Do you know the key festival dates of the year, across religious affiliations? I would submit there could be as many as thirty such days every year. I always carry the year's festival list in my wallet (not to forecast sales but to plan meetings). Does it make sense to understand how these festivals are celebrated and what their significance is? Will the festival affect sales, can it be used to drive up sales? Can we identify festivals that may not be big today but could be built up, like Akshaya Trithiya? This could be a very exciting experiment. It is not just Christians who celebrate Christmas and not just Hindus who celebrate Diwali. The festive spirit, extra cash in the wallet and a holiday can be a great combination. Just ask movie makers, many of whom time big releases to coincide with Eid or Diwali.

Big Bazaar is a truly Indian phenomenon. Kishore Biyani, the founder of Big Bazaar, speaks of how he has tried to invent new rules of the game. He gives credit for many of his ideas to the Saravana Stores of Ranganathan Street, T. Nagar, Chennai. (Saravana Stores is one huge mega mela in a multi-storey building on a hugely congested street in the busiest market in Chennai. Vast quantities of products are displayed in a way that may assault your senses but is an invitation to buy, buy, buy for the average middle-class shopper. With prices that make your jaw drop, you are bound to leave Saravana Stores with a lot more than you ever thought you would buy.) In his own way Kishore Biyani has created an Indian bazaar environment in his Big Bazaar stores. For example, for the first time in the world, Big Bazaar opted to display grains such as rice and wheat in open bags for Indian consumers to touch, feel and taste. The aisle sizes are much narrower than in stores in other parts of the world to create a crowded Saravana Stores kind of feeling. But the one interesting innovation that Big Bazaar introduced, as mentioned earlier, was to make each store go the extra mile to connect with their local shopper by appealing to their religio-festival spirit.

If religious festivals are being used to justify increased consumption, are there other areas where Indians are using religion to find a new path? Let us take a look at what I call 'auspicious puja justification'.

6. Inaugurate with a Puja—Enjoy Perpetual Prosperity

I would rather live my life as if there is a God and die to find that there isn't, than live my life as if there isn't and die to find out there is.

Albert Camus (1913–60)

I was on my way to the airport from our Chennai office in a taxi and my usual driver, Soundarajan, was at the wheel. The day's work was well done and I was all set to reach the airport on time when the normally reticent Soundarajan spoke up. 'Sir, are you planning to shift your Chennai office? This building you just visited is not auspicious. Someone committed suicide from the fourth floor a few years ago and after that people say that it is very unlucky.'

I thanked Soundarajan for his advice, and tried questioning him on his beliefs about the 'rasi' and 'not rasi' nature of buildings. In Chennai, everything is associated with rasi, or luck. Some buildings are seen as good rasi, some doctors are viewed as good rasi and so on. I failed to convince Soundarajan about the futility of believing in rasi and went back to the book I was reading. But I did dock the information in the back of my mind.

A little bit of a background on our agency's Chennai operations is needed at this point. I had started the Chennai office in 1990 in a garage. The business grew splendidly and we moved into a full-fledged bungalow in a few years. The business was set to expand further in the late 1990s and the new manager who had taken over the operations wanted an open-plan office that could be structured to suit the growing needs of the clients. The building I had visited was perfect for our purpose. And it was coming to us at a very reasonable price. Which is when the suicide story jumped out.

My colleague was given a quick update on my driver's theory and she corroborated it after discussing it with her own accountant, who in turn consulted the office peon! We knew that we would do well if we ignored all the 'bad rasi' beliefs and moved in. But the office also saw numerous visitors and it was likely they would hear of the 'unlucky' story. And these stories tend to gather steam, leading to demoralization of the team.

We had set up and built a Chennai operation, against all odds. And we did not want the operation to meet an end, thanks to some superstition surrounding a new office it was being moved to. We did not want to ignore it fully either. Was there a way out?

We figured we needed to fight the bad spirits with good spirits. Would it not be a good idea to have a really big puja to inaugurate the office? This would ensure that we have the 'good powers' on our side, and also get tongues to stop wagging.

Our situation can now be seen as a testing ground for Pascal's Wager. Blaise Pascal is familiar to us for his law on hydrodynamics. But Pascal was more than that. He invented the mechanical calculator, worked on projective geometry, economics, number theory and more. He embraced religion after leaving an indelible stamp on the scientific world. In his book

Pensees (Thoughts), Pascal presents an argument for belief in God popularly known as Pascal's Wager. It says, 'Given the possibility that God actually does exist and assuming the infinite gain or loss associated with belief in God or with unbelief, a rational person should live as though God exists and seek to believe in God. If God does not actually exist, such a person will have only a finite loss (some pleasures, luxury, etc.).' In fact, Pascal's Wager set the tone for the development of a whole new area of discovery now known as decision theory.

So though we work in a new-age communication industry populated by young business school graduates, we did go with Pascal on our new office inauguration.

The Chennai office was done up and inaugurated with a big puja. The office team was served a bountiful lunch to make the occasion more memorable.

Cut to 2013. Our office in Chennai has continued to thrive while many agencies have closed shop, including some that had offices in fancy buildings. The property that all companies stayed away from was fully occupied within a few months of our moving in; our neighbours included a pharmaceutical multinational and a large advertising agency.

I should also recount an interesting incident here. A few months after we moved in, a big red brick fell from the top of the building on our manager's brand-new car, causing significant damage. The landlord compensated and no one cursed the spirits for flinging the stone from the terrace!

Was it a rare instance of a 'bad rasi' building or is this common across the country? We are clearly living in a country in transition. In every metro there exists a large class of people who are strong believers of the rasi theory. While one section of society has embraced a form of scientific thinking with the occasional prayer thrown in for good measure, the other is still steeped in old beliefs and rituals. The concept of lucky and unlucky buildings is pan-Indian. But our solution was possibly an elegant one, going with the tide yet delivering the goods.

Indian consumers are finding interesting ways to navigate the middle ground between tradition and modernity. As a country, all of us are slave to Pascal's Wager and are taking safe bets.

It may be worth remembering that the concept of the puja was borrowed by the Aryans from the Dravidians. The word puja is derived from the Tamil word pu, which means flower, and is adapted from pu-chey, which means 'flower action' in Tamil. The early Aryan and Vedic form of worship was the rite of homa, a rite that had Indo-Iranian roots and was in essence an animal sacrifice in a fire pit. God was believed to be partial to burnt animal flesh and granted favours to those who did a homa. Following the rise of Buddhism and its call for non-violence, the Vedic homa rite gave way to a more humane form of worship, the puja.

Do only Indians perform pujas and seek divine blessings before starting a new venture? Well, it appears the most macho of all brands, Harley-Davidson, is not averse to some divine intervention either.

The iconic bike brand sought the blessings of Pope Francis for its 110th anniversary. On 16 June 2013 Pope Francis blessed thousands of Harley-Davidson riders. News reports said that nearly 35,000 bikers were present in Vatican City; 800 were allowed to park on the road leading to St Peter's Square. In return for the Pope's blessings, the company gave him two motorcycles and a black leather jacket with its trademark eagle on the back. Apparently, one of the bikes had earlier been autographed by Pope Francis's predecessor, Pope Benedict XVI. Harley had been steadily losing market share to sports bikes in Europe and possibly needed divine intervention to perk up sales. Incidentally, Pope Francis has been drawing a lot of positive press, at least from the liberal side of the fence and from the young. He addressed a World Youth Day crowd, estimated at three million, on Rio de Janeiro's Copacabana Beach on 25 July 2013. He is also the first Pope to use the word gay in his comments. There could be a bigger marketing play to attract the older, more conservative consumer, the key target audience for Harley motorcycles. There is this old joke about how the marketing agent of the Vatican went up to the Pope and said, 'We have a nice sponsorship offer from Campbell Soups. They are offering us $100 million if we change our daily prayer from "Lord give us this day our daily bread" to "Lord give us this day our bowl of soup".' The Pope thinks it is a great idea and okays it. The agent then asks, 'Father, who will tell the Modern bread company that we are dropping them because we have a bigger sponsor?'

India got its independence on 15 August 1947. But there was a twist. All of us remember Jawaharlal Nehru's speech 'Tryst with Destiny': 'At the stroke of the midnight hour when the world sleeps, India will awake to life and freedom. A moment comes, which comes but rarely in history, when we step out from the old to the new, when an age ends, and when the soul of a nation long suppressed, finds utterance.'

Though Pandit Nehru spoke of stepping out from the old to the new, the birth of the nation was mired in old traditions of 'right time' and 'place'. The British parliament had resolved to hand over India to its citizens on 15 August, which happened to be the second anniversary of the Japanese surrender that ended the Second World War. However, there was a big hurdle. Astrologers in India raised a big hue and cry saying that 15 August 1947 was an inauspicious date and a nation born on that day would break up and face unprecedented hurdles. They argued that 14 August was auspicious. But the British would not agree to advancing the date and did not want to give up their imperial authority even while handing over charge. A compromise formula that could placate the stars yet not anger the British was worked out by K.M. Pannikar, a brilliant historian and an expert in Hindu astrology. He suggested that the Constituent Assembly meet half an hour before the midnight hour and start the proceedings. Pandit Nehru's talk is mentioned as 14–15 August 1947 even in his speech notes. It is said that the timekeepers ensured that he began his speech before the midnight hour. A modern nation was born, enmeshed in age-old beliefs about good time and bad time. Again, Pascal's Wager worked out okay. The nation that most western experts did not expect to survive has continued to stay together as one country, a thriving democracy and a secular democratic nation. In its own way, it is a world economic power today. I wonder what would have happened if the Constituent Assembly had met at 9 a.m. on 15 August 1947.

We Indians not only rely on picking up the right time to bring us luck, we also use various symbols. The most popular is the swastika, the equilateral cross with four arms bent at 90 degrees. In Sanskrit, *su* is good or auspicious, *asti* means to be, and *ka* is used as a suffix. The swastika literally means 'to be good'. There is another translation—*swa* is higher self, *asti* is being, and *ka* is a suffix so the word can be interpreted as 'being with higher self'. Ironically, Nazi Germany under Hitler used the swastika, tilted at 45 degrees, as its symbol.

It appears that what started when India attained independence has continued to flourish. Our politicians still depend on astrologers to tell them when to start their campaign and when to end it. Most big businessmen have astrologers to give them auspicious periods for a new activity, be it a new factory or a new product launch. Brand names and brand logos are sometimes sent to astrologers for validation. Today, there are colour experts, numerologists as well as stargazers who come to the aid of Indian business leaders.

We need to acknowledge that Indian astrologers have learnt some valuable lessons from K.M. Pannikar. They very rarely come in the way of a big event. They often find a way out of the situation, just as Pannikar suggested starting the Constituent Assembly at 11.30 p.m. on 14 August.

Most young managers educated in the western style of management pooh-pooh these beliefs and do not profess any faith in any of them. However, they use a different set of standards when they go home and plan their sister's wedding. It may be a good idea to understand some aspects of these beliefs and ensure that a way out is found in case of hurdles. I have noticed even Christian and Muslim consumers taking precautions though their religion does not prescribe any 'good time' or 'bad time'. They probably want to ensure that they don't end up at the wrong end of the wager.

I wonder if we Indians will ever get out of this habit. A lot of it is really of no real value. But the only saving grace is that astrologers have adapted their trade to modern times. So, if there is a hurdle, they are the first to point out a suitable escape clause.

We now turn to the other movement, which has its roots in ancient India, one that has seen great tailwinds over the past two decades.

7. Planning a Home Gets the Divine Touch

Hell isn't merely paved with good intentions; it is walled and roofed with them. Yes and furnished too.

Aldous Huxley (1894–1963)

Nerolac Kansai is one of India's pre-eminent paint manufacturers. They have a whole range of paints and had launched a premium paint under the brand name Nerolac Impressions. We were discussing how we could help them build the brand through new media. This was in the early years of the new millennium and Internet and websites were the latest buzzwords. The first wave of websites were built on the belief that if you have a great website, you will automatically attract surfers. That wave soon gave way to a newer theory: you need a website that is unique and useful, but you also need engaging content for surfers to keep coming and you need to drive traffic to the website with interesting hooks.

The task given to our digital team was to think afresh about creating a website for Nerolac Impressions. The site needed to be great looking—we were after all marketing a decorative product—but it also had to be unique and useful from the Indian consumer's perspective.

It is customary to survey the market and look for the best examples globally before you build a website. What we build has to stand scrutiny across a wide cross-section of websites and, more importantly, should be easy to download, considering the relatively sluggish Indian Internet speeds.

While the task was to create a website to help consumers plan on how to paint their homes, it was felt that the site should also help them configure their own rooms and experience how it would look with different colours. But this was not enough was the view.

It was then that someone in the team suggested using a typical Indian way of determining the orientation of a home: 'Vastu on the Net'.

Once this idea was cracked, the team got down to incorporating vastu elements in the website. The site created, www.ImpressZone. com, gave visitors a quick tour on how to determine the vastu of their house and what could be done to ensure that the negative elements are neutralized (as we saw in the inaugural puja story in the previous chapter).

The website went live in June 2001 and soon garnered great reviews and industry recognition. What we had managed to do was bring elements of Indian beliefs into a modern concept of a website on interior design. It was a first. Today you can read articles on good vastu in the best of interior design magazine websites and even get online vastu advice.

Vastu, or vastu shastra or vastu veda, is based on a traditional view of how nature affects human places of living. Originally, vastu shastra was commonly used for designing temples and forts. Vastu is based on five elements that are said to make up our earth—earth or bhumi, water or jal, air or vayu, fire or agni and space or akasha. These five elements work together; by understanding how they interact, we can build living quarters that are designed for enhanced well-being, prosperity, wealth and happiness. A human place of living is called a manushalaya, a human temple. The most common format of a house for a family is composed of a 9 by 9 grid. The central 3 by 3 square is an open courtyard, left open to the sky. The corner 2 by 2 spaces are meant for specific purposes, determined by the gods who reside in them. The north-east corner is for the home shrine, the south-east for the kitchen, the south-west for the master bedroom and the north-west for the storage of grains. The space in between is meant for other purposes.

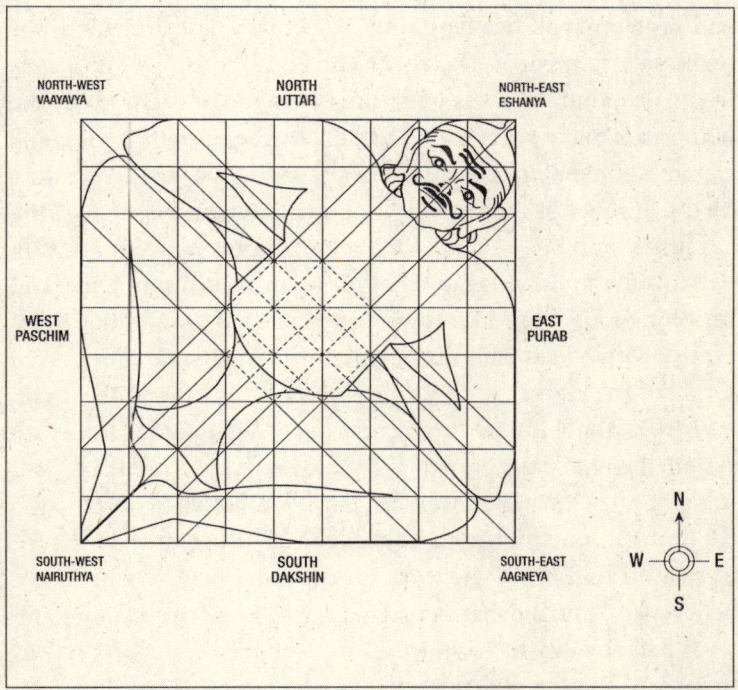

NORTH-WEST
VAAYAVYA

NORTH
UTTAR

NORTH-EAST
ESHANYA

WEST
PASCHIM

EAST
PURAB

SOUTH-WEST
NAIRUTHYA

SOUTH
DAKSHIN

SOUTH-EAST
AAGNEYA

N

W — E

S

Interestingly, even Christian church architecture has a pre-ordained form. The traditional church is composed of the atrium, the basilica, the berna, the mausoleum and the cuneiform. But this did not get adapted to home design in the Christian world.

Though the Cultural Revolution in China suppressed it, feng shui has continued to live and is now spreading its wings across continents, wherever the Chinese diaspora lives. Feng shui, which translates to wind–water, is also an ancient system of orienting buildings such as tombs and other structures in an auspicious manner. An interesting aspect of feng shui that has entered India in a big way is the feng shui bamboo. Seen as a lucky plant, these bamboos have come to adorn many homes and offices. Why is an indoor bamboo plant considered lucky? Because it combines and represents all five feng shui elements. These are wood, the bamboo itself; earth, the rocks the bamboo grows in; water, what the bamboo grows with; fire, what the pot that holds the bamboo is made with; metal, usually the bamboo pot has some element of metal in it, even if it is a clay or glass pot. Depending on the number of shoots, the bamboo plant is supposed to bring happiness and luck—three shoots for happiness, five for health, two for love and marriage, eight for wealth and abundance, and nine for good fortune. I just went and counted the bamboo plant on my windowsill, and am happy to report that I am covered for all of the above.

Just as the Chinese have rediscovered feng shui, the vastu system has seen great growth in India over the past ten years. And it is not just consumers who are fans. While I was constructing my house in Chennai, my architect politely asked me if I believed in vastu. I told him I did not. But the good man was himself a believer and told me that he had made the house vastu compliant.

What does vastu have to do with religion? Experts tell us that vastu shastra is part of the grand scheme of Hindu living, like Kautilya's *Arthashastra*. This ancient science has found new wings.

As we saw, vastu shastra is all about the wind, sun, moon and such natural phenomena. But to most Indians, it is no different from picking an auspicious date for a wedding, all enmeshed in astrological and religious beliefs. It is almost as if we are buying an insurance policy on our new house to ensure that our life in it will be peaceful and prosperous.

Vastu is, in a sense, a lot like our belief in astrology. No newspaper is complete without a daily astrology column. And though we know the daily predictions are just recirculated predictions of yesterday, many read it and hope to benefit by it. A young astrologer did tell me that there is a lot more to astrology than daily predictions, but I will leave you to draw your own conclusions.

As we become more and more prosperous, I wonder if this trend will continue or go away. We are embracing new forms of celebrations and new festivals but are also trying to ensure that we do not anger any evil force. Vastu gives us solace that we have configured our house the right way so at least evil forces will not get ready access to our family jewels, purchased during the last Akshaya Trithiya.

Now that we have bought the jewels, built the house according to good vastu principles, it is time to lock the house and go on a pilgrimage to thank the Lord above.

Before we embark on that pilgrimage, there is an interesting anecdote involving a friend of mine who was looking to buy a new flat in Mumbai. His mother had advised him that he should buy a flat only if it was vastu compliant and he too had some lingering faith in the ancient system. He engaged a sharp vastu consultant and agreed to pay him Rs 500 for each flat checked. His search continued. Each time he found a house he liked, he would call the vastu consultant, who would promptly arrive with his books and compass and declare it 'not vastu compliant'. This continued for almost six months during which more than ten flats had been seen. That was when the hapless man met another friend who is a lot more worldly-wise. He offered a possible way out and suggested that the vastu consultant be rehired on a different set of terms. It was suggested that the consultant be paid a fixed fee, say, Rs 2000, irrespective of the number of flats checked. That worked. The very next week, the vastu consultant cleared the first flat he was taken to. He did make some suggestions like where to keep the family puja idol but the seemingly insurmountable problem of finding a vastu-compliant flat had been solved with that clever vastu consultant fee plan.

8. Will Travel for God

Unusual travel suggestions are dancing lessons from God.

Kurt Vonnegut (1922–2007)

Real Image Media Technologies (RIMT) is a Chennai-based company that has been doing pioneering work in the area of digitization of movies.* The company brought AVID—among the best movie editing technologies—to India in the 1990s and got into the business of digitizing movie prints and converting cinema halls from old-style celluloid projectors to modern-day digital projectors. Today, over 75 per cent of the 10,000-odd screens in India are digital and this transformation has happened in the last five years thanks to RIMT and its worthy competitor UFO. So now movies are no longer released in just a few hundred theatres, but in thousands of theatres as the cost of prints is no longer a determining factor (digital prints cost just a fraction of celluloid prints). RIMT has a unique business model whereby it helps single-screen movie halls embrace digital cinema at an attractive cost; in exchange, RIMT gets

_____

* Full disclosure is called for here. I sit on the board of RIMT as an independent director.

exclusive rights to screen ads in those single-screen theatres.

During the 1960s and 1970s, cinema advertising was a potent force and a monopoly controlled by a company called Blaze. Advertisers and agencies had mixed emotions about cinema because it was a difficult medium to audit and monitor, but they had little choice as it was the only audiovisual medium available. And the process and cost of creating celluloid cinema prints for movie hall advertising had made advertisers almost abandon cinema advertising. The growth of national television—first through Doordarshan and its low-powered transmitters and later, from the 1990s, through the growth of satellite television—has seen television fully replace cinema as an easy and effective audiovisual medium.

It was in this scenario that RIMT created a unique cinema advertising product they called Qube Cinema Network (QCN). Through QCN, the company offered seamless cinema advertising across India in their 1500-plus screens. QCN was especially powerful in two states, Tamil Nadu and Andhra Pradesh. In fact, the company offers almost 45 per cent of all single-screen cinema halls in the two movie-crazy states. But selling to the media planners and brand managers was a challenge.

The new-age media planners and brand managers were comfortable with the simplicity of television advertising and the allure of television rating points (TRPs), which measure the percentage of viewers/households tuning into the advertising slot and can be used as a ready reckoner while planning and buying these slots. Cinema advertising was a lot more complicated in this context. The measurement system was obtuse; impact, though significantly higher than television, was unclear; and multiplexes in Mumbai and Delhi, the two cities where they had become fashionable, were too niche and too expensive to deliver significant reach.

QCN faced multiple challenges. It had a dominant position in single-screen cinema halls, but that was an animal much misunderstood by the media professional. The general view was that India had become a multiplex country (but the reality is that just around 10 per cent of the 10,000 movie screens in India are in multiplexes). Single-screen cinemas were still popular and they were no longer dingy, gloomy halls. Most were air-conditioned and were rapidly switching over to digital cinema.

The marketing team at RIMT called for a full day of brainstorming on how to achieve a breakthrough in the large and unresponsive Mumbai and Delhi markets. I was called in to moderate the discussions.

We identified the problem as threefold—media planners did not have a clear idea of how digital cinema operated, they had a mistaken notion of single-screen cinema halls and they were unsure of the impact of an ad in a single-screen hall. The only way to educate media planners was to get them to visit tier II cities and movie halls that had been digitized. It would help them realize the full potential of cinema advertising it they studied cities like Salem in Tamil Nadu or Nellore in Andhra Pradesh. There was a catch: How were we to get them to take three days off from their tight work schedule for such a trip?

That's when someone in the room came up with a truly divine idea. He said we should combine a three-day trip to upcountry Andhra Pradesh with a visit to the Tirupati temple!

Which media planner would say no to a trip to Tirupati? And if we combined a three-day visit to movie halls in and around Tirupati town, we would have achieved a win-win-win situation. Media planners would get to see single-screen cinema halls, witness digital cinema advertising in action and hopefully see their own wishes fulfilled too after praying before Lord Venkateshwara at the Tirupati temple.

Religious Tourism Map of India

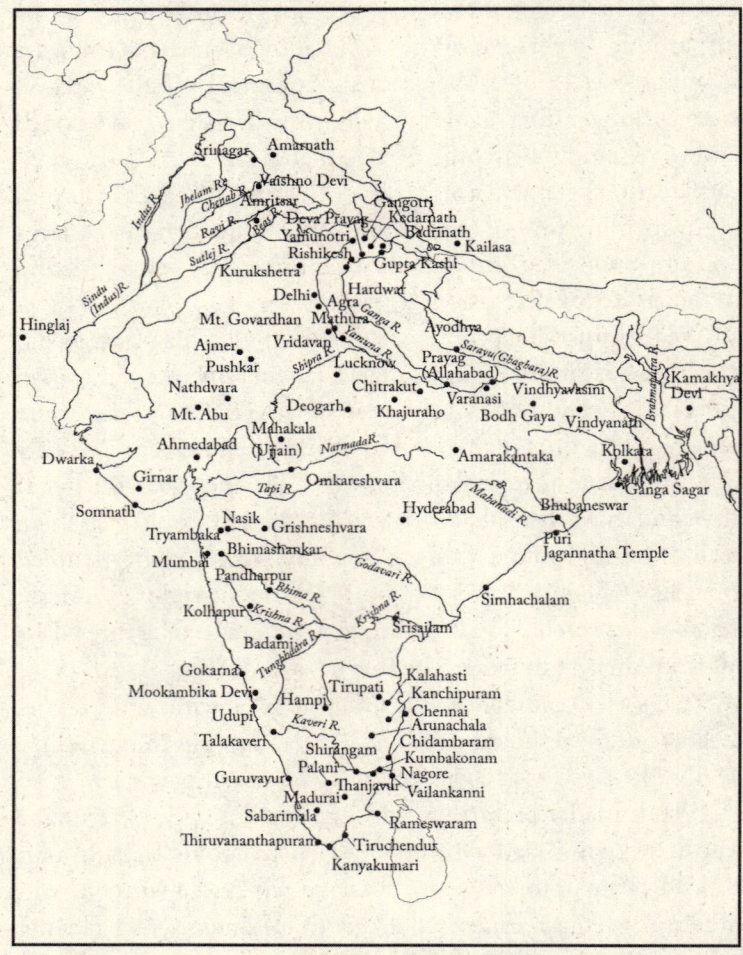

Adapted from Diana L. Eck, *India: A Sacred Geography. Reproduced with permission*

I thought the idea was terrific but some others in the room felt it needed deeper consideration. We quickly overcame these reservations by pointing out that clients and media professionals were taken for market visits to, say, Jaipur or Jodhpur with trips to general interest places like the Ranthambhore wildlife sanctuary often thrown in. The same was true of a visit to Uttar Pradesh, where the Taj Mahal was part of the package. So why not Tirupati, we argued.

The truth is that from time immemorial Indians have travelled the length and breadth of this land seeking salvation. And this trend has only increased in the past twenty years.

An estimated 851 million Indians travel every year (this would include travel for business purposes and for family functions) and our country saw some 6.29 million international tourist arrivals in 2011. According to travel industry estimates, 19 per cent of all tourist trips fall under the category of religious travel. In fact, a leading tour operator in India puts that number at 70 per cent of domestic tourist movement. The National Council of Applied Economic Research (NCAER) estimates that religious trips account for 50 per cent of all package tours while the leisure sector accounts for 28 per cent.

In her book *God Market* Meera Nanda quotes 2004 NCAER figures to say that Tirupati tops the religious tourism charts with more than 25 million visitors a year and Vaishno Devi comes in second at 17 million. On 2 June 2012 the Tirupati temple had a record number of devotees and the average waiting time was nineteen hours for a darshan. The Sabarimala temple which is open only for a few months (and a few days each month) attracted 50,000 devotees thirty years ago but those numbers had swelled dramatically by 2012. According to a *Business Standard* report (4 August 2013) which quoted the tourism ministry, Tirupati attracted 55 million visitors, Vaishno Devi 10.5 million and

Sabarimala an amazing 30 million. Even Shirdi in Maharashtra seems to have crossed the 10 million mark in 2012!

As Sudhir Kakar says in *The Indians*, 'Visits to important temples and pilgrimage places, regular fasting and turning to traditional religious practices or gurus have not declined with globalization and its worldly temptations. In fact, these have increased since the 1980s, and most conspicuously in the growing middle class.'

Ashoka's edicts speak of 'conquering the four corners of the earth'. Originally meant to be a war cry, it was soon applied to the grand pilgrimage to many shrines, circling the world (India).

With new hotels and new facilities coming up to cater to visitors, temple towns have never had it so good. And for those of us a little confused about the whole structure of religious Hindu tourism, Diana L. Eck's *India: A Sacred Geography* makes great reading. In fact, the book should be made compulsory reading for anyone involved with (religious) tourism in this country. Eck defines Hindu religious tourism under three categories—tirthas or crossings, pithas or seats of the divine and dhams or divine abodes. For those who want a full circuit of India, there are video coaches to take you on the four-dham pilgrimage—to Badrinath in the north, Puri in the east, Rameswaram in the south and Dwarka in the west. India is a land of 10,000 tirthas, according to Eck. In *The Hindus*, Wendy Doniger says tirthas are shrines where one can simultaneously cross over the river and the perils of the world of rebirth.

In *Hindu World*, Benjamin Walker speaks of thousands of holy places in India. The yatra is the 'going' and the tirtha the 'crossing'. Tirthas include the seven holy cites of Ayodhya, Mathura, Gaya, Banaras, Ujjain, Hardwar and Dwarka; according to the Hindu scriptures the seven holy rivers are the Ganga, Jamuna, Saraswati, Godavari, Narmada, Indus and Kaveri; the sacred hills and mountains include Kailasa, Paranath, Girnar, Mount Abu and Palani; the holy lakes include the Bindu in Siddhpur (Gujarat), Pampa near Hampi (Karnataka), Narayana in Kutch (Gujarat), Manasarovar at the foot of Mount Kailasa and Pushkar near Ajmer (Rajasthan). Pushkar, incidentally, is the only place which has a temple dedicated to Lord Brahma. Hindu scriptures imply that the merit of a pilgrimage is increased if the devotee chooses to make his journey more arduous, like hopping on one foot, crawling or walking on one's knees. Perhaps the concept of marrying adventure tourism and pilgrimages is waiting to happen. Walker says that though Saivites and Vaishnavites have their own designated holy sites, they often stop at the shrines of the rival group too on the way. Some also visit shrines devoted to Muslim saints, as is common in Ajmer where a Hindu visits the Brahma temple and seamlessly moves to the Ajmer dargah.

When Winston Churchill said, 'India is merely a geographic expression. It is no more a single country than the Equator,' what he did not know or acknowledge was that the land mass we call India had for millennia been united through mythology and religious travel.

Take, for instance, the travels of the ninth-century philosopher Shankara. The *Week* magazine (25 December 2011) traced his travels from Kalady, his birthplace in Kerala, to Omkareshwar on the banks of the Narmada, and also to Varanasi, Badrinath, Prayaga and Mahismati. His travels took him across the length and breadth of India, including Srisailam, Sringeri, Rameswaram and Tirupati in the south, Gokarna and Dwarka in the west, Puri and Kamarupa in the east and Kashmir in the north.

Or take the travels of Swami Vivekananda in the late nineteenth century (almost a thousand years after Shankara), again reported in the *Week* (30 December 2012). He too touched upon various corners of India, travelling to Kolkata, Varanasi, Almora, Rishikesh as well as to Alwar, Ahmedabad, Mahabaleshwar, Khandwa, Belgaum, Goa, Thiruvananthapuram, Kanyakumari, Chennai and Hyderabad.

In more recent times, the Bharatiya Janata Party (BJP) leader L.K. Advani too undertook a Swarna Jayanti Rath Yatra, which started on 18 May 1997 and lasted fifty-nine days. Advani covered 15,000 kilometres by road, through as many as twenty-one states and union territories. Starting from the August Kranti Maidan in Mumbai, the yatra covered all states, except for the north-eastern states which he covered in the second leg of his tour. The political leader addressed 750 scheduled public meetings besides speaking to the people assembled at various critical points. Just to draw a comparison, let us trace the journey: from Maharashtra to Goa, Karnataka, Kerala, Tamil Nadu, Andaman Islands, Andhra Pradesh, Gujarat, Rajasthan, Madhya Pradesh, Odisha, West Bengal, Bihar, Uttar Pradesh, Himachal Pradesh, Jammu and Kashmir, Punjab, Haryana and finally Delhi. In *My Country My Life*, Advani lists many cities where he addressed meetings. But I was disappointed not to find any mention of the famous temples he may have visited en route.

While Shankara's travels were purely religious, undertaken to rescue Hinduism from the ritualistic disrepute it had fallen into, Swami Vivekananda's journeys were aimed at spreading the word about ancient India and exhorting the continuing unity of the cultures of India. His travels were also undertaken to rescue India from its intense love affair with western civilization and its appeals.

As Indians embrace new modes of consumption, they are not giving up their ancient rites of prayer and pilgrimage. According to surveys published in two leading newspapers, 49 to 62 per cent of Indians surveyed claimed to have gone on a religious pilgrimage in 2010. No wonder religious tourism is on the top of the agenda of hotel companies. Carlson Hotels Worldwide has hotels in Katra, Hardwar, Shirdi and Badrinath. ITC's Fortune Hotel operates in Shirdi, Madurai and Tirupati to tap the growing affluent religious traveller. Some hotels even advertise luxury religious packages like this one from Leisure Hotels of Delhi: 'Make one journey an experience of many lifetimes. The Chardham Yatra, Yamunotri, Gangotri, Kedarnath, Badrinath . . . Perform an evening aarti, de-stress at our ayurvedic spa or simply wash away your sins in the private bathing ghat. Religious tourism gets the five star touch now.'

At the mass end of the spectrum, take the Mukhya Mantri Teerth Darshan Yojana offered by the Madhya Pradesh government. The state government claims to have launched this scheme to help elders fulfil their wish of visiting their dream places of worship; the advertisement lists 101 trains operated under this special scheme.

Apart from the traditional temple cities, we now have new temples getting built on a gigantic scale. The Bochasanvasi Akshar Purushottam Swaminarayan Sansthan (BAPS) has built 700 temples and 3300 centres worldwide over the past decade. In fact, the Akshardham temple in Delhi has been listed in the Guinness Book of World Records as the world's largest Hindu temple: built at a cost of Rs 200 crore over 100 acres of land, it attracts almost a lakh visitors a day. The *Hindustan Times* reported in 2008 that over 300 spanking new temples have come up in Gujarat alone in the past ten years.

Many Hindu families in India have been brought up with the concept of an ancestral village and an ancestral temple. As urbanization grows, Hindus seem to be adopting new 'kuladaivata' temples such as Tirupati and Vaishno Devi and thereby helping their numbers swell further.

Pilgrimage is not unique to Hindus.

Seven of the eight holy Buddhist sites are in India. These include Bodh Gaya (where the Buddha attained enlightenment), Sarnath (where he preached his first discourse) and Kushinagar (where the Buddha passed away). Sanchi hosts a Buddhist stupa erected by Emperor Ashoka in the third century BCE. Several Tibetan Buddhist sites in the Himalayan foothills of India such as the Rumtek monastery in Sikkim and Dharamsala, where the Dalai Lama resides, are also of great religious significance.

For Muslims, the dargah of the Sufi saint Khwaja Moinuddin Chishti in Ajmer is a major pilgrimage site. The Ajmer dargah and the dargah of Sheikh Salim Chishti in Fatehpur Sikri attract thousands of devotees of all faiths, not just Muslims. Other Islamic pilgrimage sites include the Jama Masjid in Delhi and the Haji Ali dargah in Mumbai. For the people of the Baha'i faith, the Lotus Temple in Delhi is of importance.

For Jainism, the Dilwara temples in Mount Abu as well as Paitana, Pavapuri, Girnar and Shravanabelagola are notable pilgrimage sites.

The Harmandir Sahib in Amritsar, the Golden Temple, is the most sacred gurdwara for the Sikhs.

While Protestant Christians with the exception of Anglicans do not go on pilgrimage, Catholics and the Orthodox visit places of pilgrimage, particularly during big festivals. The important centres include the St Thomas Cathedral in Chennai, St Xavier's shrine in Goa, the Basilica of Our Lady of the Mount in Mumbai and the Shrine Basilica of Our Lady of Health at Vailankanni in Tamil Nadu.

The relatively newer places of worship, which came up in the past hundred years, are the samadhi of Meher Baba in Meherabad, the Sai Baba temple in Shirdi and the Ramanasramam in Thiruvannamalai, Tamil Nadu.

Undoubtedly, the biggest of all pilgrimages is the Kumbh Mela on the banks of the River Ganga. In 1977 the bathing crowd was estimated at 1.5 crore and in 2013 this grew more than fivefold to 8 crore. This religious pilgrimage that occurs once in twelve years in Allahabad has been billed by the global media as 'the largest gathering on earth'. (The Haj pilgrimage to Mecca in 2012 saw around 3 million devotees, according to *Time* magazine.) Over fifty-five days, the administration had to manage 56 tonnes of garbage a day and set up a temporary electricity grid with 1.3 lakh connections. Besides, 250 doctors, fifteen field hospitals and 14,000 police officers were deployed to ensure the well-being of the devotees and visitors. Reportedly, the gathering at the Kumbh Mela was visible from outer space.

Many brands have been attempting to ride the religious tourism wagon. For instance, the 2013 Kumbh Mela saw brands like Lifebuoy and Tata Swach conduct special campaigns. While the former heat stamped the message 'wash your hands with Lifebuoy before eating' on chapattis, Tata Swach set up ten pure water distribution centres. Vodafone, Airtel and Idea offered special Kumbh tariff plans and Revital vitamin capsules distributed Hanuman Chalisa booklets.

The booming religious tourism does have its critics. The June 2013 disaster in Uttarakhand was of epic proportions and estimates for the death toll from the flash floods vary from 600 to 5000. *Business Standard* assessed the disaster management preparedness of four major pilgrimage sites, Vaishno Devi, Puri, Tirupati and Sabarimala. Though these sites attract annual pilgrims in millions and have annual income in hundreds of crores of rupees, some don't even have a robust insurance plan in place.

The Uttarakhand disaster has been a wake-up call. Places like Kedarnath and Badrinath have seen a fourfold increase in visitors in just a decade, the *Hindustan Times* reported in June 2013. It appears that not all centres are fully prepared to handle disasters. These disasters will become even more problematic to handle due to the unbridled exploitation of religious tourism. Seen in that light, the 2013 Kumbh Mela seems worthy of high praise and a case study at the Harvard Business School, as we will see in a later chapter.

As Indians grow wealthy they will want to travel more. The religious tourism industry is set to grow in many directions to cater to the various segments of the travelling population. Till now, the 'pilgrim crowd' was dominated by the lower-middle and lower classes. But this is set to change with the growth in the middle and upper-middle classes. Temple cities will now have a sufficient number of tourists wanting four- and five-star comforts. They will also want a more rich experience, not just a hurried darshan. So special experience centres will have to come up to keep these rich tourists in the pilgrimage city for an extra two days. There will be opportunity to combine the main temple visit with trips to nearby towns and villages, as an add-on bonus. Experts even predict the emergence of a new concept called 'religious amusement parks'. These parks will offer a lot more than just a darshan to make the trip truly memorable.

The other big trend will be numerous products piggybacking on the growth of the religious tourism industry. Just as we saw in the case of festivals, there are huge opportunities for brands here. Specially designed hotels, buses and bags are just one aspect. It is likely that mobile firms and consumer product companies will tailor special products for the religious tourism consumer. We saw mobile companies offering Kumbh Mela tariff plans. How about a Tirupati tariff plan or a Kedarnath one? Ready-to-eat food too can ride this growth wave with specially formulated food for pilgrims.

As an adjunct, we will also see the growth of 'virtual religious tours'. Online companies are today offering pujas and prayers at various religious centres.

Looking at the Indian penchant for pilgrimages, countries like Sri Lanka are repackaging their own offerings. In 2007 Sri Lanka's tourism ministry launched the Ramayana Trail, which became very popular after the civil war ended in May 2009. While Sri Lankan authorities were busy organizing 'ram kathas' and 'bhajans' for tourists, many people, including academicians and historians, were vocal in their criticism, calling the tours 'fictional' and a 'gimmick'. Though not all fifty listed sites have religious or even mythological significance, a few do stand out such as Munneshwaram, where Rama is believed to have erected a lingam as a penance for killing a Brahmin, Ravana, and Divurumpola, believed to be the place where Sita underwent her 'agnipariksha'.

Let me end with a story from my schooldays. Our school, Vidya Mandir (Mylapore, Chennai), organized an excursion for class ten students. Meticulously planned by our principal R. Srinivasan, it was an action-packed seven-day tour in a special bus. We visited Kanyakumari, Madurai, Tiruchi, Chidambaram, Tiruchendur . . . and that was when one of the boys raised a red flag. He complained that the tour had become a temple tour. Some hasty recalibration was done and RS, as R. Srinivasan was fondly called, took us to visit the elephant sanctuary at Thekkady. When I was checking the veracity of this story with my school friends recently, one friend reminded me that thirty of us had had to share a room meant for five in Thekkady.

I now realize that what our principal had planned was the ideal Indian tour, visiting various temples, tirthas and dhams. In fact, it was a perfect tour, with or without the elephants.

9. Why Do Women Pray More?

Aristotle maintained that women have fewer teeth than men; although he was twice married, it never occurred to him to verify this statement by examining his wives' mouths.

Bertrand Russell (1872–1970)

The woman in a traditional sari has her wet hair wrapped in a towel. A prayer plays in the background. Her pretty teenage daughter says, 'Amma, I want to show you something,' and lifts up her top to show the dragon tattooed on her back just above her waistline. And the pious-looking woman, much to our surprise, says, 'Nice, very nice.'

This Tata Docomo ad by our agency set up the situation of a clash between two generations by using religious music as a counterpoint to the jeans-clad teenager with a dragon tattoo.

Interestingly, someone flagged the fact that the ad could hurt the religious sentiment of orthodox Tamil Brahmins. So the company undertook consumer research to understand if there was any such danger. The ad was shown to men and women, young and old, Tamil Brahmins and non-Tamils. As expected, young women loved the ad. But, to our pleasant surprise, even older women found the situation quite harmless and humorous.

They recognized the religious music playing in the background and took no objection to it. We pray every day and our kids come with their latest problem just when we have started on our prayers, was the general drift of their feedback.

The question remains: Was it really necessary to cue morning and a traditional woman getting ready for prayer with the music? And do women really pray a lot more than men?

It is a commonly held belief that women pray much more than men and this myth is further propagated through our movies and ads. The Bollywood mom is often shown in her puja room at home and her prayers are always serene and pious. The woman dutifully prays for the well-being of the family. A woman at prayer is often meant to signify that it is in keeping with her image as a good woman, a good wife and a good mother. In contrast, when the hero prays, it is at a dramatic high point in the movie, maybe even an anticlimax. He is not praying as much as having a dialogue with god, be it the Hindi film idol Amitabh Bachchan or the Tamil icon Sivaji Ganesan. He is either complaining to god or asking for his mercy or seeking his help. The exception is when the hero is shown praying with great gusto as part of a group during festivities to celebrate the Govinda or Ganesha festival, or even a village festival organized to celebrate the local deity.

Studies reveal that both men and women pray with equal vigour in India. *Times of India*'s religiosity survey (26 November 2006) showed that about 29 per cent of men and 30 per cent of women pray every day. In another survey published in the *Hindustan Times* (25 January 2007), it was found that women were a bit more religious than men (42 per cent vs 37 per cent), but the difference may not be statistically significant. So do women really pray more? And if so, why?

What has the role of women in Indian society been and does this have something to do with their proclivity to prayer? There is no debate that women in India are given second-class treatment. So if they pray more, I would not be surprised. But how and when did we start treating our women this way?

In the Vedic period (c. 2000 BCE to c. 500 BCE), most religious rites and ceremonies were open to women, who had equal rights. They participated in all events and certain sacrifices were reserved for women, such as the Sita harvest sacrifice, the Rudrabali sacrifice to ensure fecundity of cattle and the Rudrayaga to secure good husbands. The Vedic period also produced eminent women scholars, poets and teachers. It was during the Puranic era that followed that the *Laws of Manu* came into vogue, decreeing that women had no right to read or study the Vedas. Manu also prescribed marriage customs, caste customs and more, which put an end to intermarriage among Aryans and Dravidians, as we saw in the chapter on weddings. With Manu's laws, things changed forever. The Bhagavad Gita too, revered and quoted for centuries, said, 'For, taking refuge in Me, they also, O son of Partha, who might be of inferior birth, as well as women, vaisyas, as well as sudras—even they attain to the supreme God.' This led some Indologists to say that the Gita denigrated women and lumped them with sinners and outcastes. The Taittiriya Samhita, yet another holy book, declared that a good woman is worse than a bad man. But it was possibly Manu's laws that did the maximum damage. So it can be surmised that the culmination of such disrespect and ignominious practices laid a heavy burden of guilt on Hindu women, driving them to abject submission. And maybe intense prayer.

As Mahatma Gandhi said, 'Hindu culture has erred on the side of excessive subordination of the wife to the husband. This has resulted in the husband usurping and exercising authority that reduces him to the level of the brute.'

Interestingly, Islam does not mete out such treatment to

women. The average Hindu tends to believe that a Muslim woman is not treated as well as a Hindu woman due to the imposition of the burqa, the myth of the four permissible marriages in Islam and the simple divorce procedure whereby all the man has to do to get rid of his wife is pronounce the word 'talaq' three times. But the reality is a bit different. One acid test is the sex ratio (proportion of women to men)—across the country, Muslims have a better sex ratio than Hindus. This is due in large part to the popularity of sex determination tests among Hindus in many parts of urban India. Sex determination tests are used to medically terminate pregnancies where the fetus is shown to be female, but equally abominable is the tendency of a section of Hindu households to pamper the boy child and starve the girl child. While sex determination tests are relatively uncommon among Muslims, recent data shows they too are now not averse to adopting such practices.

It is possible that Hindu women took to intense prayer as an escape route from a world that was not treating them fairly. In prayer they probably sought salvation, and in some sense this has continued to this day.

If women and men pray in equal measure, what about the young? It has been found that in many parts of the western world, especially Europe, teenagers are never to be seen near a church. This is not the case in the US and Latin America. In India too surveys show that the young are very religious. They may be a little less pious than their parents, but they do believe in many of the rituals of religion, including visiting temples, prayers and pilgrimages. In fact, self-help/health/spiritual books top their reading list (37 per cent) followed by history/current affairs (28 per cent), biographies/travel (21 per cent) and business management (14 per cent).

In the pan-India research I undertook, I couldn't find any

difference between men and women and young and old in how they perceive religion and how often they pray. Again, there is no big difference if we look at the more educated and the less educated, the more affluent and the less affluent. Across religions too there is no real difference among Muslims, Hindus and Christians. It is a myth that Muslims are a lot more religious than Hindus and Christians.

We are still left with the question of the role of women in Indian society. From the days of Manu till the Shah Bano case, how much has the Indian woman changed?

Sociologists have tried to study the changing role of women through extensive ethnographic studies. Changes have been tracked but the pace dramatically changed in the last twenty years. The role of an Indian (Hindu) woman is undergoing a dramatic transformation, both at home and outside. DraftFCB Ulka has done two landmark studies in the last decade to track the changes in Indian women. Called WomanMood I and II, the studies were done in 2000 and 2010 and involved discussions with hundreds of women across India to understand their hopes and aspirations, their fears and desires, and more. From the days that she saw her role as just a homemaker and a caregiver, the Indian woman now sees herself playing a pivotal role at home and outside. For instance, in the study done in 2000, WomanMood I, we found that a woman saw herself as a support to her husband, a caring mother to her children and an obedient daughter-in-law. Even working women we spoke to measured their self-worth through their roles at home: Is she a good cook? Does she care for her children well? Does her house look good? But when the study was repeated in 2010, WomanMood II, we saw several significant changes. From the days when women opted to work only to earn a little extra to give their children a better life (in *Audacity of Hope* Barak Obama says this is the same reason middle-class women in the US go to work), the attitude had changed dramatically. We found that almost all women, in big towns and small, wanted their daughters to study and adopt a career. They saw themselves as 'home managers' not 'housewives'. They felt that the husband should also look after their parents, and caring for the elderly should not be a one-way street. In many cases, the women were not working but had taken over a significant part of the financial management of the household. She did the banking work, paid the electricity and telephone bills, the tuition fees and liaised with the school and tutors, etc. Almost every day she went out on her own 'work'.

While WomanMood I and II highlighted the changes in Indian women, it is not as if it happened just over the last ten years. Changes had obviously been happening for a long period but our studies were done at an opportune time when the inflection point was reached.

What has brought about such a change? Are the Hindu women of India finally throwing off the shackles of Manu 2300 years later? What shape will this change take in the future?

The biggest catalyst of this change is the access to education that Indian women have had over the past five decades. The rising literacy levels of women, with a large number of them completing graduation studies, has played a major role in driving this change. The increasing penetration of television, satellite television and its myriad channels has also influenced this. In addition, I think the ubiquity of mobile phones has also been an important liberating force.

If we take the country as a whole, only about 20 per cent of women are part of the workforce; in upper-income classes, this is lower than 10 per cent. This will undergo a change in the coming decade. Many 'soft' professions are opening up for women and the presence of women in higher education is steadily increasing. It is lamentable that in leading educational institutions like the Indian Institutes of Technology (IITs) and Indian Institutes of Management (IIMs), the number of women has not changed dramatically in the last thirty years. During my days in IIT Madras, in the early 1970s, of the 250 students in my class only three were women. I am told the number is now close to 10 per cent. In my IIM-C class, women comprised 8 per cent; the number is now near 15 per cent. But the numbers are significantly better in other engineering colleges and business schools. In business schools like S.P. Jain and the Indian School of Business, where I teach, I have noticed that women comprise almost 40 per cent of the class. This is welcome and a sign of progress. It means that women are stretching out and reaching for higher levels of learning. I also think their parents have an important role in this. It is likely that the girl in a business school got the full support of her mother, who argued the case with her husband to ensure that he supported their daughter's decision to move to another city, stay in a hostel and spend big money on getting educated.

One perverse argument, as we saw earlier, is that parents are happy to send their girls to an institution of higher learning as that could reduce the dowry burden. I am not a subscriber to that point of view.

In the years to come, we will see Indian women playing an increasingly larger role in society, not just as caregivers but as workers, managers, doctors, engineers, technicians, authors, film-makers and more. This will bring new energy to a society that has for centuries subjugated her and prevented her from learning to read and write. I also hope that this will help improve the sex ratio in the country.

We started with a woman in prayer. Not let's look at another woman in prayer.

In Maharashtra, it is the custom for all family members to unite for Ganesha puja on the most auspicious day of the festival. Children working in faraway towns travel home to join in the family aarti. This ad for a telecom brand starts with a Ganesha puja. The mother is anxiously looking out of the window to see if her son has arrived. The mobile phone rings and the dad announces that the son has called to say he is stuck at the airport. Just then the son starts singing the Ganesha aarti mantras. The hymn flows into the house (thanks to the crystal-clear telecom network), and the whole family joins in, including the mother with a big smile. Would this have evoked the same sentiment if it was just any gathering? Or was the prayer needed as an emotional link between the mother and her son? You figure.

Finally, Indian society will have to decide how to treat women. Women, in turn, will have to figure out how to demand and get more rights. When our Delhi office was assigned to work on the new Hero 100-cc gearless scooter, they realized that there were already several in the market and Hero Pleasure would be yet another light scooter aimed at women. However, when they started talking to modern-day women, the eighteen-plus segment, they found that the scooter was not just a utilitarian vehicle but a great liberator. They realized that women who had a set of wheels felt equal to men. It was a clear sign to the outside world that they were in no way inferior to men. The line and the concept that finally captured her mood was, 'Why should boys have all the fun?', incidentally written by a lady creative director, Indu Pillai, an epitome of the modern, liberated Indian woman.

The days of Manu when women were prevented from learning are all but over. Let us welcome all the women of India as they join the men in this big playground of ours.

10. So Long and Thanks for All the Fish

If there is anything we are serious about, it is neither religion nor learning, but food.

Lin Yutang (1895–1976)

With due apologies to Douglas Adams, we Indians do eat a lot of fish.

It was 1998. This company had a unique product to sell. Live golden fish. These special fish were bred at a fish farm outside Chennai and the company had plans to set up sales centres across the city. It was indeed an interesting business model and a first for India. The fish farm was attached to a liquor manufacturing plant and the fish were fed from the waste generated by the unit. The business model seemed interesting and the company approached our agency for advice on how to market the fish. I was, however, not sure about the concept. First, Chennai was a largely vegetarian city and there was doubt about the potential of the product. Second, would people be interested in buying live fish?

But the sample survey we did across 300 homes told us that

over 80 per cent consumed non-vegetarian food and all of them ate fish—fresh fish that had been netted the same day and also dried fish sold in fish markets. The consumers interviewed felt that live fish was an interesting concept and were willing to try it out. This gave us the confidence to take the brand on to television and attempt a large-scale marketing campaign (though sales started picking up, the company abandoned the business since they did not feel it was scalable). Incidentally, the catchy tune for the ad was composed by a young musician called Dilip Kumar, who later went on to achieve worldwide acclaim as A.R. Rahman.

Globally, food and religion go hand in hand and we will see more of this in the chapter on the Muslim consumer. Most of us believe that India is a religious, vegetarian country. The reality is quite different from this perception. *Business Today* (10 December 2007) reports that 80 per cent of South Indians and 44 per cent of North Indians are non-vegetarian. This would come as a surprise to most Indians as the myth is that South Indians are predominantly vegetarian, probably arising from the prevalence of the idli–dosa culture and the ubiquitous vegetarian Udupi restaurants.

While the common perception is that all Brahmins are vegetarian, the Gowd Saraswat Brahmins and Bengali Brahmins eat fish at most meals. In fact, the Gowd Saraswats claim that they were given divine sanction to eat seafood when Maharashtra was hit by a bad drought.

The prevalence of greater vegetarianism in the North is indeed interesting, given the fact that Aryans were ardent non-vegetarians. Several Vedic sacrifices demanded the slaughter of bulls and pieces of the meat were eaten by the one who did the sacrifice. Beef formed a part of the Hindu diet during Vedic times even for rishis and Brahmins. In the Mahabharata, there are instances of cooks serving heroes venison and more. In the palace of Rantideva, two thousand animals were killed every day and the meat was distributed to Brahmins and mendicants. The food cooked for Draupadi's wedding included buffalo, goat, deer and fowl. The Valmiki Ramayana too says that meat was a regular item on the menu in Dasaratha's household. Rama's favourite dish was the flesh of birds and animals and Sita loved meat cooked with rice. Killing a cow to feed a guest was permitted and even encouraged, leading to the guest being called goghna, killer of cows. It is interesting that in the Bible as well the prodigal son was welcomed by his father with the slaughter of the 'fattened calf'.

The rise of Buddhism and Jainism from 500 BCE onward, and their propagation of ahimsa, or non-violence, led to a huge backlash against traditional Hindus. While higher-caste Hindus initially hung on to their beef-eating ways, rationalizing it as ritual sacrifice and the honourable way to treat a guest, the message of non-violence slowly took root. By the time Fa Hien visited India, in early fifth century CE, the upper castes had abandoned meat-eating. By the time the Puranic era started (third century BCE), a cow was seen as equal to god and believed to have been created the same day as Brahma. Killing a cow was equated to brahminicide and by the fourth century CE the Guptas had made cow-killing a capital offence. In Tamil Chola literature, there is the story of a king who executes his own son for an accidental, yes accidental, killing of a cow. Till 1947 cow-killing was punishable with death in Jammu and Kashmir. The change in the attitude towards meat may have also developed due to philosophical reasons as evident above. It could also be due to the changes in livestock breeding, grazing and ecology and a result of the changes in urban life in the Gangetic plain. The increasing uneasiness may have also been caused by the large number of animals sacrificed in larger and larger ceremonies. So the protest against meat-eating got reflected in the Upanishads, and even the Mahabharata.

So from being an ardent non-vegetarian, an Indian Hindu moved towards becoming a vegetarian or an occasional non-vegetarian who abhorred beef. I am not sure if the people who protest against beef are aware that they may still be carrying some evidence of beef-eating in their genes.

The Atharva Veda and the Chandogya Upanishad speak of three strands or qualities of matter (or gunas) woven together like three strands of a braid: lucidity or goodness or intelligibility (sattva), energy or activity or passion (rajas), and darkness or inertia or entropy (tapas). Classical Samkhya philosophy overlays this with several other concepts and says that sattva is thought to predominate in cows and Brahmins, rajas in Kshatriyas and horses, and tamas in dogs and the lower classes. Even today, yoga and Ayurvedic practitioners speak of three types of food. Sattvic food, also known as yogic food, consists of water, grains, legumes, milk, ghee, vegetable and fruits. It is seen as beneficial for mental clarity and equanimity of mind. Rajasic foods are seen as stimulant foods that create mental restlessness. They include spicy foods and intoxicating drinks. The third category is tamasic foods, also known as sedative foods, which lead to mental dullness. They include meat, fish, onion, garlic and spicy food. Yet another classification of foods in Hindu literature is 'cold' vs 'hot'. Some foods are seen as heat generating and some as cooling. For example, beans, tomatoes, sweet potatoes, yams, cucumbers and pumpkin are seen as 'cold' while white peppers, onion and garlic are seen as 'hot'. Pineapple, papaya, banana and citrus fruits are 'cold' while mango is 'hot'. This classification holds even among cereals: cooked and threshed rice, lentils, corn and nuts are 'cold'; wheat and millet are 'hot'.

We know that McDonald's had to seriously recalibrate their menu when they contemplated entering India. In fact, they had to completely eliminate beef from their menu; even lamb or mutton was moved out of most restaurants. In Mumbai, for the first time in the world, McDonald's opened an all-vegetarian restaurant.

The IT services industry, which was dominated by upper castes, had to face the vegetarian vs non-vegetarian divide in their canteens. Factory canteens have always had vegetarian and non-vegetarian food sections. In the 1980s, chicken was a delicacy served on Fridays for lunch at the Boots pharmaceutical factory in Sion, Mumbai. But IT firms stayed with all-veg menus for many years. I am told that of late they too have started offering non-veg dishes.

According to a report in the *International Journal of Consumer Studies*, consumption of seafood in India is affected by religion, family size, taste and age of family members. Religion and caste play a key role in determining our veg/non-veg orientation too. It is religion that determines some of our strange behaviour like going all vegetarian on some days. For instance, research has shown that the more religious consumer is more likely to eat seafood and other non-vegetarian food on Sundays, Wednesdays and Fridays when religion does not forbid them from eating meat. Many Hindus avoid non-vegetarian food on Tuesdays and Thursdays.

Imagine if you were in the airline industry or in the restaurant business. Or if you were running the office canteen. How will this behaviour affect your menu planning? Over time, I am sure these industries have figured out days when non-vegetarian food will have fewer takers.

Couple the veg/non-veg diet with the fasting routine and you end up with an algorithm with endless possibilities. Depending on the deity you worship, the date you observe a fast could differ. We have a colleague who fasts at least two days a week for various reasons.

There are of course the bigger fasts that are observed along with festivals like Karva Chauth, Shivratri, Lent and Ramadan.

Sociologists tell us that dress habits change fast but food habits change very slowly. We are seeing the rapid growth of new food formats in our country. The first foreign food to capture the imagination of the nation was noodles. Maggi made noodles a household name. The beef burger got modified to Indian tastes to become the chicken and potato burger, a bit like the vada pav. The next foreign food format to gain momentum was the pizza. Chances are over the next decade other forms like wraps, rolls and tacos will gain currency.

The bigger momentum will be the acceptance of non-veg food by traditional vegetarians. Till a couple of decades ago, an orthodox vegetarian would not be seen entering a non-vegetarian restaurant, at least in many parts of South India. So restaurants had to carry disclaimers of what they offered. In Chennai, non-vegetarian restaurants went by the name Military Hotel. At the upper end of fine dining, there are a few all-vegetarian restaurants in each city but you do have vegetarians going to a mixed-menu place. This will continue to grow. Modern format retail stores too are experimenting with non-veg food. Not all of them offer the whole range of meats in their cold section. They are also not sure if orthodox vegetarians will accept a pack of frozen peas if it is displayed next to cold cuts. My surmise is that this too will change. For instance, the Star Bazaar chain offers a whole range of non-veg food options in their freezer section.

India as a country, in my opinion, will become increasingly comfortable with non-veg food. Eggs will enter homes first, ideally as a special supplement for children. Other non-veg formats will follow, maybe in easy-to-cook styles. But unlike western consumers we may never accept eating non-vegetarian food at every meal. Even Muslim and Christian households in India do not eat non-vegetarian food at every meal.

As offices become the new melting pots of multiple customs, dietary habits too will undergo change, and veg and non-veg consumers will learn to coexist. I am told that the Military Hotel sobriquet is fast disappearing in Chennai as others too are relishing what was reserved for the 'military' till a few decades ago.

It is probably apt to remember here that the Government of India has mandated (through the Food Safety and Standards Act, 2006 and the Food Safety and Standards [Packaging and Labelling] Regulations, 2011) the labelling of all packaged food products—a green dot for vegetarian and a brown dot to indicate non-vegetarian. Products with milk were to carry a green dot while those with even egg in them were to sport a brown dot. I suspect this was instituted by an overzealous minister, driven by his urge to please his favourite guru. I am not sure if consumers are aware or bothered about this green/brown indication. In fact, some even believe that there is a red dot to indicate something more than egg in the product. And my submission is that all this may cease to register with the consumer in a few years as yet another item on the back of the pack, like calorific content, vitamins, etc. In fact, other labelling such as gluten-free, sugar-free, fat-free and vegan may be mandated and may crowd out these dots.

As India moves towards becoming more affluent, I see two trends taking root. The poor, who till now could not afford to eat meat, will move towards including some meat in their regular diet in addition to fish, which is their cheap source of protein. The affluent will become more and more health conscious and will swing towards vegetarianism, with maybe a touch of fish. Most Hindus, and even Muslims, do not have non-vegetarian food every day. This will not change. But I do see us becoming more homogenized in our dietary habits. Vegetarians will become more open to trying a bit of non-vegetarian food. And non-vegetarians will often stay vegetarian for purely health reasons. Interestingly, the concept of vegan, or eating products of non-animal origin, a trend that is spreading across the western world, is yet to grow roots in India. Chances are that Indians will not be able to stay away from milk and so veganism may not become a big trend in India in the near future.

During my days at IIT Madras there was a huge debate on vegetarian and non-vegetarian food. In our hostel (Godavari) mess, non-veg food was available as a special dish and you paid extra for it. Lunch was pure vegetarian, but for dinner we had fish on two days, chicken on one day and beef on two days, if my memory serves me right. This was the period 1972–77, before the Hindutva wave swept the whole country. These special dishes were served on all tables. So you could be having your all-vegetarian meal when a friend sat next to you with a plate of chicken or beef. While we had peaceful coexistence of veg and non-veg janta in Godavari, strange things were happening in the neighbouring hostel, Tapti. The vegetarians and the non-vegetarians were on a collision course and, much to the amusement of many of us, a curtain divided the mess with the two groups eating in their respective sections. I was the mess secretary of Godavari when all this was going on and could not fathom the problem. Much later, I realized that the veg–non-veg issue had become political and hence the curtains had to be drawn. Or was it the early signs of the Hindutva wave? Not sure.

Across India, fortunately, I think the curtains are being pulled away and we are embracing diversity of food habits with a lot of enthusiasm.

11. TeleRama To TeleDrama

In the Great Stories you know who lives, who dies, who finds love, who doesn't. And yet you want to know again. That *is their mystery and their magic.*

Arundhati Roy (b. 1961)

Zee TV created television history in India when it started offering Hindi entertainment 24/7. Riding the wave with programmes that tapped into Bollywood hit songs and films and engaging soap operas, Zee created a new genre of entertainment, prompting Star Plus to switch completely from English to Hindi. Years later Star Plus clawed its way back to the top of the charts with its blockbuster programme *Kaun Banega Crorepati*, and the man behind the idea of roping in the Bollywood icon Amitabh Bachchan as anchor was a soft-spoken young man from Kerala called Sameer Nair.

Zee faced a spirited challenge from Sony soon after. With some astute strategies and some course correction, Zee TV managed to rise in the television ratings game, overcoming the strong competition posed by Sony and Star Plus. In the course of ten years, Zee went on to pioneer several other genres of television entertainment in India to become India's No. 1 television network.

The Indian television market sees upheavals every five or seven years and, as can be expected, NDTV, a very successful news channel, decided to enter the choppy Hindi general entertainment waters with the launch of NDTV Imagine in January 2008. To head NDTV Imagine they roped in the same Sameer Nair.

This was the setting when the young CEO of Zee TV, Punit Goenka, called for a meeting with the agency. The question facing us was this: Would Sameer Nair pull it off again? The discussions veered around Sameer's big gambit to attract viewers of general entertainment channels. He was bringing back the Ramayana on television! This time round it was to be aired like any soap opera, four days a week, and not just on Sunday mornings.

Opinions around the table were divided. Some of us felt this was an interesting ploy to bring viewers to an unknown, new channel. Others were of the view that *Ramayan* had worked in a particular era and the current generation would not be keen on it. Some felt that religious mythologies would always work in India, given the high levels of religiosity; the increasing levels of wealth and education had not led to any reduction in crowds at temples. And there were those who said the new-generation Indians would need a different version of the Ramayana, not what was dished out by Ramanand Sagar in the 1980s.

The strategic thinkers felt that it would not be wise to jump on to the religiosity bandwagon and announce the telecast of *Mahabharat* to take on *Ramayan*. NDTV Imagine was launched with some interesting programming and *Ramayan* was expected to be their sure-fire hit. As it transpired, *Ramayan* did not evoke anywhere near the kind of response the original had.

Did this mean that Indian television viewers were now fed up with religion on television? Was Sameer Nair totally wrong? Well, the answer turns out to be a lot more complicated than that. When Star Plus launched their reincarnated second channel, Life OK (the earlier experiment with their second general entertainment channel, Star One, had flopped), it too played the religious card. But with a different god: Shiva. And what a success it has been!

The serial *Devon ke Dev...Mahadev* premiered on 11 December 2011 and soon caught the fancy of the viewers, young and old. Broadly based on the Shiva Purana, the serial has managed to give the old mythological stories a modern flavour. It has etched the character of Shiva, the ultimate macho god of the Hindu pantheon, in a more humane form. As a result, the serial has a tremendous following even in blogosphere.

Thinking back, it is possible that NDTV Imagine was on to an interesting idea but they did not execute it right. Or, as they say in show business, Life OK just lucked on to something that viewers were looking for.

Amish Tripathi, author of the blockbuster Shiva trilogy, should get a lot of the credit for bringing a modern Shiva into the collective consciousness of the English-reading public. And now that the novels are available in numerous Indian languages, he has reinvented Shiva for the modern Indian. *Devon ke Dev... Mahadev* has capitalized on the momentum he had generated and taken Shiva to the masses. It was not as if Shiva was new to television viewers. *Om Namah Shivay* was originally aired on Doordarshan in 1997 and ran across many languages for many months. So while reincarnating Shiva, Life OK seems to have done something right.

The success of programmes like *Devon ke Dev...Mahadev* is making religion sound cool to today's young Indians. Some people call it Shiva chic. The growth of the Shiva cult has had its effect on music, T-shirts and even tattoos. As Mohit Raina, the actor who plays Mahadev, says, 'People don't tell me I look divine, they tell me I look sexy. Mahadev doesn't have devotees, he has fans.' He connects across age groups. Everyone wants to own him in his or her own way.

In *Being Indian* Pavan Varma speaks of the rich legacy of mythologies and gods that Hinduism offers storytellers. The Vedas recognize thirty-three gods and the Puranas offer a staggering 330 million. The Hindu, he says, has no dearth of divinities to keep him busy; so long as they can fulfil his desires, the average Hindu is not interested in understanding the epistemological nature of reality.

In a sense, the earliest sources of stories are the Vedas, which are Aryan. The Ramayana and the Mahabharata have preserved both Aryan and local legends and the Puranas enshrine an abundance of local traditions. It is said that primitive people do not invent stories out of thin air, for their own amusement or entertainment, but often spin them to explain phenomena, preserve a tradition or justify an ancient rite. The euhemeristic theory explains that myths are really garbled versions of real events, and have their roots in history. The heroes are, in fact, cultural icons and kings of remote ages. Another theory says that myths are externalized stories of human psyche and represent the vast subconscious and other thoughts that have permeated the past.

There are other beliefs too—that the ancient gods are personifications of heavenly bodies (Surya is the sun, Rudra is Saggitarius, Dhruva is the Pole Star), that they represent terrestrial phenomena (Rudra is thunder, Rahu the eclipse) or the powers of nature such as procreation and fertility (Shakti is the force of growth, Shiva of generative power, Sita of ploughing and agriculture) and so on. Essentially, Indian mythologies are full of stories, characters, gods and devils that can be reimagined, recast and retold to make thousands of television serials and movies.

No wonder, from the original *Ramayan* to the latest *Devon...*, religious mythologies continue to be a staple feature on Indian television. Numerous characters have been assayed on television across multiple languages and this will continue. As they say in television entertainment, to launch a new general entertainment channel, you need a reality show with a big star, a couple of soap operas and one historical or mythological show. And a lot of luck.

Are mythology-based serials the only form of religion on television?

Anurag Batra, chairman of the Exchange4Media group, traces the rise of a new genre of television to 2005, the year channels like Aastha, God, Zee Jagran and Sanskar were launched. Today we have well over fifty religious channels. These 24-hour channels, telecast in multiple languages, offer viewers a range of programming with the top categories being yoga, Ayurveda, kirtan (singing), astrology and live telecasts of sermons. It has been reported that this genre grew at the rate of 30 per cent per annum from 2011 to 2013. These channels make their revenue by selling time slots to various religious organizations. A 20-minute slot is sold at the rate of Rs 2 lakh to Rs 10 lakh a month to gurus (the rates depend on the popularity of the guru). Product categories like food items, agarbattis, travel/tours find religious channels a cost-effective, targeted medium to invest in.

To get an idea of how far the Indian religious television market can grow, take a look at the biggest religious media market in the world—the United States. Trinity Broadcasting Corporation, the world's largest Christian television channel, is valued at $800 million. The channel owns seventy-eight satellites and broadcasts religious content to every continent except Antarctica. The total number of Christian radio channels in America exceeds 1500 and there are over 250 TV channels broadcasting religious messages. If the US is ahead of the game, India is doing a lot to catch up.

From 2005 to 2013, we went from zero to fifty TV channels and chances are we will get to 250 soon enough. Radio is a bit tricky since FM licences are being doled out rather slowly; if that opens up, we may well have an FM station attached to every big temple in every big town in India.

We are seeing a huge upsurge of religious content on television in India, not just on special channels but also on general entertainment channels. In a sense, these feed on each other. Can the Internet be far behind?

In April 2013 Carmelites Mary Immaculate (CMI) priests, who published the first Malayalam daily, *Deepika*, in 1887, launched a 24-hour Catholic web channel, www.livingfaithchannel.com.

With all this action, can big brother cinema be left out of the feast? The first film produced in India was *Raja Harishchandra*, based on the eponymous mythological king. From 1913, when the film was made, to now, Bollywood and regional cinema have offered viewers an endless array of religion-based films. One of the biggest superhits of all time is the low-budget *Jai Santoshi Maa* released in 1975. It chronicled a little-known goddess and made the temple, situated four kilometres from Karwar town in Karnataka, an instant must-visit destination. In recent times, films like *Hanuman* and *Bal Ganesh*, both computer animated, have managed to capture the imagination of urban children by making mythological characters resonate in a modern computer graphic avatar.

As we saw, the old Ramanand Sagaresque treatment of religious mythologies can no longer work. However, if new-age scriptwriters can spin a story that can make the godlike character connect with the modern audience, there is a higher likelihood of success. We can expect the Mahabharata to come back to us with stories spun on individual characters. A case in point is the Chhota Bheem franchise that has run on the kiddie network Pogo

Turner for an amazing 148 episodes of 30 minutes each. It has
also spun a great opportunity in franchising revenue with DVDs,
T-shirts, water bottles, toys and even food products. There is a
story to be told with Arjun or Karan or Panchali as the central
character. Who next as an animated character? Vali and Sugreev
from the Ramayana? Can youngsters be made to play a video
game that captures the Mahabharata war? Who would you play?
Arjun? Abhimanyu? Karna?

One of the biggest hits on Malayalam television in recent times
was *Sri Guruvayurappan*, a series based on the legend of the deity
in Guruvayur. In a similar vein, movies and television serials
based on Shirdi Sai Baba have worked well in Marathi television.

I would submit that there is a lot more left from where all
this is coming from. And there are astute writers digging them
all up for us. Ashok Banker probably started the trend when
he attempted to rewrite the Indian mythological stories in a
modern-day template. The first of the series, expected to go on
to 100 volumes, was based on the first part of the Ramayana.
The *Prince of Ayodhya* was published in 2003. Banker, who has
won widespread acclaim, has churned out over a dozen books
but not all have been received with equal enthusiasm. He claims
that his books have sold over 1.8 million copies.

Interestingly, thought leaders of each era have attempted to
interpret the Ramayana for their generation. C. Rajagopalachari
(Rajaji) presented the Ramayana and Mahabharata in simple,
readable format in English and Tamil for the freedom-fighting
generation. Mahatma Gandhi wrote an interpretation of the
Bhagavad Gita. So had Swami Vivekananda, a century earlier.

Following Ashok Banker, there has been a new generation of
writers who have very diligently combined religious thought with
contemporary ideas. Amish Tripathi's first book, *The Immortals
of Meluha*, did not have any takers initially since publishers

could not classify the work. Was it fiction? Was it religion? Was it a thriller? But his success has been simply astounding, and is testimony to his great storytelling style, which caters to the growing appetite for Indian writing on Indian themes, coupled with some astute marketing. Yet another writer, Ashwin Sanghi, has combined religious ideas with crime thrillers like *The Krishna Key*. Devdutt Pattanaik has also tapped the appetite for Indian mythologies. His bestseller *Business Sutras* nicely weaves traditional Hindu concepts with business strategy.

Comics are playing the game as well. Amar Chitra Katha did not reinvent itself for the modern era and is still a pale shadow of what it once was. But other publishers like Vimanika Comics have published some Shiva books and even licensed rights to the Swiss publisher Zampango Comics for publication in French and German for sale in Europe. Clamp is an all-female manga artist group that was formed in the mid 1980s. They have sold over 100 million books or tankōbon. Interestingly, the first manga was the *RG Veda*, which was released in 1989 and went on for ten volumes. The story featured elements of Vedic mythology. So don't be too surprised if Indian mythology forms the basis of the next series by J.K. Rowling.

As books and comics abound, there will be great opportunities for doing a complete 360 degree offering to the religious-minded consumer. Imagine a television series based on a temple in a remote town; couple that with a packaged tour to that town and add to that a book, music CD, T-shirts. You will end up offering full salvation. Can we take a character and make it younger? Can we take a figure and make it a magical superman, say Super Arjun? Can we take a woman character and give her special powers and immense sex appeal, Draupadi Max?

If I ever make a movie or television series based on a religious theme or temple, I would like to be in a position to offer those interested a way to get there—so a travel service provider is an ideal partner. I would also like to offer merchandise of that theme, so a retailer becomes a licensee, a radio station can become a partner if it can offer exclusivity of coverage and so can television channels. By bringing together all these players of the god market, I will be able to hedge my bets. I am sure many such plans are being hatched even as you read this book.

The combinations can be endless, and greatly rewarding.

To close this chapter on television and cinema let us recall the name of the most successful television production company in India: Balaji Telefilms, founded by Ekta Kapoor, daughter of the matinee idol Jeetendra and Shobaa Kapoor. At the entrance to their office is a large idol of Balaji, Lord Venkateshwara of Tirupati. The morning prayers are attended by Shobaa Kapoor. Obviously, her prayers are working their magic as Balaji keeps producing one mega hit after another.

12. Riding the Puja Boom

Prayer is not an old woman's idle amusement. Properly understood and applied, it is the most potent instrument of action.

Mahatma Gandhi (1869–1948)

We were assembled in the conference room of our client in Pune. The company, a global major in home care and insect repellents, was having a tough time breaking into the Indian market. The young marketing head of the company wanted our team to sit with him, his CEO and his key team members as they brainstormed. The day's discussion was air purification. The company had launched aerosol air fresheners in the Indian market and, given the price of aerosol cans, the product did not have many takers.

The company had pioneered several innovations in air freshening around the world. They had reinvented the fragrant candle category in the US, pulled it out of mom-and-pop hobby shops and taken it to mainstream stores like Walmart. They had also pioneered new concepts like electrical liquid air purifiers. But many of their products were tailored to more affluent western homes. The climatic condition and air-conditioning/heating were qualifiers that made their products big sellers in the West.

What about India?

The company had done a fair amount of research in India and it was clear that only a minuscule number of homes were air-conditioned. So windows were kept open except for a few winter months in the northern parts of the country. Given household income levels, products like fragrant candles and liquid air purifiers were unaffordable. The question came down to this: What do consumers do to make their home smell nice?

It turned out that Indians lit agarbattis every morning and every evening. The ritual was religious, the puja, but the after-effect was that the home smelt good. The CEO of this company had spent a long time in the Far East and was intrigued by this phenomenon. His experience from the Far East was that Buddhist consumers used three joss sticks when they prayed but the sticks had no fragrance. It emitted just smoke. His understanding was that the smoke rising into the air signified the human soul reaching out to Buddha. He was intrigued about the incense sticks Indians used at home.

The marketing team had collected a set of incense sticks that were brought out for burning and smelling. Price ranges were discussed and the company felt that they should compete at the top end with a product that would be made using the same technology as the joss sticks of Thailand, but with a strong fragrance.

When it came to advertising, we were told to stay away from religious overtones. The creative team came up with what I thought was a wonderful bridge position, one that could sound secular to the atheist/agnostic, and religious to the believer: Start the Day in a Positive Way with ABC Incense Sticks.

The brand was launched in attractive window packs and pouches. The initial sales response was very encouraging. Unfortunately, the company decided to pull out of India due to the global economic slowdown.

Newspaper reports estimate the global incense stick market at Rs 4200 crore and that Indian companies, mostly perfumeries and the cottage industry sector, account for 40 per cent of that. I remember reading that almost all homes burn incense sticks every day. So the market could be bigger especially if consumers start upgrading to better quality incense sticks.

The incense stick market in India has been dominated by a few family-owned firms. A few decades ago, these firms did experiment with radio advertising; brands like Sugandha Shringar may ring a bell with some older readers. The other brand that seems to have done a bit of brand building is Cycle Brand. More recently ITC managed to launch their own incense sticks, Mangaldeep, and with a dose of professional marketing made it a success. Mangaldeep has even launched a 'Fragrance of Temple-Gold Tradition' with a golden temple on the pack. The ad says, 'Add a touch of gold. Add a touch of tradition. The timeless traditions of India come alive with Mangaldeep Fragrance of Temple-Gold Tradition agarbattis. These skilfully made agarbattis give an enchanting fragrance and add serenity to your prayer.'

Incense is supposed to be one of the sixteen items to be offered as part of a typical Hindu prayer. In Islam, burning of incense is part of the prayer routine, but with no religious significance except for creating a fragrant atmosphere.

Most Indians buy unbranded incense sticks and there is a great opportunity out there—they could switch to branded agarbattis if the product offers better quality and value.

In *The Wonder That Was India*, A.L. Basham explains that the basic rite of the Vedic religion was the sacrifice (yajna or homa) and that of Hinduism is worship (puja). In general, a god is worshipped in the form of an icon (arca) that is sanctified by special rites after which it is believed that divinity has in some sense taken abode in it. While Vedic literature speaks of the Vedic sacrifice in great detail it does not discuss the puja ritual.

Central to the puja ritual is the use of an idol. Typical puja practices include invocation of the deity, bathing of the idol and an offering of fresh clothing, sandalwood paste and other unguents. Incense, flowers or flower petals, lit lamps, food and drink and other paraphernalia are also offered to the deity.

There are several opportunities in the puja market waiting to be tapped because of the number of items used in the ritual and they could all be branded.

If you thought branding incense sticks was tricky, how about *Elaeocarpus ganitrus* Roxb., better known as rudraksha beads? The seeds of the rudraksha fruit were originally found only in Nepal and Southeast Asia. Counterfeit rudraksha beads are sold near temples in India at all kinds of prices. So here's a company that saw this as an opportunity and offered authentic rudraksha beads. The brand Rudra Life has prominent advertisements for their authentic seeds. The company is reported to have organized more than 500 exhibitions in India, the US, UK, Singapore and Malaysia. To build a brand myth, the company declared itself the caretaker of the rudraksha tree of Nepal origin at Trimbakeshwar, Nashik, and is also opening a museum there to educate people regarding the various properties of the rudraksha. Their competitor, Rudra Shakti, talks of how a rudraksha has astrological relevance and can even be matched to your date of birth. I had heard of sun-sign-related precious stones, but this was the first I learnt of matching a rudraksha to date of birth.

It is likely that there will be many more opportunities to tap into the needs of the religious-minded. Puja books and CDs are already big sellers. Fabindia even sells readymade dhotis that can be used during religious functions such as pujas and festivals. I am sure manufacturers can explore the potential of puja utensils made with the right amount of copper or silver. How about a full kit that will contain all that you need for an aarti to be performed at home? Would that not make a good gift to a couple moving into a new home? There are endless possibilities with Indians wanting to move out of the traditional frugal way of doing a puja to a more elaborate, expensive way of embracing tradition.

Many years ago, the only way to perform an elaborate puja was to invite a scholarly purohit/Brahmin to come and perform it for you at your house. Then came books that gave you step-by-step instructions. Now we have video CDs that can show you what needs to be done. Soon, there will be smartphone apps to tell you the same. In the future, I suspect we could even have a purohit do a puja via video Skype. In the bigger cities of India, it would save the purohit a great deal of time. And a purohit sitting in Mumbai could well guide the devotee in New Jersey. As we start adapting, we could even have a purohit in a hologram, helping us perform the puja.

The Indian diaspora is thirsting for a quick dose of religiosity. The increasing popularity of 'online puja' and 'online darshan' could pave the way for 'online Veda' and 'online Gita'. Already, there are several services that offer online instructions in Hindustani and Carnatic music. Just as massively open online courseware or MOOCs are changing the way education is being delivered across the world, we may see MOOPs, or massively open online pujas, becoming popular.

The other day I was walking out of Mumbai's Matunga Ayappa Samaj temple and stopped to look at the products displayed at the shop abutting the temple. The shop sells most of the stuff you need for a puja—cotton dhotis, rudraksha chains, religious CDs, trays, etc. I also noticed that this shop was selling sandal powder made by P.A. Iyer's Kamala Vilas of Thrissur, Kerala. I smiled. P.A. Iyer happens to be my father's uncle. He set up Kamala Vilas to make traditional Ayurvedic medicines and beauty products well over eighty years ago. At sixteen, he perused Ayurvedic books and learnt how to make authentic products the traditional way. He started with the traditional Indian eyeliner, the kajal, and soon expanded to hair oil and other products. And somewhere down the line he also started offering products used in prayer, like sandal powder. He passed away two decades ago, having lived a full life of a hundred years, maybe aided by the many prayers people were performing with his products. His company continues to thrive, now under the management of the third generation. Will they become marketing savvy and take their products global? I often pray that they do.

13. God Okay, Gandhi Not Okay

Your idol is shattered in the dust to prove that God's dust is greater than your idol.

Rabindranath Tagore (1861–1941)

Ajay Kumar (name changed) had dropped into my office for a cup of tea and we got talking about the Gulf market and how his company was doing. He was the regional head for the famous Swiss brand of pens, Mont Blanc. He knew my love for fountain pens and was regaling me with stories about their new range. Just as he got into full flow, I stopped him and told him that I had a huge bone to pick with his company. Mont Blanc had the previous year (2009) launched a limited edition Mahatma Gandhi pen. The pen, priced at an exorbitant Rs 1 lakh, was said to have a pure silver body with a khadi texture. The company had got the endorsement from one of Gandhi's grandsons and promised to donate Rs 10,000 per pen sold to a designated Gandhian charity. I felt the company had destroyed whatever goodwill they had in the market by adopting a blatantly cheap gimmick. They should have either given away all the money to charity or kept quiet about the charity angle. I suppose it is difficult to bridge the gap between a product synonymous with luxury and exclusivity and a man who stood for simplicity and common good. As I was finishing my tirade, my dear friend and colleague Dorab Sopariwala, the founding managing director of MARG (Marketing and Research Group), who now serves as an independent consultant, walked in. I introduced Ajay as the man from Mont Blanc and, without waiting for a minute, Dorab too started a diatribe—on the very same topic.

Poor Ajay! He bore the brunt of the attack with a smile and went on to explain how this pen was the idea of Mont Blanc's Indian distributor. Unfortunately for Mont Blanc, it did attract a lot of negative press, including a scathing article in the *Economic Times* penned by the astute Vikram Doctor. A public interest lawsuit followed and the court ordered Mont Blanc to stop selling the pens in India. I was told that the pens were available in the Middle East at attractive rates.

As I ruminated over this issue, I was struck by a different thought. Why did we Indians react so violently to a Mont Blanc Gandhi pen and not to a Swarovski crystal-studded Lakshmi or a Lladro Ganesha?

When did this idol fever come to India? While some experts believe that idolatry was always a part of Hindu religion, some believe that Vedic Aryans did not practise idolatry. The Jabala Upanishad says, 'Images are meant only as aids to meditation for the ignorant.' Some experts argue that there are references to idols or images of gods in Vedic hymns. Possibly, the Vedic Aryans learnt of idols from Indians and in due course became full-fledged idol worshippers. The Ramayana mentions idol worship. While early Buddhism frowned upon idol worship, it soon accepted the image of Buddha as an idol to be worshipped, albeit in a less elaborate fashion than a Hindu puja described earlier. Apparently, Hellenic influences had a role in the mass production of Buddha images in North India. Hindu scriptures speak of the special qualities of the material used for making idols—each piece of wood or stone or metal or mineral has to have specific virtues and special invocations are to be made before an idol is created.

Idolatry has been roundly condemned by religious reformers, including Periyar of the Dravida Kazhagam, the party that gave birth to the two leading political parties in Tamil Nadu. But idolatry has had its fans even among the intelligent. Gandhi, who was a true child of Hinduism, had little distaste for idolatry and justified it as a harmless aid to worship. Swami Vivekananda too justified idol worship saying 'human beings hav[e] the need to perceive via the senses'.

While Islam abhors idolatry, Indian Christians do have a penchant for images and idols, but to a lesser degree than their Hindu brethren.

It is but natural that, with increasing affluence, Indians are also willing to splurge on expensive idols, not necessarily the types described in the holy scriptures.

Leiber, a fashion brand, recently arrived in India with the Ganesha minaudière, a handbag studded with 12,000 Swarovski crystals and priced at an eye-popping Rs 2.6 lakh. The Spanish porcelain luxury brand Lladro claims that religion as a segment contributes to about 30 per cent of their total sales in India. Their Spirit of India collection includes the goddess Lakshmi, the Veena Ganesha, Bansuri Ganesha, Dancing Ganesha and the Radha Krishna priced between Rs 55,000 and Rs 2.5 lakh. Ma Passion, which makes idols with precious stones, has a Ma Passion Ganesha idol in adventurine (popularly known as Indian jade) for, hold your breath, Rs 25 lakh. Indian jewellers always knew of the potential of gods cast in gold and silver. Now, we are seeing international brands too jumping on to the religion bandwagon with all kinds of materials, not just gold and silver.

The Austrian brand Swarovski has offered their crystals to producers who want to decorate religious figurines.

The Gitanjali lifestyle group seems to be experimenting with the religious gifting market in earnest. It has even created a brand with a foreign-sounding name, Adler & Roth, to tap the growing premium idol market. Adler & Roth has a divinity collection and the advertisement says that the images are 'Handcrafted by generations of Master Craftsmen, using resin and the finest clay from the riverbeds of the holy Ganges and the purist (sic) of pure sterling Silver and brass. The Divinity Collection brings a rich heritage of traditional elegance to the beauty of your home.' It is a bit like the apparel brand Peter England, which was created in Bangalore by Madura Coats and is close to 10,000 kilometres from England. Chances are that many other jewellers will also jump on to this exotic bandwagon.

In yet another innovation, Gitanjali Gems has set up an ATM-type vending booth in Mumbai's Siddhivinayak temple. The vending machine dispenses gold and silver coins of various sizes with the images of the temple's reigning deity. This is an interesting experiment since it capitalizes on the immediacy of a temple visit with the purchase of an expensive gold or silver memento. Till now, the temple used to sell ceramic and marble figurines. While they used to have on sale small coins with the Ganesha figure on it, setting up a dispensing machine is a first. I only wonder if the purchase of a god-themed gold or silver coin from a vending machine can by any stretch of the imagination be construed as a sign of piety. But then we are living in a fast-changing, tech-savvy material world. We collect our Lakshmi, the goddess of wealth, every week from an inanimate machine, the ATM. So why not a coin with a Lakshmi impression on it? Those of you who have been to Las Vegas would have been fascinated by the array of slot machines that greet you at the airport. So here is a suggestion, how about a Venkateshwara coin vending machine at Tirupati airport, just in case you forgot to pick up a coin for your friends at the temple!

If crystals are already here, can luxury watches be far behind? Century, a luxury brand from Rodeo Drive, has launched a Lord Venkateshwara watch and here are its specifications: red gold 18 carat; white dial set in diamonds, rubies and emeralds; Swiss movement/automatic; leather strap; gold deployment clasp; and limited to just 333 pieces; price available on request.

While Hindutva activists are quick to raise a red flag against Valentine's Day, they seem to have no qualms with a Ganapati that is probably handcrafted by a beef-eating Spaniard.

The market for luxury goods with a religious-theme is going to explode in India and Lladro seem to have latched on to an early trend. When Indians want to indulge in luxury goods, it is likely that they also look for some indication of value. So a premium watch which is silver or 18 carat gold gets better acceptance. By bringing in a religious angle, luxury marketers can bridge this value chasm in the mind of an Indian consumer. For instance, a premium handbag with an inlay of a silver Lakshmi could work miracles. Similarly, a premium silverware brand could tap this idol fever by coming out with an Indian mythology collection.

There is yet another big opportunity that religious-themed gifts are harvesting. People in positions of power get a lot of expensive gifts. A friend who runs a Swiss brand of watches in India speaks of the absurd volumes they sell to contractors who have to keep a lot of people happy. If you run over a pothole in monsoon-hit Mumbai, remember the pothole was probably 'covered' with an expensive Swiss watch. But a watch can be passed along. So a lower-level babu in the government can gift that watch to a big babu and so on. Interestingly, religious figurines are a lot more difficult to give away. You would notice that most homes sport numerous Ganesha figurines, and chances are that more than half are gifts received from friends and relatives. Even in corporate settings, it has become quite okay to gift a religious-themed object like a Ganesha or Saraswati idol. I don't remember seeing such gifts in the past, but then gifts those days were at best boxes of sweets and pens.

This brings us back to the original question: Why did a section of society react so violently to a Mont Blanc Gandhi pen? I doubt we would have reacted the same way if Mont Blanc had launched a Ganesha pen or a Saraswati pen.

I suspect Mont Blanc blindly chose to ride a horse and discovered, much to their chagrin, that the horse was a wild one. If they had launched a range of Indian god-themed pens, they may have had a success and not red ink on their hands.

14. Every Fifth Indian Will Be Muslim

The extinction of race consciousness as between Muslims is one of the outstanding achievements of Islam, and in the contemporary world there is, as it happens, a crying need for the propagation of this Islamic virtue.

Arnold J. Toynbee (1889–1975)

'Mr Rafi will see you now,' said Ravi, the long-serving assistant of M.M. Rafi, founder-chairman of Light Roofings Ltd, a Chennai-based company specializing in economical roofing sheets for low-cost houses, poultry/cattle sheds and small-scale industrial sheds. I knocked gently and walked in. I had made it a habit to meet with senior client executives at least once in three months. Mr Rafi smiled, and said, 'Sir, please sit down, I will be with you in a moment,' and went back to what he was doing. I observed he was working with a calculator and was jotting things down in a small black notebook. After a few minutes, he closed his book, smiled and offered me the usual cup of tea. I accepted and went on to speak about the general economy and the state of the industry. After we discussed market dynamics, the building market and his diversification plans, I was all set to leave. But I could not help myself and had to ask him, 'Sir, what were you so busy doing when I walked in? If it is confidential, I apologize.' Mr Rafi responded by asking me what I knew about his religion, Islam. I confessed that though my branch head in Hyderabad was a Muslim as was my neighbour in Chennai, I knew very little except that they prayed five times a day and their festival Ramadan. Mr Rafi proceeded to patiently explain the concept of zakah or zakat, the purification of wealth, practised by prosperous Muslims. He said his religion prescribed that each Muslim contribute 2.5 per cent of his annual wealth to the poor and needy. Interestingly, he combined this with his annual tax routine and while his auditors computed the taxable income he worked out the 2.5 per cent zakat and the charities that he would contribute his money to. These were noted down each year in that little black book.

I was so enamoured by the concept of zakat that I decided to become an honorary Muslim by contributing 2.5 per cent of my annual income to charities that my wife decides on.

Many months later, I thought back on that incident and realized how little I knew about the customs of our Muslim brethren. According to the 2001 Census, Muslims number around 160 million, and comprise 13.4 per cent of the total population of the country. The population of Muslims has grown from around 10.7 per cent (Census 1961) to 13.4 per cent in 2001 and to 14.6 per cent in the 2011 Census, says the Cogito India 2061 report. The report estimates Muslims will make up 19.3 per cent of India's population by 2061; the *Economic and Political Weekly* (10 March 2007) estimates that by the turn of this century Muslims will account for 20 per cent of the country's population. Among the states, in Jammu and Kashmir, Muslims comprise over 60 per cent of the population and according to the 2001 Census Muslims make up more than 20 per cent of the population of Uttar Pradesh, Assam, Bihar and Kerala or are fast approaching those levels. So it makes sense for any business to understand a bit more about Islam.

The first Muslims arrived on the coast of Malabar in the eighth century and settled down as traders and proselytizers. Punjab was conquered by the Turks in the eleventh century, and the first sultanate in Delhi was established in the thirteenth century. But Islam probably took root in India with the founding of the Mughal Empire by Babur in 1526. The imposition of the jaziya, the tax to be paid by all non-Muslim males, may have also helped in the growth of Islam.

Islam has five key pillars—Shahada, the declaration of faith that there is no god but Allah, and Muhammad is his messenger; salat, or five daily prayers; saum, fasting during the Ramadan month; zakat, which Mr Rafi explained to me; and Haj, the pilgrimage to Mecca which is to be performed by Muslims once in their lifetime if they can afford it, financially and physically.

In terms of numbers, India has the third largest Muslim population in the world (after Indonesia and Pakistan). Almost 80 per cent of Indian Muslims belong to the Sunni school of theology, but we also have the largest population of Shia Muslims outside Iran. So not only are we a multicultural, multi-religious country, we seem to have a nice admixture of schools coexisting even in each religion.

The increase in global Muslim population and their growing wealth has been the subject of debate in western media. Global estimates put the number of Muslims at 1.8 billion and, given their growth rate, the global ad agency Ogilvy estimates that Muslims will comprise 50 per cent of the world population by 2050.

Marketers are trying to understand the phenomenon of the Muslim consumer and there are numerous reports in the media on the size of the markets and their potential. Ogilvy did a fascinating study, Ogilvy Noor, in partnership with TNS, a leading global marketing research firm. The study covered the four key Muslim markets of Malaysia, Egypt, Saudi Arabia and Pakistan and highlighted the growing confidence of Muslim consumers and their willingness to 'adapt' their religion to individual needs.

Financial markets are getting their arms around what is known as Islamic banking. The basic principles of finance under sharia law prohibit any transaction that involves paying interest and ban investment in certain economic sectors such as gambling and pornography. Under the law, investors and recipients of the investment must share any risk, and transactions have to be underpinned by tangible assets. *Newsweek* reported (2 November 2009) that some 300 Islamic banks and investment firms were operating in more than seventy-five countries, overseeing banking services totalling close to $500 billion, which is about 1 per cent of the global market. But the Islamic finance industry's value is growing at around 15 per cent per annum and could reach $4 trillion in five years, Moody's Investor Services reported in 2008. Dr Hussein Hamid Hassan (*Economic Times*, 3 December 2007), popularly known as the father of Islamic banking, quotes an old Egyptian proverb while commenting on bankruptcy laws in Islamic banking: conventional banking is like 'giving the key of the food store to the cat'. 'But in Islamic banking, the lender is not giving money to you to buy equity in your name or your wife's name. Instead, it will buy an aircraft and lease it to you for 10 years, in return it gets a fixed rental and also gets a variable as a percentage of the profits,' he said. I wonder if this approach would have saved Indian banks from the Kingfisher Airlines fiasco.

The concept of Islamic banking is yet to gain ground in India and some experts are of the view that this should not be encouraged since it will further alienate the Muslim populace from the mainstream. In a study I undertook with Professor R.K. Srivastava regarding financial behaviour of Jains and Bohra Muslims (who belong to the Shia sect) in suburban Mumbai, we noticed some differences in the financial instruments these two communities invested in. The Muslims were more aware of the religious restrictions on their financial transactions, though most banked with traditional banks and had fixed deposits, etc. But the area we noticed a significant difference in was insurance. Of the Muslims we studied, only 30 per cent had life insurance as compared to 85 per cent of the Jains surveyed. This came as a surprise. I decided to cross-check this with our client LIC and they too confirmed this phenomenon.

Interestingly, the UK-based Salaam Halal Insurance offers an Islamic (takaful) car insurance that complies with sharia law. The risk is shared among policyholders and surpluses are returned to consumers as a discount on their next renewal (*Hindustan Times*, 2 August 2009). If the insurance majors are keen on unlocking the 15 per cent potential that Muslims offer, they need to rethink their strategies and tailor their products to entice the community. It may involve lobbying with religious leaders to redefine some of the rules to suit modern times. This aversion to insurance may be related to an overall belief of Muslims that the outcome of their actions is God's will; in fact, in studies conducted in Mauritius and the US, Muslims have been reported to be more risk-taking and innovative in their shopping behaviour than other communities. US studies indicate that among shoppers Jews and Muslims are open to experimenting with new and innovative products. In my studies in India, I did not notice any significant difference between Muslim, Hindu and Christian consumers.

Recently I came across a magazine called *Islamic Tijara*, which claims to be India's 'premier Islamic finance magazine'.

In its January 2013 issue, it listed 211 companies in India that it considers sharia compliant. Industries and business activities that are excluded based on their primary filter are banks, alcoholic beverages, pork and non-halal products; advertising, media and casinos; and film production companies. Their secondary filter includes factors like leverage, liquidity ratios and interest income. I could not decode what they have against advertising and media!

Dr M.Y. Khan, former adviser to the Securities and Exchange Board of India (SEBI), says, 'Islamic Shariah recommends the elimination of Gharar or uncertainty and establishes the concept of economic efficiency, fair and equitable distribution and good governance of human activities including business activities and accountability towards social and ethical values.'

While widespread acceptance of Islamic banking may still be some years away in India, we may see halal products entering India in a bigger way. In simple terms, halal in Arabic means permissible. The opposite is haram, which means harmful. According to Islamic rules, all products, especially food products, have to be halal—that is, the food must come from a supplier that follows halal practices. Specifically, the slaughter must be performed by a Muslim, who must invoke the name of Allah before the kill. This is done most commonly by saying Bismillah (in the name of Allah) and then Allah Hu Akbar (God is great) three times. The animal must be slaughtered with a sharp knife (so it does not feel pain) by cutting the throat, windpipe and the jugular vein, causing death without cutting the spinal cord. Lastly, the blood from the veins must be drained. This final step is performed because blood can harbour harmful bacteria and also to ensure that there are no blood clots, thus keeping the entire body safe and clean to be eaten. Muslims must ensure that all foods (particularly processed foods), as well as non-food items like cosmetics and pharmaceuticals, are halal. Frequently, these products contain animal by-products or other ingredients that are not permissible for Muslims to eat or use on their bodies. Alcohol, pork and crustaceans are seen as haram.

There has been an amazing growth of halal products around the world. *Time* magazine (25 May 2009) estimates the global halal food market at $632 billion (the Jewish kosher food market is estimated at $12 billion in the US). In fact, the global food major Nestlé has been catering to this growing market from the 1980s through facilities where halal and non-halal products are manufactured separately. Of their 456 factories, 75 are geared for halal production. McDonald's, KFC and Domino's offer halal foods in Islamic markets and even select outlets in western countries. In April 2007 McDonald's started testing halal Chicken McNuggets in its Southhall outlet. KFC is going a step further by testing halal-only stores in Muslim-dominated areas in the UK. The Subway sandwich chain has halal franchisees across Britain and Ireland.

The halal wave is not just gripping the global food market. Several other products have also gone halal to woo the devout Muslim consumer. For example, Wipro Unza, one of Malaysia's largest cosmetics companies, has a halal-compliant cosmetic brand called 'Safi' which has seen tremendous growth over the last five years. The brand offers a whole range of products such as skin care creams and lotions.

IndiGo, one of the best-run airlines in India, has ensured that all the non-vegetarian food served on its flights is halal compliant. The menu carries this disclaimer in small type: All non-vegetarian meals are certified halal on all flights of IndiGo. Chances are most international airlines operating in the Middle East/Africa/Asia region have a clear disclaimer regarding halal-compliant food. I had not noticed this on any Indian menu cards, which is why the IndiGo disclaimer immediately caught my eye.

Why is this of any relevance to marketing professionals? I believe Muslim consumers in India are a growing segment, with their literacy and affluence levels set to grow over the next decade. If marketers can understand their desires and tailor their products for them, they are bound to reap rich dividends.

There is a global trend that is gaining ground in India, and you may have noticed it too. The global ad agency JWT describes the Muslim market thus: 'It's young, it's big and it's getting bigger.' Other studies point out that 62 per cent of Muslims are proud of their religion. As against the traditionalist segment (religion connects me, religion centres me, religion purifies me), the futurist segment is larger and has a more positive outlook towards religion (religion individuates me, religion enables me, religion identifies me). The Atticus 2011 report says that the futurists are creating their own cultural contexts on a daily basis, synthesizing different worlds and opinions in the way they choose to live. Seen collectively, they are the new Muslim consumer. They are at once welcoming and challenging, and need to be approached carefully, with knowledge and flexibility.

The big question remains: Are Indian Muslims different from the Muslims in other countries? Thomas Friedman believes they are. He says Indian Muslims have been integrated into the mainstream and have no or very little desire to idolize terrorists as 'martyrs' as most Arabic media seems wont to do. The journalist and columnist Aakar Patel also asserts that the subcontinent's Muslim is influenced more by Hinduism than by Islam. Rama Bijapurkar, the pre-eminent market and consumer strategist, says that Muslims in India are not one homogeneous body; a Tamil Muslim is more like a Tamil Hindu than like a UP Muslim. And you can find Muslim flower sellers outside the Madurai Kamakshi temple. Dorab Sopariwala is of the view that the increasing visibility of Muslim women in Mumbai is because of the diktat issued to Shia women (Bohris and others) by their religious leaders to wear a burqa. This single move, initiated a decade or so ago, suddenly made these women stand out in the general populace. Be that as it may, we are seeing a burst of confidence in Indian Muslims. Young Muslim men in white-collar professions are sporting a beard, confidently. These are signs that the young Indian Muslims are futurist in outlook.

As an adman and marketer, I am excited by the prospect this opens up for us—to tailor new products and services for these proud young consumers. The starting point is to understand them a little bit more, and I do hope this chapter will get you to embrace this growing consumer segment.

A regular Hindu has several misconceptions about the Indian Muslim driven by the portrayal of Muslims in Indian movies. Rachel Dwyer, a film scholar associated with the School of Oriental and African Studies in London, has traced the trajectory of the 'archetypal' Muslim in Bollywood films down the ages. She lists ten such archetypes—veiled beauties (*Chaudhvin Ka Chand, Mere Mehboob*), tawaif and nawab (*Pakeezah, Muqaddar Ka Sikandar, Mere Huzoor, Nikaah*), emperors (*Mughal-e-Azam, Jodha Akbar*), loyal sidekicks (Pran in *Zanjeer*), poets and qawwals (*Mere Mehboob, Amar Akbar Anthony*), intolerant Muslim (*Gadar: Ek Prem Katha*), the gangster (*Agneepath*), the Pakistani (*Ek Tha Tiger, Kurbaan, Sarfarosh*), the terrorist (*Fanaa*) and the rare modern Muslim (*Chak de India*).

Given the fact that non-stereotypical Muslim characters are rarely presented on screen, the average Indian believes all Muslims are polygamous. As S.C. Dube points out in his wonderful book *Indian Society*, not all Muslim men have four wives. The incidence of polygamy among Muslims in India in the decade 1931–40 was 7.29 per cent, in 1941–50, it was 7.06 per cent and in 1951–60 it had dropped to 4.31 per cent. Comparable figures for Hindus during the same period are 6.79 per cent, 7.15 per cent and 5.06 per cent respectively. The other myth revolves around the treatment of women by Muslim men. We earlier saw the inferior status accorded to women in Hindu holy scriptures. In comparison, Islam makes no distinction between man and woman. While the burqa system may appear antediluvian, Muslims in India accord equal status to their women. One acid test is the sex ratio among Hindus and Muslims. In every state of the country Muslims have a better sex ratio than Hindus.

There has also been a gradual marginalization of Muslims from mainstream society in India. Bigger cities are becoming zoned out for Muslims. It is reported that a Muslim will not be able to buy an apartment in South Mumbai for all the money in the world. In many other parts of Mumbai, societies have devised their own way of keeping out Muslims by 'vegetarian' or 'no-meat-eating' restrictions. In rural India, the separation is a lot more geographic. In Uttar Pradesh, there are villages and clusters of villages that are Muslim dominated and some where Muslims are 'not allowed'. The fact that Islam is casteless has kept the majority of poor Muslims from the reservation largesse. So, if one were to look at the problem dispassionately, we need to be worried about how the problem will get solved. Unless Muslims are embraced with open arms by the rest of the population of the country, we will continue to see flashes of trouble.

Economic growth finally could serve as the big equalizer. An orthodox Hindu household will still permit a Muslim electrician to walk in and repair the lighting system of their puja display. While eating at a restaurant, a Brahmin has no idea if he is being served by a Hindu or a Muslim.

The National Sample Survey (2009–10) report lamented that 46 per cent of Muslims in urban India are self-employed (a term used by demographers for petty craftsmen, skilled and unskilled daily labourers, etc.), the highest for any religious group. This, the report said, indicates that Indian Muslims are unable to join the organized workforce like the other religious groups, especially the Christians. I expect this to change in the next three decades driven by three movements: increased education of the Indian Muslim, increasing number of Muslim women joining the workforce and the shortage of skilled manpower across all sectors. I also expect them to set up innovative companies in the technology sector, given their proclivity for technical education.

Marketing companies have an interesting challenge before them. By trying to create Muslim-friendly products and services do they run the danger of driving away Hindu/Christian customers? By offering halal food, will IndiGo deter Hindus/ Christians from ordering non-vegetarian food? Similarly, when a bank offers a sharia-compliant product or service and displays that on its walls, will it be sending a negative message to non-Muslim customers? These challenges will get played out in multiple sectors acros India over the next few decades.

Multinational companies have ways of segmenting their messages to suit the majority population, but if the numbers of the minorities are going to grow exponentially in India, and soon Europe, we will see the need for some innovative thinking. This will put pressure on various societal groups to rethink their positions. For instance, is a non-Muslim permitted to refer to his god as Allah? No, said a Malaysian court on 21 August 2013, ruling against a Catholic newspaper that used the term Allah to denote God. In one of Istanbul's most famous mosques, I read 'Allah raised 124,00 Prophets and Messengers to guide humanity, from Adam the first Man and Prophet, followed by Noah, Abraham, Moses and Jesus, finally to Muhammad, the Last and Universal Prophet (Peace be upon them all). All the

Prophets were Muslim and they preached the Religion of Islam in its various stages throughout human history.'

Global brands have tried to walk the thin line by using religious festivals in ads. For instance, Coca-Cola has made numerous commercials linking its product to the process of celebration and festivities. The company's ads based on the concept of sharing food during iftar have always been very popular. But a Coke spokesperson is quoted in *The Economist* (4 August 2007) as saying, 'We don't segment our consumer based on religion.'

I would love to call those 'famous last words'.

15. Thank God, He Created 'Nothing'

Promise—large promise—is the soul of advertising.

Samuel Johnson (1709–84)

In 1999 Jose Dominic of the Casino Group, Kochi, called us for a discussion on how to market their latest acquisition: the Bangaram Island Resort. The Casino Group had bid and won a long-term lease on the island and were planning to build an eco-friendly tourist resort there. As Jose unveiled his plans, we realized that this was indeed going to be a unique resort: no telephone, no television, no carbonated beverages. A resort that would take you as close as you possibly could to nature! The strategy was to target affluent international travellers and Jose felt he would be able to achieve this by roping in travel agents and international travel magazines and television channels.

There was, however, need to attract the top-end Indian traveller as the international tourist could be expected only during a few months of the year. The budget for advertising was very limited and we could not afford a long-running campaign. The target audience was in the metro cities of Delhi, Mumbai,

Bangalore, Kolkata and Chennai. With his annual budget, the best we could get was a half-page colour advertisement in the *Economic Times*. To put all the annual budget into one ad was a great risk. But Jose was willing to go for it. The team felt the ad should present the island resort as stunningly beautiful and invite customers to write in for details. Those were the days of direct mail, well before email, Google and YouTube. Each customer who wrote would get a VHS tape of the resort. The strategy was all set. It was now in the hands of the creative team to conjure up a miracle. The copywriter came up with a great line: Thank God, He Created 'Nothing'. The body copy went on to explain the attractive features of the resort.

The advertisement attracted over 2000 enquiries and the resort was sold out for one full year. God really came to our rescue.

There is a strong connection between god and nature in the ad world. When Kerala wanted to position itself as nature's paradise, it went for the slogan God's Own Country. Conceptualized by the then Kerala tourism secretary Amitabh Kant, it is possibly the most recognized tourism line in the country.

God also comes into advertising when the brand wants to project a feeling of awe. One remarkable use of this metaphor was for the Bajaj Avenger. The bike, which is a cruiser that can be ridden sitting erect, showcased some wonderful landscape (again nature), the dread roads of Leh, with the tagline Feel Like God.

In the Superbowl ads of 2013 in the US, the most remembered was one by Dodge Ram. It featured part of a famous speech, 'And God Made a Farmer', delivered by a radio host, Paul Harvey, at a 1978 Future Farmers of America (FFA) convention. The television commercial showed snapshots of farmers at work, set to the immortal words of Harvey. Resonating with emotion and wonder, it makes you truly believe that god made a farmer to help us live. A must-watch, the ad was produced in collaboration with the FFA. Dodge agreed to donate $100,000 for every 1,000,000 views that the YouTube video of the ad received, setting itself a limit of $1,000,000. This goal was reached in less than five days. Again god featured close to nature.

The other genre of advertising that uses god or religion are brands that want to convey they are pan-Indian. The famous Hamara Bajaj film, which ran in movie theatres and television screens in 1989, showed several religious communities and prayer situations, including Sikhs, Parsis, Hindus and Muslims. In the words of the creator of the ad, the film showed three Indias, the traditional, the modern and the middle. Come 2001, the company had changed dramatically and its product lines were also totally different. So when the company made version II of the Hamara Bajaj film, the attempt was to show the new India, an India that was revelling in the new breeze of change, a 'naya hai kal', 'tomorrow is new', ethos. One way the film-maker captured the intermingling of modern and traditional India was by showing young men and women on motorcycles, displaying signs of traditional worship—the young man carrying a guitar pauses to pray in front of a street temple and the young couple avoids riding over a rangoli on the road. In the Veedol lubricants ad, the marketer chose the worshipping habits of truck drivers belonging to the many religions of India; aptly enough, as all highways in India have a temple or a place of worship every 100 kilometres.

The third area where religion and gods come in useful is to signify celebration. In an ad for Tanishq jewellery, the company Titan and its agency Lowe experimented with a multi-religious setting—a Muslim man rejoicing at getting a Diwali discount. Karva Chauth was featured in a Hyundai car commercial which shows the loving husband driving home in a hurry in his new Accent car to join his wife to look at the moon.

The fourth area is where religious groups are used as cultural stereotypes; for example, a Christian pastor conveys authority. In an ad for a detergent powder, Amitabh Bachchan played a school principal/father sporting a sparkling white cassock; obviously, the church used the best detergent powder. Parsis are used to show their love for things old. Hindu gurus have been parodied in numerous ads—fans have made them levitate and sweets have made them speak in funny languages.

The fifth area is ads using mythological characters to deliver the message. Imagine a nice-looking house that has just been painted. Yamaraj, the Hindu god of death, comes visiting, seeking the soul of the owner of the house. The owner in turn asks for one wish: he is willing to go with Yama as soon as the paint on the house fades a tad. Unsuspecting of any mischief, Yama agrees. But the wily home owner has just painted his house with Nerolac Excel, and that paint never fades, come sun, rain or hailstorm. So poor Yama is made to wait for years and finally gives up and disappears. This ad for Nerolac was a big hit and we had no protest group outside our office objecting to the trivialization of the god Yama.

I am sure there are many other cases of Indian agencies and marketers using religion, god and mythological figures in their communication. I would suspect one in every ten ads has an element of one or more of these three.

I am not sure if advertising in any other country has such strong underpinnings of religion and god. The Dodge Ram ad is an exception to the general trend in American advertising. If at all, advertising in the western world may feature a festival like Christmas, but without any strong religious undertone. In contrast, when Indian ads show festivals, they do not shy away from showing a puja or an aarti. In Europe, it probably is anathema to show religious symbols or worship. In the Middle East too, while cultural cues are all Islamic, religion stays in the background.

Here is an interesting sidebar. Pakistani television would discourage ads being made in India, not just because we were so obsessed with god and religion but also because they did not want their marketers to route their advertising production money to India and to Indian models. Television authorities in Pakistan insisted that none of the actors were of Indian origin. When Indian agencies made ads for their Pakistani partners, they had to ensure the actors had non-Indian passports, copies of which had to be sent to Pakistan for approval.

Why are we in India so comfortable showing religion and worship in advertising? I suppose it is simply because we are quite open about our religious practices and beliefs. This open display of religion and religious practices is but a natural outcome of our own new brand of religiosity that is celebratory rather than exclusionary. I would like to believe that in the coming years, we will continue with the trend but will also see more cross-religious messaging. We will celebrate our multi-religious culture more openly in advertising as we are doing in movies and television.

Recently, Hindustan Unilever got its agency Lowe to make a documentary-like film that ran on YouTube. The film starts with a young village boy running out of his small house. He sees palm marks on the ground outside his home. He tries walking on them and then sees his father walking on his hands further ahead. He starts following his dad. As the man struggles to walk on his hands, the villagers look on in wonderment and some start following him. A local music troupe joins the entourage and elders follow too. A bus stops and a young, obviously city-bred, woman gets down with a camera in tow. She too follows the man walking on his hands. He is sweating and struggling to move ahead, but continues up the steep incline, over muddy fields and rocks. Then he finally reaches his destination, the village temple. The temple priest smiles and receives him with an aarti to the village deity. The city girl is piqued and asks one of the elders why he is doing this penance. The old man replies, he is celebrating the fact that his son is now five years old. All this for five years, asks the girl. And the old man says, none of his children have lived beyond five, they have all died at an even younger age. The girl is awestruck. And the message from the company flashes: in rural India millions of young children die due to poor hygiene, and regular washing of hands with a germicidal hand-wash soap can prevent numerous illnesses.

Would the film have worked without the temple? I guess not.

Going forward, advertisers will continue to use religion and various metaphors and analogies to stir emotions in Indian consumers. The stories may change, as we saw in the earlier film. But the use of religious motifs will continue and may even increase, now that the Indian media is no longer trying to be pseudo-secular. As multiple religions and multiple festivals spring forth, the opportunities for using them in advertising will also increase. For instance, thirty years ago, doing an ad with a Ganesha festival would have appealed only in Maharashtra. Now, it is a pan-Indian festival. Similarly, Durga Puja was primarily centred in Kolkata, not any more. As mentioned earlier, there was an ad that celebrated both Eid and Aadi discount in a Tamil newspaper. St Valentine's Day is now an occasion for Gujarati jewellers to bring out big ads.

Increasing religiosity and the increasing festival spirit should open up opportunities to create advertising that will resonate with new Indians. Since loosening purse strings is the job of advertising, it will find echo with the new-age religious, festival-crazy Indian consumer.

16. Burqa Ke Peechhe Kya Hai?

A woman's dress should be like a barbed-wire fence: serving its purpose without obstructing the view.

Sophia Loren (b. 1934)

I was having dinner with my mentor Subhas Chakravarty, an advertising veteran and keen observer of consumer behaviour, in Kolkata at, where else, a restaurant called Oh! Calcutta. I asked him what surprised him the most about how modern consumers were navigating the dual path of affluence and religious piety.

Subhas had a great story to tell about Bangladesh, a country he visited often since he had several consultancy assignments in Dhaka. As it was an Islamic country, wearing a burqa was common. But, to his surprise, he realized women took off the burqa when they entered their workspaces. So the woman wears a burqa while in the car, scooter or bus but it is cast off once she enters her factory or office. Under the burqa, the Bangladeshi woman wears the most sophisticated clothes, clothes that would be the envy of girls in Kolkata. It may be of interest to you that Bangladeshi women have a huge range of apparel to choose from. Consider this: 5500 garment factories are licensed in Bangladesh, the world's second largest manufacturer of garments after China; 80 per cent of Bangladeshi garment workers are women, some four million of them; 78 per cent of the total export earnings of Bangladesh is from garments, around $18 billion.

We discussed the reason for this transformation. Aren't the women supposed to wear the burqa all the time? Interestingly, the modern Muslim woman has interpreted the burqa as a way of hiding her face and all other features from strangers. But once she is in the safe space of her own office or workspace, she is happy to take off the burqa and show off her designer wear and trendy hairstyle.

In Turkey, Mustafa Kemal Ataturk, the liberator, banned the Islamic face veil and turban in 1934 and successive governments have upheld this decision. With the growing population of Muslims in Europe, there has been concern regarding the burqa and facial veil and whether it 'demeans' a woman and takes away her rights. The burqa has not been allowed in French public schools since 2004 and this has to do with the display of religious symbols; Christians too are not allowed to wear clearly visible religious symbols in French schools. Nicolas Sarkozy banned the burqa in France in 2010, and the government has not backed off despite occasional protests. Sarkozy said at a joint session of the two houses of France's parliament, 'In our country, we cannot accept that women be prisoners behind a screen, cut off from all social life, deprived of all identity.' In the UK too there has been some public outcry against the burqa, and polls indicated that over 65 per cent of British people supported the burqa ban.

Interestingly, in places like Belgium and Italy, the ban on the burqa had more to do with the identification of the person from the security point of view rather than religious or the emancipation of women. Italy banned the burqa as far back as 1975, Belgium in 2010 and the Netherlands in 2012.

Islamic countries have adopted different dress rules. Some like Saudi Arabia have rigidly enforced the burqa for all women in their country, irrespective of their nationality and religion. Some have been liberal about it, mandating the hijab, a headscarf. In *Religion and Globalization* John Esposito and others say that the Quran does not stipulate the veiling and seclusion of women although it does say that the wives of the Prophet should speak to men from behind a partition. The requirement of the hijab has been interpreted differently by various scholars. Even in Old Delhi, the custom at one time was for young women, unmarried or in the first few years of their marriage, to wear a burqa. In Pakistan, the practice was more prevalent in the Pashtun territories in the north. Wearing a burqa was common even among Hindu and Christian women in some parts of Pakistan in the past. In Israel too a section of orthodox Jewish women once wore the burqa.

Newspapers report that there has been a growth in the number of Muslim women wearing burqas in India over the last twenty years. In Kerala's Malabar districts, which have a large Muslim population, the percentage of Muslim women wearing the burqa went up from around 5 per cent in 1990 to over 30 per cent in 2010. In Mumbai, Bohri Muslim women who did not wear a burqa some years ago are today wearing their traditional attire, a form of burqa called 'rida'. Unlike a burqa, the rida comes in many light colours and is decorated with lace. Bohri Muslim women are not expected to keep their face covered all the time while wearing a rida.

So, why this increase in the number of women wearing burqas? There are some religious reasons, such as decrees by the local religious leader. But I came across an interesting explanation in a blog by a woman activist and it did ring true. The blogger has observed that more and more women today are venturing out of their homes to go to college, to take up employment, etc. Apparently in some conservative Muslim households, the head of the household comes under pressure from his daughters, ably supported by their mother, to let them attend college and pursue higher education. The burqa is then offered as a condition for allowing the daughter to go out. Given the incidents of harassment on Indian roads and buses, it looks like a win-win for the girl and her parents.

It is true that Muslim women are today venturing out a lot more than in the past, at times in a burqa—interestingly, their burqas are a lot different from the traditional black burqa. The modern burqa comes in many shades, leading to interesting business opportunities. Designer burqas are making a big entry into India. They have been in existence for many years in the Middle East, as have designer hijabs. In cities like Patna, Muslim women are willing to spend as much as Rs 8000 for a designer burqa. There are burqas available with zarkan work; some are even embedded with American diamonds.

When Big Bazaar opened its store in the predominantly Muslim area of Bombay Central, it had a tough time convincing the local populace it understood their needs. The local management decided that one way of showing their 'understanding' of the local populace was to stock ready-to-wear burqas. But that did not work. The store had to revisit its inventory strategy and bring in better quality burqas, made of fine fabric with delicate embroidery work, and slowly the tide started turning. The affluent Muslims in the locality stopped feeling insulted and started loosening their purse strings. The mistake the store made was in painting all burqas with the same brush, given the growing buying power of Muslim consumers and their increasingly exacting tastes.

The veteran consumer researcher Hema Viswanathan has said that Muslims are more innovative and ready to try out new products—echoed in international studies as well, as we have seen. Her hypothesis was based on the fact that Indian Muslims have a strong connect with Middle Eastern countries and have always enjoyed imported products. This extended to burqas too; they have seen what is available in places like Dubai and Muscat and affluent Muslim women often have an imported burqa or two in their wardrobes. A few decades ago, every Indian youngster aspired for an imported pair of jeans. And many of us would treasure the imported pair of Levi's we got from our cousin visiting from America. Now it is the turn of the burqa.

We are going to be seeing more and more products being tailored to suit the needs of the affluent Muslim woman. Pious Muslim women have to pray five times a day. And they have to wash their hands five times a day. Manicures have long posed a religious problem. Traditional nail polishes have been off limits since they prevent nails from getting in contact with water. A new 'breathable' nail polish from a Polish company, Inglot, is changing that. While Islam does not forbid nail polish, some Islamic scholars have said that water must touch the nails as part of the cleansing ritual. Some women would apply nail polish after the last prayer of the day and take it off before the first prayer. Now with the new nail polish which has been tested by an Islamic scholar in the US for its permeability, fashionable Muslim women can have their nails coloured and do their prayers as prescribed in the religious texts. It is not just burqas and cosmetics that are being tailored to suit the modern Muslim woman's needs. *The Economist* (4 August 2007) reported a full coverage swimsuit. The Australian apparel company Ahiida, founded by a Lebanese immigrant, has created a burqini, which as the name suggests is a cross between a burqa and a bikini; made with synthetic materials, it has been designed in accordance with Islamic law which requires Muslim women to dress modestly. Lady Gaga, the singing sensation who has become a fashion icon because of her bizarre dress sense, has taken to appearing in various Islamic clothing. Her pink burqa created quite an uproar, and so has her song 'Burqa' with its sensational lyrics.

I am sure over the next decade we will see the rise of halal cosmetics, new types of burqas and more innovations aimed at the affluent Muslim woman.

There is a view that after the invasion of the Mughals Hindu women in North India were forced to cover their faces with a ghunghat before all men except their husbands. They were to use the pallu or the loose end of their sari to cover their face. This continues till date as young newly married girls in some sections are told to wear a ghunghat while meeting elders. Did upper-caste Hindus invent the ghunghat as a way of protecting their women from invading Muslims? Or did they invent it as an answer to the Muslim burqa—if we can't see your women, you can't see ours? It is to be noted that the ghunghat habit is widely prevalent in Rajasthan, Uttar Pradesh, Haryana, Madhya Pradesh, Jharkhand, Bihar and parts of West Bengal but absent in other parts of India.

On the contrary, some experts say that the burqa was derived from the ghunghat. Interestingly, carvings and paintings at all ancient Hindu temples show women without a ghunghat; maybe the only exception is the Nalanda painting, but even there the woman's face is seen. While women in North India wore their sari in ghunghat style, lower-caste women in many parts of India were not allowed to cover the top half of their body.

Here's a sideshow regarding the burqa and its unique appeal. All over India we are seeing young women become more mobile with their own set of wheels. This has led to the rebirth of scooters, especially the gearless kind. During summer, across India, girls on two-wheelers are dressed in burqaesque fashion. They wear gloves that completely cover their hands. They wear a helmet that covers their hair. And they also wear a mask that covers their face, except for their eyes. Maybe there is a market for a burqa designed for the scooter-driving woman!

If you thought the burqa is really a sign of female bondage, think again. In 2013, Pakistan discovered a new side to the burqa. The country and its kids have fallen for a new superhero, the Burqa Avenger. This masked crusader takes on villains like Bandooq, a Talibanesque character trying to close down her school, and Vadero Pajero, the corrupt politician. In the cartoon series, a demure class teacher, Jiya, takes on the role of an action hero by donning a burqa at night. While kids are lapping up the animation series on Pakistan TV, it has stirred debate elsewhere. People are questioning if it is right to make a burqa look 'cool' to children and to brainwash girls into believing that the burqa is an empowering costume and not a sign of subjugation. Well, as the debate rages on, kids are enjoying the adventures. Will the little girls watching the cartoon series one day agree to wear a burqa to go out to buy vegetables? Only the future will tell.

17. Pray for Better Health

*Health is the greatest gift, contentment the greatest wealth,
faithfulness the best relationship.*

Gautama Buddha (563–483 BCE)

Jaslok is one of India's most respected hospitals and its clientele
includes the who's who of the country. Set up in 1973 by the
philanthropist Lookomal Chanrai, the hospital has some of
the best doctors in the country consulting with it. When Jaslok
approached our agency in the late 1990s for branding advice,
we felt truly honoured. The hospital is run by a not-for-profit
trust that shunned any form of publicity. But the world around
was changing with the entry of for-profit hospitals and the
hospital management felt they needed to spruce up its image for
the twenty-fifth anniversary celebrations for which the prime
minister was invited.

Our team felt the first step was to give the hospital a new,
modern identity. The designer working on the assignment, Ravi
Madkaikar, and the business manager handling the assignment,
Basudev Biswas, pondered on what identity would suit a hospital
brand. An analysis of international hospital brands revealed that
most of them stressed on heritage, history and science in equal

measure. Jaslok boasted of tremendous research facilities, but the team was not sure if the Jaslok brand should be anchored mainly on research.

What happens when a person enters a hospital? What is their state of mind? What are they thinking of? What are their worries? What are the worries of the people accompanying the patient? What should the hospital be telling them, verbally and non-verbally?

We knew that Indian patients treat doctors like gods and this has been an age-old custom. When a patient enters a hospital, he is not walking in like he walks into a hotel or a mall. He is walking in with a lot of trepidation. And often he is also thinking of higher powers.

One of the earliest works relating religion to well-being was by Emile Durkheim, the French philosopher who is also called the father of sociology. In his work *Suicide* he linked suicide rates to religion and religiosity. While the research has had its critics, his primary argument, backed by data, was that increased religious contact among Catholics in Germany had reduced the incidence of suicide. Following in Durkheim's footsteps, there has been a great amount of work done in the recent past linking religiosity and subjective well-being.

If religion and god can play a role in the psychological well-being of a client, can the hospital's identity cue some aspect of this? The team at the agency did not want to designate the hospital as belonging to any one particular religious faith. But was there a way of projecting a soft religious faith, without really openly showing one?

Finally, it was vital that the hospital did not send out a message of 'cold science'. Indian patients need more hand-holding than a well-educated European or American patient. So it was important to cue 'caring' in the identity of the hospital.

Keeping all these considerations in mind, Ravi Madkaikar came up with an identity design that presented the hospital name in a nice old-style typeface. He added three flowers above the logo. These multicoloured flowers signalled caring, but also puja or worship, something anyone entering a hospital is thinking of, irrespective of the kind of care and treatment he will get once he is inside the hospital. The design was presented to the management of the hospital and was loved by one and all. Till this day, Jaslok continues to sport the three-flower logo. Religion and god are intrinsically enmeshed with our sense of health and well-being. Research done in the US holds some interesting lessons. Consumers ranked religious affiliation of a hospital (Catholic, Protestant, Jewish, etc.) as very low in influencing their choice of hospital. However, hospitals of a particular religious affiliation were more likely to be recalled, preferred and selected by people of the same religious affiliation. Even in quality of care measures, religious affiliation influenced hospital evaluations. The researcher Syed Saad Andeleeb advises that hospital marketing professionals should be aware that the religious affiliation of a hospital may be an important marketing variable that could provide an edge in this highly competitive industry. In this regard, the similarity attraction theory has interesting implications from a positioning perspective.

The lessons outlined above are things that our doctors know for sure. They know that if you are operating in a Muslim area, you should be a Muslim or sensitive to the Muslim patient's issues. The gods displayed in the little clinic could also be modified depending on the clientele. This does not mean that I am endorsing blatant exploitation of human frailties. I think the display of a suitable religious totem helps the patient derive some solace, however little.

Now think back. Have you ever been to a hospital in India

that does not display a big idol of some Hindu god? Christian hospitals always have a picture or a statue of Jesus Christ or Mother Mary. Muslim hospitals and even Muslim doctors often display a photograph of the holy Kaba at Mecca. The religious idol is often accompanied by a collection box, a hundi, and there are regular pujas performed at these hospital-mandirs every morning and evening.

The e-magazine *Psychology Today* speaks of the many ways religion could be good for your health—religion is a source of hope and optimism, it promotes feelings of belonging, boosts self-esteem and provides protection from existential threats. Other fascinating findings on the relationship between religion and health include the following: Jews and Mormons, who are in general more religious, are the healthiest (among them too, the more religious are more healthy); doctors believe that religion plays a role in patients' health; changing religious groups can take a toll on health; religion aids recovery in traumatic brain injury victims; religious thoughts reduce stress in believers and increase stress in non-believers; and being diagnosed with a terminal disease does not reduce one's religious beliefs.

There is also evidence of patients using religion to cope with negative events like disasters, accidents, illnesses and even marital abuse. Even here there is a difference in the way god is perceived: as a benevolent, all-forgiving god or as a punishing or indifferent god. People subscribing to the first kind of god tend to cope with stress and health issues a lot better than those subscribing to the second kind.

We have not done any such research in India but I would submit that Indians too would be using religion and god to cope with illnesses and trauma. Is it not a practice in all Indian homes to take the newborn to the temple? While Hindus do not have a formal baptism like the Christians, you can count over a hundred babies being brought to Mumbai's Siddhivinayak temple every day. Each of the babies is handed over to the priest who places it at the feet of the Ganesha idol for a second, while the rest of the devotees smile in recognition of the ritual.

Interestingly, we also have different types of medical treatments in India aligned to different socio-religious groups. For instance, Unani medicine is closely aligned to the Muslims while Ayurveda is more Hindu. Siddha, the third form of traditional medicine practised in India, is found in Tamil Nadu. As allopathic medicine gains ground, these older forms of medicine are becoming less common. It would be a tragedy if they were to vanish. It is therefore heartening that companies are doing research to identify the active ingredients in the natural roots and herbs prescribed in Siddha and Ayurveda.

One success of a brand crossing barriers erected by allopathic medicine is Himalaya's Liv 52. It is prescribed by all kinds of doctors for illnesses related to the liver such as jaundice. Another interesting product is the green tea offered by Organic India. To stand apart from the clutter of green tea brands, it is labelled 'Tulsi Green Tea'. The product description refers to tulsi as 'Holy Basil', which is supposed to have 'life enhancing properties according to ancient scriptures'. In the ingredient listing in addition to green tea two varieties of tulsi are listed, Rama tulsi and Krishna tulsi. I wonder if this product can have a global appeal. Curiously, I noticed a brand of tea called 'Rishi Tea' labelled as organic masala chai in the gift catalogue of the December 2011 issue of *Oprah* magazine. The company claims to be a leading seller of organic tea, but I suspected the combination of tulsi/basil with green tea is a very alluring product offering. And I would submit that there are many more such gems waiting to be discovered.

In *Hindu World* Benjamin Walker speaks of the Hindu myth that the science of medicine is derived from Lord Brahma, who instituted it to allay the pains of gods and lesser gods. This treatise on Ayurveda written in one lakh verses describes the cause (hetu), symptoms (linga) and remedy (aushadha) of all diseases and was handed down to Prajapati, then to Daksha and so on. The most well-known authors on Ayurveda were Charaka who lived in the early years of the Common Era and was a court physician to the Kushan kings, and Sushruta who lived in the fourth century CE in Banaras. Sushruta is believed to have written on complex surgeries, including hernia, cataract and plastic surgery.

There is the apocryphal story about two western doctors, Ellis and Anderson, who in the nineteenth century had to resort to a trick to get tradition-soaked Indians to accept vaccination: they composed verses in Sanskrit and had them transcribed on old paper and convinced the local public that it was an ancient practice. I am not sure how true that story is, but it makes an emphatic point about how medicine is so closely intermingled with ancient beliefs and customs.

The other major area where religion and health overlap is in the domain of fitness. And the biggest global import from India is probably yoga. In Vedic Sanskrit, the common meaning of the word 'yoga' is 'to add', 'to unite' or 'to attach'. While yoga was born in the Indus Valley civilization, dating back to third millennium BCE, the originator of yoga is supposedly Yajnavalkya. It was documented in the early years of the Common Era by Patanjali as Yoga Sutra. Today, traces of yoga can be found in Hinduism, Buddhism, Jainism and Sikhism. The Bhagavad Gita too devotes an entire chapter to traditional yoga practices, including meditation. The Gita also introduces three other prominent types of yoga—karma yoga (the yoga of action), bhakti yoga (the yoga of devotion) and jnana yoga (the yoga of knowledge). Explaining the essence of yoga, Lord Krishna tells Arjuna, 'Be steadfast in yoga, Arjuna. Perform your duties and abandon all attachment to success or failure. Such evenness of mind is called yoga.'

There are several forms of yoga, depending on whether we are looking for liberation, samadhi, mental energy, siddhis or physical powers. Each form of yoga has different levels or stages. So there are fifteen stages of raja yoga, sixteen stages of mantra yoga, nine of bhakti yoga, ten of laya yoga, and so on. The key yoga form is hatha yoga and it has eight stages—yama or restraint, especially external control like non-injury and continence; niyama or internal control like meditation; asana or bodily postures, the most common form; pranayama or breath, again a popular stage; prathahara, control of senses; dharana or meditation; dhyana or contemplation; and finally samadhi or superconsciousness. The highest form of yoga is traditionally raja yoga, which stresses on mental and spiritual rather than physical well-being. Even higher is the raja athiraja yoga, the king of kings yoga. It is a yogic form which has no eternities. It is the pure contemplation of the supreme principle by means of which the mind is freed from anger, lust, fear, greed, jealousy and melancholy, something that should be made compulsory for our political leaders.

It was Swami Vivekananda who took yoga to the western world in the late nineteenth century. And today we see various forms of yoga gaining ground, including 'hot yoga' and 'cold yoga'. Is yoga essentially Hindu in nature? Practising yoga was essential to Vedic rituals, especially the breath control needed to chant Vedic hymns, but today is yoga really 'Hindu'? When a school in San Diego, California began offering yoga to its students, a Christian civil liberties group took it to court. The judge after hearing the appeal decided to let the school continue the practice. The school on its side claimed it had developed a simplified form of yoga, shorn of its Hindu symbols; even the postures/asanas were made kid-friendly with names such as 'gorilla', 'turtle' and 'peacock'. The group that petitioned believes that the battle is not yet over since yoga may travel to other parts of the US seen as hotbeds of Christian religiosity. While the judge has favoured the school, the 20 million American practitioners of yoga do encounter these issues and more. For instance, yoga is all about the body being a vehicle for reaching consciousness with the 'divine'. This is fundamentally at odds with the Christian teaching of eternal heaven and hell as a system of rewards and punishments in an afterlife. In an interesting story in *Newsweek*, with the sensational 'We Are All Hindu Now' headline, over 24 per cent of Americans claim to believe in reincarnation. Other practices like vipassana are also growing in popularity across India and the western world. Derived from Theravada Buddhism, vipassana meditation seeks to achieve inner peace and solitude. Employing breathing techniques and extended periods of silence, this form of meditation has been adopted by not just laypeople but also leading industrialists.

While Indian doctors are raising the standards of medicine, including complicated surgeries of the heart and eyes, I think they face strong resistance in one area—psychiatry. In India, even the more affluent use religion as a mode of achieving mental peace. Various religious gurus too perform this role with great results. In addition to religious gurus, astrologers and numerology experts seem to be performing this role for the rich and famous. From just listening to the woes of day-to-day life, religious gurus also provide counsel, pretty much like a psychiatrist. I wonder if Indian psychiatrists display religious symbols in their consulting rooms, or if they see these as 'competition'. As India embraces the problems of the developed world, it is possible that we too may go their way with a weekly visit to the psychiatrist. It would be interesting to observe if psychiatry visits are more for the less religiously inclined. To those going to temples, churches and mosques more often, it may be that visits to psychiatrists are not required. Now add to that a bit of meditation, yoga and even vipassana and you get the full treatment from ancient Indian forms of healthcare.

I have another prediction. Today, doctors in India are rarely sued for medical malpractice. Experts tell me this is because of the slow legal system and the fact that it is almost impossible to get a verdict in any reasonable time. But I believe patients will not be willing to take their doctor, who they see as 'god', to court even if our legal system improves and medical cases are fast-tracked. You don't take the religious guru to court, you don't take the local temple to court, so why the doctor? I think the fact that medical malpractice is so rare in our country is helping our doctors innovate with new ways of therapy and surgery. Sushruta performed cataract surgery in India almost two centuries ago, and Indian doctors have innovated cost-effective forms of cataract surgery, carrying forward Sushruta's legacy. Many more such innovations could follow, if patients treat doctors with regard and respect.

From the days of Durkheim to vipassana, there has been a close relationship between spirituality and good health. India has a lot to offer to the world from yoga to meditation and more. Global movements like transcendental meditation, or TM, have been triggered from India. With the world and its citizens caught between petty desires and wants and struggling with their own inner consciousness, Indian forms of meditation and exercises offer great potential. In India too there are going to be numerous centres offering yoga classes and more. Medicine will also discover the hidden gems in Indian traditional medicine and meditation.

Religion and health are closely intertwined and those who are in the business of healthcare need to understand this. Consumers do believe in the power of science to cure them of their illnesses but they also believe in some divine intervention. I would submit that the reason for low medical malpractice litigation in India is the direct result of the closer interaction between illness and religious faith. Smart doctors use this to their advantage, asking the patient to pray for speedy recovery.

18. Religious Music Can Rescue Ads

Next to the Word of God, music deserves the highest praise. The gift of language combined with the gift of song was given to man that he should proclaim the Word of God through music.

Martin Luther (1483–1546)

Voltas is India's largest air-conditioning company with a strong presence in the home and institutional segments. The company decided in the mid 1990s to enter the booming consumer durables arena, known as the 'white goods' arena. The launch of Voltas refrigerators was handled by our agency and the brand gained instant support from trade and consumers given the Voltas brand pull and the Tata association. The company wanted to expand the basket by offering washing machines. The Indian refrigerator and washing machine market had exploded in the 1990s when the Indian government reduced the excise duties from the absurd levels of 160 per cent to a more modest 15 per cent. The story goes that a member of Parliament from a left party objected to this drastic reduction in washing machine duties saying that the Indian government was going to render jobless millions of maids who earned a living washing clothes. The then prime minister, the normally reticent P.V. Narasimha Rao, is reported to have replied, 'Would the honourable member of Parliament prefer that we continue to be a country of maids?'

Voltas saw great opportunity in the fast-growing washing machine market. But unlike refrigerators, washing machines were not that popular as they needed both electricity and continuous water supply. However, to sell the bottom-end semi-automatic washing machines, the manufacturer had to build its image as an innovator at the top end of the product pyramid. Voltas therefore decided to tap the top end of the market with a powerful product offering, with the promise of a full range in due course. The model picked out to advertise was the biggest in its class, with a 7 kilo capacity. The planning team had come up with an interesting name for the model, the Voltas Mega Laundrette, signifying powerful cleaning as in a laundry. The teams brainstormed on the creative idea and it was felt that the 7 kilo capacity needed to be communicated powerfully and visually since it meant nothing to a consumer.

The idea was crystallized with a very large family of men and kids dressed only in towels, all waiting for their clothes to be washed. The creative team thought the film should show these men and kids challenging the women of the house by singing, 'no washing machine can wash so many clothes'. The creative director, Subodh Poddar, had written a song pretty much saying that—'Yeh nahin ho sakta, kabhi nahin ho sakta' (this is not possible, definitely not possible). The words were set to tune and the account director, Shireen Cama, played it to then head of the agency, Anil Kapoor. They heard it a few times and Anil pronounced that the tune was not working. The creative director was requested to try something else. Cut to two days later. Same scene, same result. Cut to two days later. Same. Same.

It was then that Anil and Shireen started a serious discussion on what they wanted from the music. Anil said he wanted the music to stir emotions of incredulity, not fun or frolic. He remembered that some form of old Christian religious music could produce such an effect. Shireen, who was quite an encyclopedia on operatic and western classical music, said she would rummage through the family music collection and return the next day with some options. Finally, they discovered the music they wanted: it was the Gregorian chant. This form of music is a monophonic, non-instrumental, sacred song of the Roman Catholic Church dating back to the ninth and tenth centuries Europe. Pope St Gregory the Great has been credited with its invention.

Armed with the tape, the creative director rushed back to the studio and the recording was done and dusted just a couple of hours later. The ad for Voltas Mega Laundrette featuring men dressed in towels singing a Gregorian chant-like song went on to become a big hit. Washing machine sales peaked and the ad went on to win numerous industry accolades.

That was the case of religious music rescuing an ad.

Marketers have also used religious music to build consumer contact. Castrol, which was a big advertiser on radio, discovered that truck drivers, a key target audience, could be reached more cost-effectively through free music cassettes of various genres. Their research revealed that contrary to their image as philanderers, truck drivers were happiest while listening to religious music. So they decided to distribute religious music cassettes with cans of Castrol lubricants.

Religion and music go hand in hand in most parts of the world. We saw how the form of music called Gregorian chant was in fact created by a pope. Christianity also has the tradition of gospel music; it continues to be popular and is seen as a joyous expression of faith in god. Famous gospel singers include Aretha Franklin and Mahalia Jackson. There is a fairly large following of Christian religious music in India too. Traditional gospel singing has evolved to embrace other forms of music including pop, blues and even rock. There are several rock bands that only play religious music. In mega churches in the Midwest, religious music is a critical element of weekend services. Music is blasted through state-of-the-art music systems and the congregation joins in the singing. It is no wonder that god features in numerous popular music albums. From Janis Joplin's crooning of 'Oh Lord, won't you buy me a Mercedes Benz' and John Lennon's 'Imagine' to Bob Dylan's 'With god on our side' and Louis Armstrong singing the ever-popular hymn 'When the saints go marching in . . .' many music legends have sung of god and religion.

Similarly, the Sufi music form was created by Sufis, the followers of the mystical dimension of Islam. The most famous Sufi poets were Hafiz, Rumi and Bulleh Shah. The qawwali performed by matinee idols in numerous Hindi films is really a form of Sufi music. The Sufi form of music is central to the Sema ceremony of the whirling dervishes in Turkey; their performance is bewitching and highly spiritual in many ways. Nusrat Fateh Ali Khan of Pakistan took Sufi music to the western world, a bit like Pandit Ravi Shankar taking Indian classical music and the sitar beyond Indian shores. He provided music for the Hollywood film *Dead Man Walking*. The music blends in seamlessly, building the tempo of the film about a Christian nun reforming a confirmed murderer on death row. Without that superb Sufi music, I am not sure the film would have had the great spiritual uplifting appeal that it did.

In *The Wonder That Was India*, A.L. Basham gives a background of the origin of religious music in India. He says there is evidence to show that the Aryans knew the heptatonic scale (seven notes) and the hymns of the Sama Veda were rendered in a liturgical style which has been preserved fairly accurately across three or more millennia. The sage Bharata is believed to have composed the Bharata Natyasastra, the earliest authoritative treatise on the three arts of music, drama and dance. Consisting of some 5600 verses, it is sometimes referred to as the fifth Veda (the other four being Rig, Yajur, Sama and Atharva). The Natyasastra represents the synthesis of ancient and more modern Hindu religious traditions and continues to be a living treatise of the art forms. Mythologies tell us that Narada invented the veena, a musical instrument that has inspired numerous other stringed instruments over the millennia.

However, the central idea of Indian music is sabda or sound. The human voice is seen as the highest form, hence intoning, chanting, recitation of mantras and singing are seen as the most effective expression of sound. The Ramayana and the

The Dancing God, Nataraja. Adapted from the Vedic Diary published by Srinivasa Print Works, Sivakasi. *Reproduced with permission*

Mahabharata are both presented in musical form. They have been adapted to various Indian languages by Tulsidas (Hindi/Avadhi), Kamban (Tamil), Ponna (Kannada) and others. In North India, the Ram Lila and Ras Lila recreate Rama's and Krishna's legends in folk idiom. Yakshagana in Karnataka and Kathakali in Kerala also take up religious themes. Episodes from the Ramayana and the Mahabharata have inspired most classical dance forms of India such as Bharatanatyam, Kuchipudi, Mohiniattam, Kathakali, Odissi and the devotional form of Kathak.

It would be impossible to speak of Indian music without referring to the whole genre of Bhakti poetry. *Ramcharitmanas* by Tulsidas, Surdas's padas, Kabir's sakhis and Meera's bhajans have shaped Indian music and Hindu religious orientation. Muslim poets like Rahim and Raskhan, in addition to Kabir, have written on Hindu religious themes. There has been religious music and poetry in every Indian language, an influence that continues to resonate. These include the abhangs of Tukaram (Marathi), vachanas of Basava (Kannada) and the kritis of Thayagaraja (Telugu). As the Bhakti tradition grew, new forms of singing such as group singing flourished. The kirtan tradition was strengthened by Chaitanya. Qawwali incorporates works of non-Muslim mystics and saints too.

I have always wondered how some of the most legendary Hindustani musicians, who often sing songs with Hindu themes, became Muslim. Namita Devidayal's book *Music Room* gives some answers. It was not as if Hindustani music came to India with the Mughals. In fact, Mughal kings, especially Akbar, embraced Hindustani music and persuaded the biggest Hindu singers and gurus to convert to Islam. So, encouraged by the visionary king, they converted to Islam but continued to sing the songs of Rama and Krishna. Classical Hindustani music is mostly sung in a language called Braj Bhasha and modern exponents do not pay as much attention to the lyrics as to the way the raga is explored. Aakar Patel writes in *Mint* (3 August 2013) about the historical figure Niyamat Khan, who under the pen name Sadarang pioneered the khayal form of Hindustani classical music which till then featured only dhrupad and qawwali. Niyamat Khan's father sang in the court of Aurangzeb and Niyamat in the court of Muhammad Shah. Niyamat apparently addressed the emperor as 'rangile', the colourful, since he was usually in an ebullient mood. Poor Muhammad Shah has also been called the Nero of Islam, since it was during his reign that Nadir Shah sacked Delhi. So much for music lovers.

In South India, Carnatic music continues to flourish. Almost all songs in Carnatic music have religious underpinnings. The greatest of Carnatic composers, Saint Thyagaraja, is believed to have composed thousands of songs in praise of Rama. I remember asking my IIT humanities professor R.K. Gupta why so many songs in Carnatic music were composed in Telugu. His short answer was that it is the 'sweetest' of Indian languages. Carnatic music transcends religions. One of the biggest exponents of the instrument nadaswaram was Sheikh Chinnamoulana Sahib. Yesudas, a Christian singer and disciple of Chembai Vaidyanatha Bagawathar, my grandfather's friend if I am permitted to add, has sung numerous songs in praise of all Hindu gods. Many years ago there was a big controversy when he requested to be permitted to perform in the Guruvayur temple.

If it was Pandit Ravi Shankar who took Indian classical music to the western world, it is John McLaughlin who brought Indian fusion music into mainstream jazz. The group he helped found in 1975 was aptly titled Shakti with John McLaughlin. Among others it featured L. Shankar on the violin, Vikku Vinayakram on the ghatam and Zakir Hussain on the tabla. John McLaughlin's first dedication to Indian music was the name he gave the jazz super group he founded in 1971—the Mahavishnu Orchestra. The group broke up in 1976 and was reconstituted by John in 1984. The original Shakti albums and the Mahavishnu Orchestra albums are must-haves for jazz fans around the world. I am sure all of them are also aware of the origin of the band's name and its dedication to a Hindu god.

When it comes to music we Indians are willing to overlook religious affiliations. The only two other areas where we can do this are cricket and films.

Advertising films and radio jingles have used music with religious connotations in multitudinous ways. Operatic music has been used by brands such as Titan and Indigo cars. Fair and Lovely used a Sanskrit mantra-like chant to launch their Ayurvedic formula fairness cream. In the Tata Docomo ad featuring a young girl with a new dragon tattoo, the creative director used the music of 'Venkatesa Suprabhatam', sung every morning to wake up Lord Venkateshwara in Tirupati.

Religious music is big business in India. Close to 40 per cent of the music sold in India would be religious in nature, say reports (obviously after we exclude film music). People are not just lapping up religious music, they are also buying CDs of mantras, shlokas and wellness music. Times Music claims that 50 per cent of the music they sell could be termed religious. The production cost of such an album is a fraction of the royalty charged by a Hindi movie banner and sales continue for a long time, unlike film music which tends to taper off soon after the release of the film. Hungama, a large mobile music provider, also claims that 45 per cent of the music they sell is religious in nature.

Religious music sales also get a boost from what is happening in other media. The hit television series *Devon ke Dev...Mahadev* is bound to have driven up sales of music related to Shiva and shloka music. Similarly, the popularity of Amish Tripathi's books on Shiva would have led to a surge in sales of Shiva music.

The last decade has seen the revival of rock bands of Indian origin. Bands like Indian Ocean and Parikrama have a big following across India. I suspect there is great opportunity for rock bands to blend religion into their offering. So there can be a rock band that marries Sufi music with rock and jazz for instance. Sushila Raman is an American jazz singer of Indian origin who is innovating with Carnatic songs sung in jazz format. Prasanna is using the electric guitar to innovatively present classical Carnatic songs. I am sure there will be pop, rock and jazz bands that can create music by bringing in Sufi, qawwalis, ragas and other forms of music.

The discussion on the revival of Indian rock bands and fusion music would be incomplete if we don't delve into the phenomenon of the Internet, YouTube, television, fusion and music coming together to create some great music. Coke Studio originated in Brazil as an online fusion music experiment some ten years ago. The multinational cola major Coca-Cola took the idea to Pakistan and created the Pakistan Coke Studio which was conceived as a music show in 2008 and featured musicians from across the spectrum, with Abida Parveen, the amazing Sufi singer, and Javed Bashir, a classical singer who hails from a family of qawwals, teaming up with mainstream Pakistani pop music bands like Strings and Zeb & Haniya. The show became a huge hit and the videos continue to garner millions of views on YouTube. Coke brought Coke Studio to India in 2011. Its media agency Lodestar UM did a unique tie-up with MTV and brought the show on the pop music channel. In 2013 the show was on its third season and had featured several singers from the religious music firmament, including the Tamil folk singer Chinnaponnu. Coke Studio MTV has garnered numerous industry awards and has triggered a strong fusion wave. Unlike the past fusion waves, which just combined instrumental music, the music this time is going to new places. In addition to *Coke Studio* on MTV we now have *The Dewarists* on Star World, *Sound Trippin* on MTV and *Sound Trek* on Fox Traveller. For *Sound Trek,* producer Ranjit Barot worked with the qawwals at Nizamuddin dargah. *The Dewarists* featured Harigovindan, who was born into a temple musician family and plays the edakka, a traditional Kerala percussion instrument. So, in a sense, these new shows are unearthing new talent and also making room for a fusion of traditional religious music of India to meld with western pop, rock and jazz music. Seeing the growth of these programmes, viewers too are clearly enjoying the feast.

In India, film music dominates the scene. This is followed by religious music and then classical music. Indian folk music, rock music and modern forms of music like fusion and jazz figure later in the list. In the future, there will be opportunities to combine these and create popular new music formats. Just as in television, where serials like *Devon ke Dev* and *Chhota Bheem* have created new markets for old heroes, in music too there could be new interpretations of, say, old ghazals rendered in new formats. Similarly, songs that are devotional in nature, specific to particular pilgrimages, could get reconfigured in modern formats. In television, we are seeing channels that cater to specific markets and tastes, for instance comedy or action. The religious genre could get further divided into religious music, religious travel, religious discourses, etc. There are several religious channels and I am sure we will have religious music channels in the future. Similarly, there will be websites streaming religious music, much like WorldSpace.

Talking about WorldSpace, it was a wonderful service. This satellite-based radio had over thirty channels spread across different genres. In this age of FM music that plays only the latest Bollywood hits, WorldSpace was manna from heaven.

I was an early subscriber and used to listen to their jazz and rock channels as well as to Shruti, the Carnatic music channel. It also had a few religious music channels, though Carnatic music could be classified religious by some readers. For a fee of Rs 1200 per annum you could get 24 hours of uninterrupted music. Unfortunately, it could not sustain the initial excitement and stopped operations in India in 2009, in spite of some heavy duty endorsement from people like A.R. Rahman. I just wonder if WorldSpace got the strategy all wrong. Rahman, the genius that he is, was the wrong ambassador. What if the company had got the top ten religious gurus to endorse the channel?

Would they have succeeded? I think god would have ensured their success!

19. Parsi-owned Car Sells in a Jiffy

Drinking beer is easy. Thrashing your hotel room is easy. But being a Christian, that's a tough call. That's real rebellion.

Alice Cooper (b. 1948)

Katy Modi was in a quandary. And she wanted some advice. Her father had passed away a few months ago and she was in the process of giving away his old possessions to the needy. She knew that her father has been very fond of his car, a Morris Minor, bought when it was introduced in 1952. Should she sell it, and if so how? Or should she keep it? What were the issues to be taken into account? Her friends around the lunch table in office were spewing ideas, as is wont with people in advertising. Someone said she should keep it and charge people for a ride. Someone else said she should send it to London's car museum. Another wise guy said she should sell it to a car collector. Finally, Katy realized that maintaining an old car was difficult and so it was best to sell it. But who would buy an old car and how was she to sell it? The next day the folks around the lunch table were again brimming with ideas. She should advertise in specialist car magazines, not the usual classified ad in the *Times of India*. No, said another person, she should list it on ebay.in. What should the ad say? Well, Morris Minor, 1952 model, in mint-fresh condition, single owner, well maintained. Was that enough?

It was then that a wiser soul in the room asked a question, Katy, you are a Parsi, right?

The group realized that they had missed out on an important sociological trivia. In the Indian automobile market, a Parsi-owned car always fetches a better price. A Parsi is supposed to be someone who loves history and tradition.

So the final ad read: A Parsi owned Morris Minor 1952 Model for sale. Single owner. Self-driven, self-maintained. Mint fresh condition.

The car was sold in one day.

What is it with us Indians and our religious stereotypes? A Sikh is supposed to be hard-working and good with his hands. A Christian nurse is the best in caring for her patients. When we made the first television advertisement for Tata Indica we had to show a wedding. The story was about a girl asking a young man in an Indica for a lift. The man looks at her and starts dreaming, of romancing her, eloping with her, getting married to her, having children with her and so on. The film titled *More Dreams Per Car* had a crucial wedding scene. The cast was all Indian and the film was shot in Ooty. But how about the wedding? Should it not be a nice Hindu wedding? We decided to go for a Christian wedding. The belief was that the Christian wedding has a sense of largeness, scale and style, not present in a noisy Hindu wedding.

If we were to go by demographics, more than 75 per cent of our cars would be bought by Hindus. Less than 5 per cent would be Christians. However, we opted for a Christian wedding, since it gave us a sense of scale—and remember only in a Christian wedding do the bride and groom drive away in a car (not strictly true as an elaborately decorated car is now a must-have accessory in Hindu weddings as well; Hindus have borrowed that from Christianity). The film was a big success, and post-campaign research confirmed what we had guessed. Indian consumers were quite happy seeing a Christian wedding. It was not perceived as alien.

In the 1960s, the American advertising agency legend Bill Bernbach turned the religious targeting taboo on its head when he wrote the lines 'You don't have to be Jewish to like Levy's. Real Jewish Rye'. The series of ads featured many characters, including a Native American, an Asian boy and the famous comedian Buster Keaton. The 'Levy's Real Jewish' could not really be called Jewish. It was a common thick bread baked in old-style stone hearths, Russian style. The founder of the company, Henry S. Levy, had learned those skills in Russia and turned them into a New York family fortune. Levy's bakery, located at 115 Thames Street, was a successful family business even before it was immortalized in advertising. When asked why he called it Jewish bread, Bill Bernbach is reported to have said, 'Levy is such a Jewish name, no one will mistake you for a Christian.' The advertising campaign has gone into history books and to museums. But it has also been called a racist campaign, a campaign that used our baser instincts to sell.

It may be of interest to readers that the Jews in Bollywood used to hide their identity. In the early days, film-makers were hard-pressed to get women to act in movies. Dadasaheb Phalke even tried to convince women from red-light areas to act in his film, but he failed. This is where Jews stepped in. Jewish women from progressive families were among the earliest movie actresses and the first genuine superstar of Indian cinema, Ruby Myers, better known as Sulochana, was a Jew.

Racial and religious stereotyping is used in marketing

communication to telegraphically code values that would be difficult to input into a small ad format. A tailor who looks Muslim speaks more than words (immortalized by the late Bollywood actor A.K. Hangal, who has played the Muslim tailor in numerous films). A nurse called Mary again telegraphically says she will be caring (a nurse called Shakti does not sit right). The sardar truck driver sits well (a truck driver who looks like a Jain does not fit). A Goan Christian is fun-loving as depicted in the Bollywood films *Bobby* and *Amar Akbar Anthony*.

In communication we try and use these short codes to tell the story in nanoseconds. But there is the danger of pressing some wrong buttons if we are not careful. Religious groups can take objection to the way a member of their community is portrayed. Similarly, groups can take objection to the way certain products are advertised. In Pakistan, for instance, there was a big hue and cry over a condom campaign that featured a famous Pakistani TV star. The film shows a bride who makes a neighbouring couple jealous by pampering her husband. Finally, the neighbour asks the rather nerdy-looking husband how he keeps his glamorous wife so sweet and he answers, 'Bring Josh into our life.' Josh being the brand name of the condom.

Objection to advertising could come from many quarters and could be driven by different agenda. International studies have tried to find out the relationship with religious affiliation and type of product advertised. Grouping 'objectionable' products/ services into four groups—gender/sex related (condoms, underwear, contraceptives, sanitary napkins), social/political groups (religious denominations, political parties), addictive products (cigarettes, alcohol) and healthcare products (weight loss, sexual cure), a study looked at Muslims, Christians, Buddhists and non-religious, across Malaysia, Turkey, the UK, China and New Zealand. Research shows that there are differences across countries and across religions. All religious groups found gender/sex-related products and addictive products advertising objectionable. Devout followers of Islam were the most sensitive to all these four types of advertising.

A study of this nature is yet to be done in India, but my submission would be that even devout Indians would be tolerant of advertising messages from objectionable products. We have had sanitary napkin and condom ads on television for decades now. Similarly, we have shown various religious stereotypes on television for years—a Hindu doing puja to a scooter, a Parsi fondly cleaning the logo of his mobike and so on.

The religious diversity of India offers opportunities for advertisers to use religious typologies to short code their messages. As S.C. Dube says in his wonderful little book *Indian Society*, there are eight major religious communities in India: Hindus, Muslims, Christians, Sikhs, Buddhist, Jains, Zoroastrians and Jews. We also have tribals who have close affinity with Hindus, though traditional Hinduism did not recognize them. Many of them are being actively converted to Christianity and Islam. Interestingly, all major religions and even minor ones have subdivisions, offering more typecasting opportunities. According to the 2001 Census, Hindus are 80.5 per cent of the population, Muslims 13.4 per cent, Christians 2.3 per cent, Sikhs 1.9 per cent, Buddhists 0.8 per cent, Jains 0.4 per cent and others (including Jews, Zoroastrians, undeclared) 0.6 per cent. Add to this the regional typecasting and the melting pot just became even bigger. But watch out!

There are two contradictory trends we will see as India develops. More and more Indians will start dressing similarly. Even today in villages you see men dressed in trousers. In an urban white-collar setting or in a call centre, workers are all dressed in similar clothes. You can't make out who belongs to which religion or caste (the vanishing bindi adds to the mystery). Paradoxically, Indians are also embracing their religions with renewed vigour. Many Muslim men are growing beards and some have taken to wearing traditional clothes as well. Wearing sacred threads on the wrist is becoming more and more common among Hindus. How these two trends will pan out is anybody's guess. Will the Muslim cap become more popular or less popular? Will the traditional Sikh attire vanish or continue or come back in a new, more modern form? Will the thread that a Brahmin wears become increasingly rare?

Here is a question: By looking at a person in your office can you guess his religion or caste? Chances are that this is highly unlikely. Even if you get him to speak for one whole minute on any topic, you may not be able to guess his religion. At best you might be able to guess his state of origin. Young Indians too are reflecting this mood by saying that they are Indians first (61 per cent), according to a study by *Hindustan Times* (15 August 2013). So will we not be able to use religious stereotypes in the future? I am not sure of that since each of us reverts to our stereotypical behaviour and dress once we enter the home zone. So if you visit your colleague at home, you may be able to guess his religion by looking at what he wears. Of course, if you attend any function at his home, a naming ceremony or a house warming, you will see him in his religious attire. So we will have enough opportunities to continue to use religious stereotypes in advertising like Levy's Bread.

It is here that I would sound a cautionary bugle. The Advertising Standards Council of India (ASCI), set up by the Indian Society of Advertisers and Advertising Agencies Association of India, a self-regulatory body, wants to widen its scope. It has several public activist groups in its complaints committee and is actively soliciting complaints from the public about objectionable ads.

The Indian government too is considering setting up its own ad monitoring body. Chances are that ASCI will be given extra powers to impose bans and maybe even fines. Before this becomes a reality, advertising in India needs to become more sensitive to the religious sentiments of the various groups. Socio-religious stereotyping will have to be done more carefully, without any derogatory nuances. Advertising 'objectionable' products will also have to be handled with care.

But I am sure a Parsi-owned car will always triumph over a Goan Christian-owned mobike!

20. Timeless Religious Art

God . . . invented the giraffe, the elephant, the cat . . . He has no real style. He just goes on trying things.

Pablo Picasso (1881–1973)

We work with ICICI Bank's International Business Group (IBG) to support their marketing efforts in countries such as Canada, the UK and the US. The bank has a very successful track record in these countries and its clientele goes beyond the Indian diaspora. The ICICI IBG team is always looking for ideas to better connect with their customers through numerous direct marketing campaigns, television advertising, merchandising efforts and more. A few years ago, they felt the time had come to do something they had not done before. Keeping the Indian diaspora in mind, they asked the agency to think of a desk calendar that would resonate with them.

Ulka was famous for its Hongkong Bank calendars in the 1980s. Many of those calendars became coveted gifts. My favourite was the one which featured six antique chess sets from the exquisite collection of the Ulka founder Bal Mundkur. Other calendars featured rare artefacts, statues and jewellery from collectors, ancient manuscripts, etc. But those wall calendars were aimed at the upper echelon. We now had to target the Indian diaspora on foreign shores, people who weren't necessarily in the upper levels of those societies. Chances were they hardly had a work of art in their home, unlike the Hongkong Bank customers in tony South Bombay homes in the 1980s.

Coincidentally, the design director who was faced with the ICICI Bank challenge was the same person who had worked on the Hongkong Bank calendar as a young trainee. What could unite the Indian diaspora and also be appealing to non-Indian customers?

When in doubt the team did what all Indians do: they sought divine inspiration.

The first year they decided that the desk calendar would feature exquisitely illustrated images of the most famous temples of India. They picked out six temples that would qualify as beautiful architectural monuments. They identified a line illustration artist, who was asked to sketch them in the old 'pen and ink' style. The artist, Pushpa Gandre, took almost three months to do the illustrations. At the end, the team had six wonderful images. Each image was accompanied by a short biography of the temple. To the devout, the image of the temple conveyed a sense of blessing whenever he looked at the calendar. To the non-Hindu, the illustrations by themselves were beautiful and the buildings looked like wonders of the world.

The religious theme has continued for several years with different themes and different art styles. One recent calendar featured watercolour illustrations of various goddesses from the Hindu pantheon, each with its own message and blessing. Again something that would cut through religious boundaries.

Almost all artistic remains of ancient India are of a religious nature or made for religious purposes. It is not as if secular art did not exist. We know our ancient kings lived in sumptuous palaces replete with wall paintings and sculptures, though a lot of these have vanished. The nearest Sanskrit equivalent for the term art is shilpa, which means diverse or variegated. It was first used to describe decorative arts and subsequently for all forms of skills such as archery, architecture, painting, cookery and even the sciences. While arts were discussed in the Vendangas and Upa-Vedas, the chief manuals were the Shilpa Shastras created around the second century BCE.

Experts tell us that Indian art is somewhat different from the art of medieval Europe. Temple towers, though tall, are solidly based on earth. Gods and demigods alike are young and handsome, their bodies are rounded and well nourished and, often by European standards, effeminate. While they are occasionally grim or angry, they are generally portrayed as smiling. With the exception of the dancing Shiva, they are always firmly rooted, either fully seated or standing with both feet on the ground. In Indian temple sculpture, Hindu, Buddhist and Jain alike, the female form is made full use of as a decorative motif, often scantily clad and always in accordance with the Indian definition of beauty.

While Indian art had its own styles, with the arrival of the Mughals and Europeans, alien designs became fused with indigenous styles; it is not easy to unravel all the influences. The term 'Hindu art', experts warn us, is difficult to decode. As early as the fourth century BCE, Indians were expert imitators. Indian sculptors worked wonders with Achaemenid, Hellenistic and Central Asian art forms, as seen in the Ashoka columns in Sanchi and other places. There is an apocryphal story about how an artist in Shah Jahan's court reproduced a European painting and presented six copies before experts and no one could identify the original.

It is to be noted that ancient Indian religious art differs significantly from religious literature. The latter was created by men with vocations, Brahmins, monks and ascetics. Religious art was created by skilled craftsmen, who worked according to priestly instructions and rigid iconographic rules (we saw vastu earlier) and loved the world they lived in, expressing themselves in many lively ways. As a result, Indian art is not a ceaseless search for the ultimate truth but a manifestation of the delight in the world as the artist saw it, and is infused with that sensuous vitality.

Is that what binds religion and calendar art in our country? For decades, images of the goddesses Saraswati and Lakshmi have been defined by their portrayal on calendars which reproduced illustrations done by Raja Ravi Varma. In fact, some of those original calendars are now collector's items. Original lithograph prints of calendar art have been in great demand at exhibitions. Religious-themed calendars are still a rage all over India and are featured internationally as kitsch art. There are calendars that appeal to other religious groups, featuring the Golden Temple, Mother Mary and the Kaaba of Mecca.

As *The Economist* says, 'Religions have a rum relationship with calendars. They invite people to enter a reality that transcends all the limitations of time, space and finitude; yet faiths are often disputatiously obsessed with pinning down the precise moment at which certain cosmically important event occurred or should be celebrated.'

In fact, the connection between religion and calendars is not so much about art; it is about pinning down the dates for various celebrations. In the Hindu calendar, the tithi, the lunar day, is of prime importance to determine the good days and the bad days.

Various types of calendars are popular totems across India. As we saw earlier, Kalnirnay, the calmanac published by the

Salgaonkar family, claimed a total printrun of over 1.4 crore across languages at its peak. The family managed to create several advertising properties around the calendar and generated substantial revenues from marketers of daily consumption products.

In Kerala, the most popular calendar is the one brought out by the Manorama group of publications, which is used by all religious groups. In Tamil Nadu, daily tear-away calendars are more popular.

As religion goes hi-tech, these calendars are available in downloadable forms that can sit on your laptop or tablet computer. iPhone and Android apps too are freely available, keeping the tech-savvy in touch with tithis.

Closely linked to the calendar mania in our country is the obsession with astrological predictions. No newspaper or popular magazine is complete without an astrology column. Brands compete to support these astrology columns. The lesser-known fact is that astrologers too fight over these columns and are willing to offer the columns free provided their photograph and name are prominently mentioned.

While more literate, worldly-wise Indians move to centre stage, we don't see them giving up on any of these trappings. Capitalizing on this trend, companies are able to market amulets and rings to suit various astrological signs. Every jeweller has a selection to satisfy the astrologically minded.

Moving back to religious art, some of the most famous Indian painters of this era have painted religious figures. M.F. Husain's Durga paintings are world famous. Jamini Roy's paintings of gods and goddesses are prized collector's items. S.H. Raza's tantric themed 'dot' paintings have a broad religious underpinning. Their paintings are much valued by art collectors around the world, and most of them know that these paintings have strong religious significance. However, the master of religious-themed paintings is, of course, Raja Ravi Varma, who has painted innumerable mythological characters and gods and goddesses. Many young painters are also exploring new ways of presenting religious art.

Anjali Kale is a wonderful artist who decided to experiment with wood and paint. She conceptualized a new art form that I would call 'wood art'. It is a hybrid form of art which uses three-dimensional wooden forms mounted on a frame and painted in great detail. In her first exhibition, held a couple of years ago, she experimented with several artistic themes such as nature, symbols and religious figures. Interestingly, her most popular art piece is Shrinathji, based on the image of the seven-year-old Krishna as depicted in the temple at Nathdwara near Udaipur in Rajasthan. I got her to make one for my home and she continues to get requests for custom-designed Shrinathji pieces, the latest being a five foot by eight foot mural commissioned by an art lover and Krishna devotee. The Paris-based Raza visited Kale's exhibition after reading about it in the paper. Great artists often see art in things that we commoners see as mundane objects. Campbell soup cans were seen as art by Andy Warhol. Piet Mondrian saw art in lines and squares. Jackson Pollack saw art in paint dripped on a canvas.

I think there is going to be a big boom in religious art in the country. Growing affluence, improving design and art sense are bound to create a market for religious-themed art. Paintings, wood art, metal sculptures, ceramics, all are going to be in demand. There are thousands of temples around India and each one houses hundreds of ideas for art. There are several books on art and sculpture in Indian temples. Shilpi, an artist who worked for the Tamil magazine *Ananda Vikatan*, spent a large part of his life sketching temples and temple sculptures all over

South India's temples. Recently, the magazine brought out a two-volume, 1000-page compilation of his work.

A few years ago, a friend gifted me the 'Vedic diary', containing over 200 line drawings of religious idols done exquisitely by the artist Ganapathi Satapathy. While most diaries find their way out of the house once the year is over, this one continues to live in my bookshelves. That is the power of religious art.

I would strongly recommend that those of you planning to paint or draw take a field trip through books on sculpture and religious art, then plan a real one to some of the beautiful temples dotting the country. Then start painting. Either way you will end up a lot richer.

21. Religion Goes Hi-Tech

Science is a differential equation. Religion is a boundary condition.

Alan Turing (1912–54)

India has been the beneficiary of the IT boom, the early pioneer being Tata Consultancy Services (TCS). From tapping the potential of the lower cost of software professionals in India to unlocking the power of the global delivery model and now to a networked model that works on the cloud, TCS and its Indian cohorts have done the country proud, creating many millionaires and providing job opportunities for millions of Indians along the way.

While Indian IT majors leveraged the potential of trained computer programmers and the global delivery model, they also pioneered the creation of well-oiled matrix organizations. These organizations created verticals that specialized in specific industry domains like manufacturing, retail, telecom, banking and healthcare. Simultaneously, they also created practice silos such as e-commerce, ERP (enterprise resource planning), accounting and human resources. If the Indian IT industry benefited from the global boom of banking and telecom automation, it should now wake up to the opportunity offered by yet another growth industry: religion.

Cloud computing in the next decade will get a divine touch with religion touted to be the next big boom industry for IT service companies. The global consultancy company Gartner estimates that the size of religion-driven IT will be more than $40 billion by 2017. Religion-based IT services would cover banking, equity trading, mutual funds and financial services (including Islamic banking, takaful insurance and the Dharma Global Index, where the performance of companies selected is based on dharmic religions such as Hinduism and Buddhism). Each of these areas needs new applications, products and customized solutions. IT companies will not only need programmers, they will also need religious domain experts.

There were reportedly 125 million Indians on the Internet in 2012; of these, 38 million use the Internet for online transactions, the biggest application being train and airline tickets. A new breed of entrepreneurs is planning to tap the online medium and offer unique religious products and services. The types of businesses envisaged include online darshan and prasad from temples across India, retailing of specific products like pilgrimage kits for Haj and Umrah, religion-specific products like turbans for Sikhs and online distribution of books, music and videos based on religious mythology. A Hyderabad-based online venture, for instance, provides a full kit for Haj and Umrah. It consists of twenty-three products, including the unstitched cloth used for covering the body called ihram, prayer beads and maps of the pilgrimage site. A site called silkturbansonline.com is seeing demand from places like the UK and Australia. It also hopes to see increased demand from India soon.

One of the biggest potential winners is onlineprasad.com. The site offers to do a puja and send prasad to you. They have made on-ground arrangements to do pujas in thirty well-known temples across India. These include Vaishno Devi, Palani

Murugan, Shirdi Sai Baba, Lord Venkateshwara (Tirupati) with rates starting from just Rs 501. The venture started by the Birla Institute of Technology and Science (BITS) alumnus and former Bain & Co. analyst Goonjan Mal was recently picked up for investment by the pedigreed serial investors K. Ganesh and Meena Ganesh, founders of the hugely successful Tutorvista. Meena and Ganesh have picked up a 35 per cent stake in the venture and will help the company go for scale. They plan on expanding the number of temples on their roster to a hundred. The plans are to tap into the growing $1 billion religious spends by Indians on the Net, both from India and abroad.

I believe there could be a great opportunity for Online Prasad to offer an off-line darshan version as well, in partnership with a travel portal.

Religious organizations are also reaping the benefits of technology in very many different ways. It was reported that 15,000 devotees get their head tonsured at Tirupati every year. The hair is collected by the temple and sold to wig makers from the US, France and Italy as well as some Asian countries. In September 2011, temple authorities conducted an e-auction for the first time and managed to get Rs 133 crore as against Rs 105 crore collected the previous year. In 2013, temple authorities asked a government-owned metal trading company to help out with the auction and managed to net Rs 250 crore.

Temples and religious gurus are using the online medium to spread the message far and wide. However, social media is still a bit of a novelty. At least the Catholic Church is trying to get its hands around the social media animal. Reports say that the resignation of Pope Benedict was also an opportunity for the Catholic Church to rebrand itself for the age of social media. Apparently, communicating daily with the masses is not new to the Vatican. Pope John Paul II was well into his seventies when he inspired millions of people to see him and he communicated a daily message to the Catholics through SMS, the Twitter of his day.

In India, it is estimated that the mobile will be the most important medium for online communication, surpassing the computer. And if smartphones are going to be in many more hands, smartphone apps cannot be far behind. Free apps like the Hanuman Chalisa are already quite popular. It is possible many other such apps will find favour. You may get live kirtans or religious hymns whenever you want them. All this for a small monthly fee.

Indian software developers and IT companies are set to reap rich dividends if they get on this religious tech bandwagon early. Given the multiplicity of religions in our country and the trained software manpower, India can lead this wave of technology even more definitively than it did the earlier wave. Imagine apps that are aimed at Catholics, Protestants, Shia Muslims, Sunni Muslims, Hindus, Sikhs, Buddhist, Jains . . . chances are that you can get software programmers belonging to each of these religions to do your app development. So you are doubly sure that the app developed is halal or Hindu or Jesus compliant.

We started the story with Indian tech firms tapping the religious IT opportunity. To tap this global opportunity they need to send Indian tech guys to the US. And for that they need H1B visas. It is here that Visa Balaji comes in. I was in Hyderabad visiting a friend and we got down to our children's career plans. His daughter had completed her engineering course and joined an IT major in the city. Her employer was sending her to the US for an extensive job assignment. She had never been to the US and was hoping she would have no problems in getting her visa. Her insurance was Visa Balaji!

The Chillur Balaji temple outside Hyderabad has gained an

awesome reputation as Visa Balaji. Devotees start gathering outside the temple at 7 a.m. As an applicant put it, 'I would feel terrible if my visa was rejected and I had not come here to pray.' The temple on some days sees as many as 500 visa applicants visiting it. 'Visa is not under my control. It is all luck. The only way to change my luck is through god,' the temple priest says.

22. Honesty, Charity, Religiosity

Sorting out what's good and bad is the province of ethics. It is also what keeps priests, pundits and parents busy. Unfortunately, what keeps children and philosophers busy is asking the priests, pundits and parents, 'why?'

Thomas Cathcart and Daniel Klein,
in *Plato and a Platypus Walk into a Bar*

You may remember this famous ad. A woman is trying to balance her shopping bag and it falls, scattering all that is inside on the pavement. A small boy, a stranger, rushes to her help. He picks up the oranges, apples, soap packs and more as she reassembles her shopping bag. Just as she is about to leave, he notices a pack of his favourite brand of biscuits lying under a car. There is also a pack of agarbattis with a Ganesha on the pack. The lady seemed to have missed picking up the packets. The kid is in two minds, it is his favourite biscuit. The lady is about to walk away. What should he do? Pick up the biscuit packet and give it to her? Or let it lie there and pick it up only after she crosses the road?

I played a little trick just now. In reality the ad did not have a Ganesha in it. The little boy listens to the devil playing games with his thoughts, but the angel in his head wins. He picks up the small biscuit pack and rushes to give it back to her. The woman smiles and asks him to keep it, adding a bar of chocolate as well.

Now think back. Did the Ganesha agarbatti pack do anything to you when you were reading the story? Did you have any guesses about the way the kid would behave? What would have determined his behaviour? The Ganesha? His upbringing? The home he lived in? The socio-economic class he belonged to?

Chances are that you would bet on the fact that he is from a caring, religious home. But why? What has honesty got to do with our religious practices and beliefs?

Dan Ariely, professor of psychology at Duke University, offers an interesting course on the MOOC platform Coursera. I took a course offered by him titled Beginners Guide to Irrational Behaviour. He explained in one lecture how religion can make us think in more ethical terms. According to an experiment he and his research scholars conducted, a consumer made to think of god and religion will behave more ethically. She will not lie and will not cheat—to a large extent.

So I inserted a Ganesha agarbatti pack in the above story to test if you could spot the implication.

This is not the place to get into a debate on the larger purpose of religion, but research has shown that religiousness does have a role to play in ethical behaviour. In the western, largely Christian setting, religiosity is measured across two dimensions: intrinsic religiosity (prayer and self-meditation) and extrinsic religiosity (going to church, societal activities involving religion). It has been shown that intrinsic religiosity is a strong determinant of consumer ethical beliefs, but extrinsic religiosity is not related to those beliefs. In a sense a person who is internally religious seems to be a lot more honest than a person who may be outwardly more religious.

In their light-hearted take on philosophy, *Plato and a Platypus*

Walk into a Bar, Thomas Cathcart and Daniel Klein speak of the proverbial golden rule: 'Do unto others as you would have others do unto you.' Emanuel Kant called it the supreme categorical imperative. George Bernard Shaw wryly said, 'Do not do unto others as you would have others do unto you; they may have different tastes.' Cathcart and Klein find instances of this golden rule in the Mahabharata, the Babylonian Talmud (Judaism), the Dadistan-i-Dinik (Zoroastrianism), the Tibetan Dhammapada (Buddhism), Analectus (Confucianism), the Sunnah (Islam), the Hidden Words (Bahai'i) and, of course, the Bible.

So, if all religions tell us to uphold ethical behaviour and never do unto others what we would not have them do unto us, why, despite our high religiosity, both intrinsic and extrinsic, are we seeing so much unethical behaviour in India? The explanation may come from the role of money ethic, or love of money. It has been found that strong money ethic negates the positive impact of intrinsic religiosity, encouraging unethical behaviour. Yet another explanation comes from a study published in *The Economist*. Analysing data from the World Values Survey covering eighty-seven countries—the survey asked consumers about their religiosity as well as acceptability of a range of infractions like littering to adultery—it was found that people whose religion includes an omniscient, judgemental god (Christians, Muslims, and so on) regard the whole range of such transgressions more harshly than those such as Buddhists whose religions don't have a strong judgemental god (maybe Hindus fit in this bracket?). Is it therefore right to assume that Hinduism does not have any role to play in the honesty or lack thereof of Indians?

There are no systematic treatises dealing with ethics in Hinduism though norms of moral conduct are scattered throughout Sanskrit writings and even in the Tamil *Thirukkural*. Hindu literature speaks of purushartha, or human object or aim of human existence, having four dimensions. These are artha or wealth or material power and possessions which is the domain of politics, statecraft, economics, etc.; kama or physical love, the domain of eroticism and the *Kama Sutra*; dharma or righteousness, concerned with ethics and law; and moksha or salvation through spiritual knowledge, the domain of religion and yoga. Moksha is therefore spoken of as the paramartha or supreme wealth. While there seems to be no single work called the Dharmashastra, like *Arthashastra* or *Kama Sutra*, the Upanishads mention several virtues such as non-injury (ahimsa), truth (satya), non-stealing (asteya), continence (brahmacharya), friendliness (maitri), duty (dharma), compassion (karuna), fortitude (virya), self-restraint (dama) and purity (saucha).

There is the famous story of Da found in many Hindu texts. The Brihadaranya Upanishad outlines three virtues through this story. Gods, men and demons went to their common father Prajapati and asked for guidance in the matter of the chief virtue. Prajapati gave a monosyllabic answer, 'Da.' The gods took this to mean dama or taming, the men took it to mean datta or giving, charity, and the demons took it to mean daya or mercy. The Upanishads say that when thunder says 'DA DA DA', the gods, men and demons hear it as 'self-control, charity and mercy'.

Unfortunately, da does not seem to connote charity for Indians any more. Look at yet another data point. Indians donate huge sums to temples and religious gurus (these may be attributed to favours received) but Indians rank a poor 133 of 150 in the World Giving Index. Interestingly, the 'Muslim country' Bangladesh ranks 109 and the 'Hindu country' Nepal 115.

As a share of GDP, private charity contributions are only 0.4 per cent in India, compared to 1.3 per cent in the UK and 2.2 per cent in the US.

Why is a country so high in religiosity and full of gods and godmen ranked so low in a list of giving to the needy and the destitute? Will this change as Indians become more and more wealthy? Will they make significant contributions to charitable causes?

There is no denying that many temples and trusts run by gurus are doing good work in terms of running schools and hospitals. But they are really proverbial drops in the ocean. There is possibly an opportunity for NGOs to leverage religion to their own advantage and get Indians to unzip their purses. World Vision is a global body that supports children. Though it is Christian, it does not differentiate between who receives charity from it. While discussing the group's marketing strategy many years ago, I realized they found that advertising in women's magazines worked best for them. They also felt that showing children worked better than showing a mother and child. In a similar vein, other NGOs also need to figure out what will work for them. I would submit that using religious symbols could also help in increasing commitment. Parivaar is an NGO based in Kolkata, started by an alumnus of IIM-C. Parivaar tries to reach its donors before big festivals like Durga Puja and Diwali. While it sends out its emails as timely reminders, I don't get such reminders from other NGOs that I know. Several other charitable organizations in India such as the Ramakrishna Mission do not have a strong marketing, fund-raising arm. They are sitting on a potentially great opportunity.

One of the biggest Indian not-for-profit fund-raising organizations in the US is the Sankara Eye Foundation (SEF). The foundation collects money in the US to fund eye surgery for the needy in India through the Sankara Eye Care institutions. What Dr R.V. Ramani started as one hospital in Coimbatore is now present in ten states and is set to grow to twenty states across India. SEF raises funds through the NRI community in the

US and some of its biggest fund-raising occasions are religious festivals and events at the local temples. Indians in the US have absorbed the American ethos of giving and have managed to help thousands of poor Indians regain their eyesight. When my colleague and I visited the Coimbatore branch of the Sankara Eye Care Institution, I was curious to know why they had chosen the name Sankara. There is the Sankara Netralaya in Chennai, also doing yeoman service. Dr Ramani explained that he was a general practitioner and had started out with a small clinic to serve the poor. It was the Kanchi pontiff who advised him to focus on eye care given the high incidence of cataract-related blindness in India. Simultaneously, Sankara Netralaya also drew inspiration from the Kanchi seer's desire to eradicate avoidable blindness from the country. Both these Sankaras do great service to society and are expanding their reach to cover the whole nation. I would submit that intense religiosity is a driving force for the Sankara institutions.

Unfortunately, we don't have too many such examples in India itself. It is possible that Indian businessmen are just about seeing real wealth and are in the process of building new hospitals, educational institutions, etc. across the country. One community that has set high standards in giving are the Parsis, who account for less than 0.1 per cent of India's population. A simple enumeration of the institutions they set up in the last century will convince you: Indian Institute of Science, Tata Memorial Hospital, Tata Institute of Fundamental Research, Tata Institute of Social Sciences, Jehangir Art Gallery, J.J. Hospital, National Centre for Performing Arts, Grant Medical College, among others. I am hopeful that in the coming decade we will see hundreds of hospitals, colleges and universities coming up across India, powered by spirituality and charity.

Moving to non-governmental social service organizations, we

do have numerous NGOs and some are doing great work. But we need them to scale up so that they can make a more sizeable impact. It is possible they are not using the power of religion to help them grow.

Over the last five years I have been hearing a lot about what is known as conscious capitalism, a form of capitalism that is not rooted in exploitation but in sharing of wealth. In line with this ethos there have been two new trends in India. The growth of social service and corporate social responsibility awards and the growth of what is known as social sector businesses. We Indians love awards of any kind. In the last three years, I have attended at least five awards that recognize NGOs and social sector organizations. These awards recognize several different types of social sector groups in the sectors of healthcare and education as well as the not-for-profit, for-profit, part of a large company/group, government-owned or -run segments and the like. I am yet to see religious social sector as a category. It would be worth looking at this and to evaluate which temple, which mosque and which church is using its funds in the best possible manner. Are they serving the general public by spending the money they collect every year from the devotees in a prudent manner? Are they running charity hospitals? Are they running schools for the poor?

If we can build some consciousness among the educated middle class about how donations to a temple are actually getting used for the social good of society, perhaps we can get them all to become more Muslim and give zakat to their local temple. I am not sure if this can happen in my lifetime, especially since most Hindus see their contribution to the temple as going to their favourite god for favours rendered, but it is worth a try. And maybe we can really get Indians to give away 2.5 per cent of their annual income to charity. That would be something big.

It is thus fitting that the biggest philanthropist in India is Azim Premji, who is setting new standards in giving. Looking at him, others too are picking up the baton. Educational institutions are coming up funded by philanthropic industrialists around the country. Hospitals too are being built.

The tone was set by the industrialist J.N. Tata more than a century ago when he donated half his wealth to set up India's first institute of science, the Indian Institute of Science, Bangalore. That move is now hearing echoes around the country. As they start ringing, temple and church bells can also join in the celebrations.

The loftiest dharma is one's duty performed for its own sake, says the Mahabharata. Yudhishthira says, 'If I do not look for the reward for my conduct, it is because I do not trade in virtue, or greedily seek the fruits of my righteousness. I follow the paths of those who have lived wise and holy lives because I consider it my duty to do so.'

I am sure the Indian rich too can be made to give—not because they are expecting any fruits for their virtuousness but as a simple conduct of righteousness.

23. Can Spirituality Lift Business Education?

A thorough knowledge of the Bible is worth more than a college education.

Theodore Roosevelt (1858–1919)

I have the privilege and honour of sitting on the board of governors of my alma mater, the Indian Institute of Management-Calcutta. It is India's oldest institute of management and has blazed many new trails. I believe it is not just another business school but a pioneer in many important fields. IIM-C was probably the first management institute to realize the new imperatives of business management, over three decades ago. It set up the Centre for Human Values in 1991, probably the first management school in the world to do so. As Professor S.K. Chakraborty says, 'I read research papers from other Asian countries—which showed emphatically how all of them have struggled to build the "soft" side of management on the strengths of their own religio-spiritual cultures.' SKC, as he was known, taught us finance and control in the years 1977–79 and began a course called 'management and Indian ethos'.

There has been a whole lot of debate on the need to reform management education, not just in India but around the world. There is widespread fear that MBA education breeds number-crunching clones who are programmed to make money and little else. In the fascinating book *Rethinking the MBA* three Harvard Business School professors, Srikant Datar, David Garvin and Patrick Culien, say that business schools need to teach their students that principles, ethics and attention to details are essential components of leadership and they need to place greater emphasis on leaders' responsibilities and not just rewards. The economic and financial crisis of 2008 has made such reforms critical for the long-term survival of business schools around the world.

If management education is set to prepare a new generation of managers to face tomorrow's challenges, it is really a moot point if they should know how religion will interact with business. We examined the potential rise of Islamic banking in an earlier chapter. We saw the opportunities offered online to serve the religious millions. But I believe that is not the only purpose of adding religion to business school curriculums.

In *The Clash of Civilizations* Samuel Huntington prophesied that future clashes will not be between countries but between cultures as defined by religion, race and language. Not necessarily geographic borders. As the young decode religion in their own way, global religiosity is showing no signs of decline. And with Africa set to join the group of developing zones, we are set to see even newer challenges.

Harvard Business School sent a whole team to study the Kumbh Mela phenomenon in Allahabad in 2013. The paper they plan to publish is expected to cover the challenge of creating a megacity in double quick time and dismantling it soon after. In addition, I do hope the study also covers what drives the millions to visit the holy site. Will their numbers continue to rise as India becomes increasingly prosperous? If so, what will the challenge at the next Maha Kumbh Mela be? Will there be a five-star devotee wanting a helicopter darshan? The study was supposed to study devotion, design, health and finance coming together. I also hope it looks into the future of all these dimensions as well.

There is a growing 'God in Business' school of thinking emerging in the US. Sample this:

A conference at the business school of Santa Clara University, a Jesuit institution in Silicon Valley, California, begins with the melodious strain of a Tibetan bowl, a reading from the Sufi mystic Rumi and a few moments of silent meditation.

The commencement address at Stanford University in June 2013, which I attended, was opened by a Christian pastor and closed by a Jewish rabbi, and they made the best speeches that day, not one word of which was a sermon.

A lecture series called Faith@Work is organized in Firth Avenue Presbyterian Church in New York City attended by senior business leaders.

In India as well business leaders are embracing religiosity and other forms of spiritual awakening. Vipassana meditation, the journey of discovery with long periods of silence, has some big followers. Business conferences attract spiritual leaders as keynote speakers. I was at the 2012 Ad Asia conference in Delhi which featured eminent speakers drawn from the biggest global corporations. But wonder of wonders, the only speaker to get a standing ovation was Swami Sukhbodananda! Sri Sri Ravishankar too was well received when he spoke at a Pan IIT Alumni conference in 2006. I have been to Jaggi Vasudev's talks and he frequently gets a standing ovation. In a first-of-its-kind initiative, he partnered with the business thinker Ram Charan in early 2012 to offer a three-day retreat for business leaders at his ashram.

If all this is happening in the business world, is it not necessary to prepare the young in business schools, asks the management guru Warren Bennis. There are others who argue that spirituality will eventually find its place in work for one simple reason—it works. Spirituality, the belief that all individuals have dignity, that we are all interconnected, that a transcendent force defines our purpose, fits in well with what contemporary management thinking says about great companies. These successful companies do not use people as machines, they do not buy eight hours a day but are sensitive to human wants and deploy interconnected teams of people who strive for excellence in all that they do. These companies encourage listening, learning and sharing. And they have a mission that is beyond the bottom line.

As Hamilton Beasley who teaches at George Washington University says, 'Spirituality is in convergence with all the cutting-edge thinking in management and organizational behaviour. It creates a higher-performing organization.'

Bennis has lamented the fact that religion is not a part of business school syllabi. All business schools claim that they are creating global minds but how complete is that global mind if it knows nothing about global religions, he asks. Shouldn't they know about the rise of capitalism in Europe along with Protestant Reformation (Weber's Protestant work ethic)? Should they not know about the growth of Islam as the youngest global religion? Should they not know of Hinduism and its creeping presence in the US? And what will the growth of religion do to the Chinese work ethos?

Bennis recounts an interesting anecdote in an article published in *Business Week*. He attributes it to Groucho Marx, a Jew himself. A famous New Yorker, Otto Kahn, a Jew and a phenomenally wealthy one who had donated huge sums of money to many institutions including the Metropolitan Museum, was good friends with Marshall P. Wilder, a hunchback and an actor of great repute. Kahn and Wilder were one day walking past a newly constructed synagogue on Fifth Avenue. Kahn remarked, 'You know, I used to be a Jew!' To which Wilder replied, 'Really? I used to be a hunchback.'

Would a dose of religion help the new generation of managers understand this complex world?

I undertook an elaborate search for such a course across all leading global business schools and could not find any specific course dedicated to world religions. I did not even find a course that could be termed anthropological in nature and covered religious issues. I suspect business schools may be a little wary of bringing in religion into the curriculum given the incendiary nature of religion in Indian and global politics. But it may be a good idea to offer management and anthropology as a subject or 'cultural issues of management' as a compulsory course for all business school graduates. This one- or two-credit course could cover the basic aspects of the key religions of the world, including their origins, key religious underpinnings, growth and population around the world and their managerial implications.

I suspect religion could have implications in human resource management, in marketing, both domestic and global, environmental management, covering lawmakers, shareholders, stakeholders and the media, etc. Understanding of global religions is going to be all the more critical given the changes expected in Arab countries after the Arab Spring of 2012. The course should have case studies that could touch areas like a Christian CEO's first day in a Hindu country, or launching a halal product in a Muslim country, or HR issues arising out of religious practices of minorities (a simple holiday list can become a thorny topic, if not handled well). I think Indian business schools can be real pioneers in this domain. Already, some like S.P. Jain and the Narsee Monjee Institute of Management Studies (NMIMS) have created innovative learning opportunities like making their students spend two months with an NGO. This exercise is aimed at helping privileged business school students understand the challenges facing the underprivileged and also to help them think of innovative ways of applying management principles to the social sector. In a similar vein, I think Indian business schools can innovate by creating course outlines that can teach students the fundamentals of world religions and how they can impact business. Given the multi-religious nature of our country, we can help create case studies and exercises that can be used by business schools around the world.

As more and more Indian companies start operations around the world, it will become important for Indian managers to understand the cultural differences. In his pioneering study across countries, the Dutch social psychologist Geert Hofstede identified five dimensions of national culture—power distance, individualism–collectivism, masculinity–femininity, uncertainty avoidance and long-term orientation. This seminal study was done more than three decades ago and is still widely used to understand cultural differences across countries. For instance, his study showed that eastern societies like India and China are more collectivistic: we consult with many people before taking any decision. We also sport high power distance: there is a big social divide between the higher and lower classes. Many business schools have a course that covers these issues well. But, in addition to these issues, it may be necessary to educate young managers about religious differences. As Mareike De Mooj says in *Consumer Behaviour and Culture*, 'If we trace the religious history of countries, what religion a population has embraced seems to have been a result of previously existing cultural value patterns more than a cause of cultural differences.' Be that as it may, with changing population structures, the challenges the future will pose will indeed be daunting. And knowing the local population's cultural and religious values can help an Indian company achieve miraculous results.

Let me recount the story of Galaxy Surfactants, a Rs 2000 crore company in the business of speciality chemicals used in personal care products, and its Egypt plant. The plant had been on the anvil for many years but when construction finally started, disaster struck in the form of the civilian uprising against the long-time political leader Hosni Mubarak. Indian managers who had been sent to Egypt to oversee the construction had to be called back in a hurry. When normalcy returned, they volunteered to go back and get the plant going. Soon, it was the month of Ramadan. What the Indians did then was amazing. They partnered with local labour contractors to help workers observe the religious fast. But they also got the labourers to agree to work extra hours after sunset, under artificial lights, so that the project delay could be compensated. This was achieved because the Indian managers made serious attempts to integrate themselves with local religious customs and practices. What was achieved was indeed a miracle.

In a similar vein, when Wipro acquired Unza, a Southeast Asian cosmetics company with a large team in Malaysia, it made an effort to invite the Malaysians, many of them Muslims, to India to help them understand the ethos and value systems of the company run by a large number of Hindus. In the process, the Wipro team dispelled any fears the Malaysians may have had regarding the practices and culture of the Indian major.

As Indian businesses increasingly become part of the global ecosystem, our managers will have to understand cultural and religious differences. They will have to learn to deal with executives from very different backgrounds. Understanding cultural differences can play a very useful role. So will understanding religious differences.

24. The Last Word

Aandavan solran. Arunachalam seiran.
(God tells. Arunachalam does.)

Rajinikanth (b. 1950) in the movie *Arunachalam*

Mumbai Mirror ran an irreverent joke a few months ago. A school teacher asks her class, 'Children, can you tell me what is common amongst Rama, Guru Gobind, Mahavir, Prophet Muhammad and Jesus Christ.' One kid shouted from the back of the class, 'They were all born on government holidays.'

That joke exaggerated the reality of the situation. It is possible that kids in most of our schools know very little about the multiple religions that coexist so vibrantly in our country. The only thing they probably know is that we have school holidays on the birthdays of the gods and gurus. I suspect that is an exaggeration of sorts though I should admit I did not learn about any religion other than Hinduism in my own school, a liberal-minded albeit conservative Brahmin institution. Over the last fifty years, I suspect schools have become a lot more 'liberal' and it is possible they teach more than just one religion in moral science classes.

But I think my son's school in Mumbai too did not teach him

much about any religion other than Hinduism, specifically the Arya Samaj belief systems. My son learnt a bit about religious leaders and the Puranas thanks to his addiction to Uncle Pai's famous Amar Chitra Katha series of comics. I suspect the absence of knowledgeable grandmothers is also hurting religious education. Given the growing trend of nuclear families and other preoccupations of busy grandmothers, it is likely that that mode of religious education has been shut forever. Amar Chitra Katha could use mobile apps to boost their fortunes. Fortunately, television and popular books are still serving up mythologies and keeping religious fires burning bright.

The situation in some parts of the world is much worse. The *Financial Times* proclaimed in 2001 that brands are the new religion. People turn to them for meaning. It also declared that admen and women are the new missionaries. So, in a way, it predicted that I would write a book on religiosity. Be that as it may, researchers have compared the behaviour of committed Apple fans to those of people belonging to religious cults, and almost eerie resemblances have been noticed. It has also been found that consumers primed on religion react differently to brands compared to those not primed on religion. So some researchers have concluded that brands are the 'opiates of the non-religious masses'. This conclusion was arrived at after research proved that consumers who had been primed on religion, like reading a religious passage, were quite happy opting for a less visible brand of a consumer good than a well-known brand. The research concluded that when made to think of religion, consumers are a lot less brand-centric.

Does this mean that the more religious consumer is less brand oriented across the world? Well, what I found in my research does not confirm that in any way. Indian consumers are by and large more religious than international consumers, especially those in Europe. The more religious Indian consumer, based on international research, should be less brand oriented. Being non-religious would mean the consumer is more brand oriented. In fact, what we found was just the opposite. Among Indian consumers, the more religious ones were in fact more demanding. They want brands, they want the best features, they want the best price, etc. So, in a sense, these consumers are more demanding on their god as well, praying more often, going to temples more often, etc. Studying Indian consumers' religious proclivities and how these affect their day-to-day life is indeed a fascinating journey. And I do hope you enjoyed the journey you have undertaken with me this far.

We started our journey with an exploration of the bindi and mangalsutra, and concluded it at a business school. Along the way we explored television programming, music, films, books as well as other topics like auspicious dates, weddings, tourism, micro-religious typecasting, information technology and more.

As I draw the curtains, I realize that there are many unexplored areas still. For example, we saw that women pray a little more than men. We also saw that the young pray a little less than adults. But we did not delve into inter-religious differences in prayer behaviour.

We considered how advertising is using religious symbols and religious music to sell but did not consider whether a more religious consumer is any different from a less religious consumer.

We did look at Muslim consumers in some depth, going beyond the purdah, but did not see they are any different from their Hindu neighbours in terms of consumer behaviour. Even Christian consumers are no different. It is, however, true that Muslims are a little more religious-minded than Hindus and

Christians. They do claim to pray more often and read religious books more frequently. But these are claimed responses, one has not done an observation study. One little indicator is Ramadan fasting, which I believe is a lot more prevalent among Muslims than fasting during Lent among Christians or ritualistic fasting among Hindus.

We looked at some interesting stories about Jews in two chapters. We did not examine whether they are any different as consumers from Christians, whether Catholic or Protestant. But yes, they are different. They are more innovative and risk-taking. So are Muslims.

In every chapter, I tried to bring in my own personal experience relating to religiosity and aspects of religiosity that were impacted. I also attempted to suggest ways of using data to further business interests. From tourism and travel to durable sales and apparel, there is a bit of religion in many products. From the person we are married to and the way we design our living spaces to holidays and the timing of our purchase of durables, there is a little bit of religion in all that we do.

I believe that we are in a unique situation in India. I don't see religious fervour dying in the near future. High religiosity will coexist with high consumerism. While political forces try to create wedges using religious and caste lines, these fissures should disappear in a couple of decades. The modern-day office has made caste lines vanish; with increasing literacy, better skill development, I would submit, religious lines too will slowly vanish. We have proved Max Weber wrong with our economic growth because we have allowed skills to move up and down caste and class hierarchies. Religion will also become a great force multiplier in the years to come. The multi-religious nature of our society, the intense celebratory fervour we bring to every religion, will help us grow as a country.

What can you do to help yourself, at home, at work and in society at large? I think you can improve your life if you make some effort to know a little more about the major religions of our country. Understanding key aspects of each of these will make you that much more sensitive to differences and also similarities across religious lines. This greater understanding should help you connect better with society at large, maybe greet the shopkeeper a little more politely or offer Eid greetings to your Muslim neighbour. Overall, I think you can become a more sensitive human being by knowing a little more about all religions.

Finally, I think knowing about world religions makes us better human beings. We realize how religious typecasting is a blemish on society and learn to read between the lines that appear in popular media and political sabre-rattling. I also believe that English-language publications we read often varnish the scene in monochromatic shades of secularism. The real India is revealed when you pick up an Indian-language publication and read the religious stories they tell. I would strongly recommend that all of us in corporate India should develop the habit of reading at least one vernacular publication. You will notice how all of them provide a glimpse of what English-language publications hide: the religious India and its myriad colours and celebrations. The second step is to understand what is behind the celebration. And the final step is to enjoy every religious festival like your own.

It may be my intense sense of optimism speaking but I do believe that high religiosity is a positive driving force for us Indians. It is up to each of us to see it as a blessing. And benefit a bit in the bargain.

So go ahead, start your journey of discovery, pick up that book, start on that pilgrimage, perform that puja, that prayer. And may the Force Be with You!

I leave you with some parting words from Rabindranath
Tagore:

> When I go from hence
> let this be my parting word,
> that what I have seen is unsurpassable.
>
> I have tasted of the hidden honey of this lotus
> that expands on the ocean of light,
> and thus am I blessed
> —let this be my parting word.
>
> In this playhouse of infinite forms
> I have had my play
> and here have I caught sight of him that is formless.
>
> My whole body and my limbs
> have thrilled with his touch who is beyond touch;
> and if the end comes here, let it come
> —let this be my parting word.

Acknowledgements

The idea for the book was probably sown in 1999 when Professor P.L. Arya (then director of K.J. Somaiya Institute of Management Studies and Research, SIMSR) asked me why I should not seriously think of doing a PhD, given my interest in teaching and writing. The idea got a booster shot when Professor Suresh Ghai took over as director of SIMSR and called me to say that I could register for a PhD with Mumbai University through SIMSR. This was in 2006; little did I then know that it is a six-year journey with a number of unexpected speed breakers, one of which starts the book.

Over the course of six years my PhD guide, Professor R.K. Srivastava, was a pillar of support; I also got a lot of help from my IIM-C batch mate and friend Professor Meera Venkatraman of Suffolk University. Many others helped me navigate the terrain of religion and consumer behaviour and they all have my deepest gratitude.

After I completed the defence of my PhD thesis, the idea of converting it into a book was put into my head by Professors R.K. Srivastava and Suresh Ghai.

My search for a publisher got me in touch with Penguin (thanks to the generous introduction from Prakash Iyer) and before I could put down the phone Anish Chandy was sitting in my office demolishing my idea of converting the thesis into a book.

After two meetings and many email exchanges we agreed that the lay reader cannot be expected to read a thesis-laden book. Fortunately during my PhD I had read more than fifty books and over a hundred articles on religion and consumption. Anish and I started discussing some of the surprising facts I had uncovered during my thesis work. Seeing the potential for a very different book Anish started nudging me towards writing a book on religion and consumer behaviour, but one that is richly anecdotal and packed with interesting information about how religion is shaping consumption, and vice versa. The result is in your hands.

I owe a deep sense of gratitude to many people who were generous with their time, support and encouragement. Amish Tripathi, one of India's most popular fiction writers, agreed to write the foreword in a blink. The idea of the book (and my thesis work) was discussed with many friends including Professor Julien Cayla, Dorab Sopariwala, Hema Viswanathan, Meena Kaushik, Devdutt Pattanaik, T.R. Gopalakrishnan, Renuka Narayanan, Professor Arvind Rajagopal, Santosh Desai, Harish Bhat, Prakash Iyer, Shanta Kumar, Subhas Chakravarty, Professor Sridhar Samu and Rama Bijapurkar.

Special thanks to Professor Diana Eck of Harvard University for permission to use a map from her wonderful book *India: A Sacred Geography*, and to Srinivas Fine Arts for permission to use some wonderful illustrations from their Vedic Diary.

DraftFCB Ulka is where I have worked for almost twenty-five years and many of my colleagues (and clients) you would have met in the book. My assistant Jensy George helped in the compilation of the book. Our studio team led by Hemant Ranadive and Aditya Dighe helped out with the illustrations.

This is my first stab at non-fiction; all my previous efforts were in the 'professional' book domain. It was Anish Chandy who played a key role in shaping the content. My copy editor Jaishree Ram Mohan and her colleague Paromita Mohanchandra have done a great job of not only editing the book but also pointing out mistakes; they and their team deserve my utmost gratitude. Thanks are due to the sales and marketing team at Penguin led by Rahul Dixit, Hemali Sodhi and Vaarunya Bhalla.

Finally my wife, Nithya, and son, Aditya, are always a great source of support and criticism. It is but natural that the name for the book, 'For God's Sake', was suggested by Nithya, ably seconded by Aditya as we were crossing the road, interestingly in the Mission District of San Francisco (it was here that a Spanish priest named Father Francisco Palóu founded Mission San Francisco de Asis on 29 June 1776).

For God's Sake was made possible because of what we see around us in India. A country that is facing the challenges of modernization and consumerization, yet clinging on desperately to its myriad religious beliefs and rituals. It is indeed a fertile hunting ground for interesting stories and business ideas. May that continue for a long long time. And For God's Sake may many more books bloom.

Religion:
An Essential Vocabulary

Acharya	A spiritual or religious teacher.
Adi Granth	The 'First Sacred Book' of the Sikhs, compiled by Guru Arjun in the sixteenth century, of the hymns and teachings of Guru Nanak and his successors as well as selections from Kabir and other bhakti and Sufi mystics.
Advaitavedanta	Philisophical system: Knowledge of the identity of the individual self (*atman*) with the universal self (*brahman*) brings salvation; most prominent representative: Samkara.
Agastya	Legendary sage, credited with bringing Vedic dharma from the north to the south.
Agni	God of fire; many hymns are addressed to it in the *Rig Veda*; personification of three forms of fire, the sun, lightning and sacrificial fire.
Ahimsa	The doctrine of non-violence, or non-injury to animals or men. Of uncertain origin, it gained popularity in the sixth century BCE among Jains and Buddhists and was later adopted into Hinduism.
Ahl-i-hadis	Originally the jurists who laid greater emphasis upon *hadis* (the traditions of the Prophet) than upon

their own interpretation; in later days, in the sub-continent, the school which does not bind itself to any of the recognized schools of jurisprudence and believes in independent interpretation; the school is commonly called ghair-muqallid, 'those who do not follow others'.

Ahmadiyya	A nineteenth and twentieth century Muslim reform movement centring about the figures of Mirza Ghulam Ahmad; also referred to as the Qadiani movement.
Akali Dal	A Sikh party of the Punjab, founded before Independence, advocating a separate Punjabi speaking state that was established in 1966.
Akhara	'Regiment' of ascetics, gymnastic center.
Aligarh Movement	A Muslim movement in the latter half of the nineteenth century encouraging Western education for Muslims and leading to the founding of the Anglo-Oriental College of Aligarh in 1875.
Ananda	Bliss, happiness. The sublime bliss of oneness with Brahman
Ananta	Endless. The name of the coiled serpent on which Vishnu rests in between the aeons of time.
Annapurna	Goddess of 'Plenteous Food', Shiva's consort, especially in Varanasi.
Aranyaka	'Wilderness text', supplements to the Brahmanas with esoteric interpretations of the sacrifice rituals; related to the Upanishads.
Arati	The circling of oil-lamps before the divine image; used also to describe the entire sequence of honour offerings made to the deity.
Arhat	A Jain saint.
Arjuna	One of the five Pandava brothers in the Mahabharata, who in the Bhagvadgita is taught by Krishna

about the path to salvation.

Artha	'Wealth, power, purpose'; one of the four purusharthas, the aims of life.
Arunachala	Dawn Mountain, place of pilgrimage associated with Shiva linga of light and, more recently, with the sage Ramana Maharashi.
Arya Samaj	A religious movement founded by Swami Dayananda Saraswati in 1875, that tried to effect social and religious change through the elimination of caste, the denunciation of rituals and idols, and promotion of the Vedas as the ultimate source for religious authority.
Arya	'The hospitable', self-description of the Indo-Iranian tribes that invaded southern India in the second millennium BCE.
Ashivins	Gods of healing.
Ashoka (d.232 BCE)	Mauryan emperor who came to power c.269 BCE and expanded the empire until after the conquest of the Kalinga, when he became deeply influenced by Buddhism and developed a policy of non-violence and tolerance.
Ashram	Forest retreat, dwelling place of sages, yogis, and their students.
Ashrama	Stage of life, traditionally four: student, householder, forest-dweller and renouncer.
Ashvamedha	Vedic horse sacrifice; a rite of fertility and creation, performed also at the consecration of a king.
Asura	Beings that oppose and compete with Gods (suras or devas). Demons, but not always wicked.
Atharva Veda	The fourth and last of the Vedas compiled later than the other three and containing many non-Aryan elements such as spells and incantations employed in popular rather than ceremonial religion.

Atman	Essence of life, identical with Brahman and refers to that essence within the person.
Aurangzeb or Alamgir (1618-1707):	Mughal emperor and orthodox Muslim who began ruling India in 1658 after he had deposed his father Shah Jahan. He extended the empire to include Bijapur and Golkunda, yet his administration was unstable, partly because of his religious intolerance, and even before his death, the Mughal empire began to disintegrate.
Avarna	Casteless
Avatara	'Descent', manifestation of Vishnu and other gods.
Axial Age	The term used by historians to denote the period 800-200 BCE, a time of transition during which the major world religions emerged in the civilised world.
Ayodhya	One of the seven cities of liberation; traditional birthplace and capital of Rama, as such, the focus of late-twentieth-century communal politics.
Ayurveda	Traditional Indian art of healing.
Ayyappa	A local hero-deity of Sabrimala, Kerala, created from the union of Vishnu and Shiva.
Baditeej	A rite celebrated on the third of Bhadrapada of the Vikram Samvat year when women pray for the longevity of their husbands.
Badrinath	Himalayan pilgrimage place, where Vishnu as Badri Narayana is honoured. One of the four dhams of all India and also of the Himalayas.
Balaji	Popular name for Vishnu as Shri Venkateshwara, honoured at the hilltop shrine of Tirupati.
Ban Yatra	Also Vana Yatra, the pilgrimage through the groves and forests of Krishna's homeland in Braj, in north India.
Baniyas	Banians, Hindu traders.

Bar/ Bat mitzvah	The rite of passage for boys (bar mitzvah) whereby they become full members of Israel who are able to read and interpret Torah; in modern times a parallel rite for girls (bat mitzvah) has been established in some forms of Judaism.
Bhagavad Gita	Lit. 'Song of the Lord', regarded by Hindus as the very word of God, a philosophical interlude, forms part of the famous epic Mahabharata; completed sometime in the second century it received its present form in the third century. It is a dialogue between Arjuna and Lord Krishna on the eve of the battle of Kurukshetra. The central theme of the Gita is that one must do his duty in complete disregard of the consequences.
Bhagavata Purana	One of the eighteen major Puranas, its tenth section being one of the most extensive sources for the life and lore of Krishna.
Bhagiratha	King of ancient Kosala, whose austerities brought the River Ganga from heaven to earth. Thus, one of her names is Bhagirathi.
Bhairava	'Atrocious, terrifying', form of the god Shiva.
Bhakti	Devotion to god, the love of the worshipper for a personal god, whether understood to be a form of Vishnu, Shiva, the Goddess, or the formless one.
Bharat, Bharata	Land of India, named for an ancient king, Bharata— not to be confused with Bharat, the brother of Rama.
Bhima	One of the five Pandava brothers in the Mahabharata, who are distinguished by immense strength.
Bhimashankar	A Shiva shrine and *jyotirlinga* in Maharashtra at the source of the east-flowing Bhima river.
Bhuvana Kosha	'Dictionary of the world' or 'Atlas of the world'; texts in the epics and Puranas that describe the whole cosmos, including the cultural geography of the land of India.

Bodhisattva	'Enlightenment being', Buddhist saint who renounces his salvation to help other beings to salvation.
Brahma	Creator god, having four heads, one to look in each direction. Brahma has no independent cult but is especially honoured at Pushkara in Rajasthan.
Brahman	All-souls, absolute, highest spiritual principle, a Veda word.
Brahmana	Genre of texts that connect with the Samhitas and contains prescriptions for carrying out and explaining sacrifical rituals.
Brahmin	The priestly class or a member of the priestly class, charged with learning, teaching, and performing rites and sacrifices.
Brahmo Samaj	Society of the worshippers of God, a movement founded in 1828 by Rammohan Roy. The movement was eclectic in its religious outlook and style of worship, and it respected human reason. After the death of Rammohan Roy the movement broke into several factions.
Brhadaranyaka-Upanisahd	'Big-Wilderness-Upanishad', belonging to the Satapathabrahmana, pre-Buddhist.
Buddha-Gaya (Bodh-Gaya)	The site in modern Bihar in which Siddhartha Gautama received enlightenment; a sacred pilgrimage center for Buddhists (not to be confused with neighbouring Gaya, a Hindu pilgrimage site especially important for final rites offered on behalf of deceased relatives).
Caliph (Khalifa)	A representative or successor, the title adopted by the rulers of the Islamic community indicating, that as successors of Muhammad, they were both spiritual and temporal leaders. After the destruction of the Abbasid Caliphate in 1258, the title was held by various rulers, including the Ottoman sultans; the

office is referred to as the Caliphate or Khilafat.

Catholic   Those churches that define their Christian authenticity through apostolic succession.

Chaitanya   A Bengali Vaishnava saint whose hymns and
(1485-1533)   poems extol the love of Radha and Krishna. He preached that through love, song and dance, man could experience the personal presence of God and asserted that true religion transcends barriers of caste and sect.

Chandogya-   Upanishad of the Chandogya school, belonging
Upanishad   to the Samaveda, pre-Budhist.

Char Dham   'Four abodes' where the divine dwells, most widely construed as the compass points of India: Badrinath (N), Rameshvara (S), Dvaraka (W), and Puri (E) ; other fourfold pilgrimages also have this name.

Christ   From Greek translation of the Hebrew word meaning 'messiah' or 'anointed one', title Christians apply to Jesus of Nazreth.

Circumcision   The cutting of the foreskin of the penis as a sign of the covenant of Abraham.

Constantinianism   View of the unity of church and state, in which the state exists to rule over and protect the church as the official religion of the empire.

Covenant   The agreement between God and the people of Israel whereby they are chosen to be God's people; God agrees to guide and protect them; the people agree to follow God's commandments (halakhah).

Daksha   Creator demigod, father of Sati, who insulted Shiva by not inviting him to a great sacrifice.

Dana   Ritual gift, often a charitable donation.

Dargah   Memorial tomb-shrine of a Sufi saint or martyr.

Darshan   In ritual and pilgrimage, the 'auspicious sight' of the

	deity; also a 'point of view', or a school of philosophy.
Dasam Granth	(Lit. Tenth Granth.) It was written by the tenth and the last guru of the Sikhs, Govind Singh (1666-1708). Guru Govind Singh knew Sanskrit, Persian and Arabic and wrote inspiring poetry of great literary excellence in Punjabi.
Dayabhaga	One of the two principal divisions of Hindu Law, the other being Mitakshara. Dayabhaga by Jimutavhana (tenth century) is a commentary on the Srutis, especially on Manu.
Dayananda Saraswati, Swami (1824-1883)	Founder of the Arya Samaj in 1875 that claimed ultimate religious authority resided in the Vedas. Dayananda and his followers opposed idol worship, untouchabiilty, child marriage, subjugation of women, and hereditary caste because they were not taught by the Vedas.
Deopatan	City in Kathmandu Valley with the national shrine of Pasupatinatha (Shiva).
Devanagari	Northern India syllabary; used today for Sanskrit, Hindi and Nepali, among others.
Devi Bhagavata Purana	The Purana with the most extensive treatment of the lore and theology of the Goddess, usually considered an Upapurana, not one of the major eighteen Puranas.
Devi	A goddess; refers to the thousands of local goddesses as well as to the consorts of the great gods and the Great Goddess, called Devi or Mahadevi.
Dham	'Abode', 'dwelling' of God. A sacred place where the divine is said to dwell.
Dhammapada	(Lit. meaning: the Law Path), the best known of the Buddhist canonical texts. It is a collection of over four hundred aphoristic verses collected from the sayings of Buddha.

Dharma Shastras	Ritual canon; whole body of scriptures dealing with the religious and ceremonial practice of Hinduism.
Dharma	Signifies code of conduct of the individual or group as found in the Dharma Shastras, law scriptures.
Diaspora	The dispersion of a religious people outside their geographic homeland, where they must live as a minority among others.
Din-i-Ilahi	'Divine faith', an eclectic religion established by the Mughal emperor Akbar in 1582 that included elements of Hinduism (fire sacrifice ceremonies), Zoroastrianism (fire worship), Christian (baptism), as well as Islam. The cult, centring around Akbar himself and stressing a simple monasticism, rapidly faded away after Akbar's death.
Draupadi	Daughter of King Drupada of Panchala and the wife of the five Pandava brothers who accompanies them in their forest exile.
Dravidian	A large language family of the Indian subcontinent. Completely unrelated to Indo-Aryan, although there has been some mutual borrowing of sounds and vocabulary, it includes the four major languages: Tamil (Tamil Nadu), Telugu (Andhra Pradesh), Kannada (Mysore), and Malayalam (Kerala) as well as Toda and Kota (Nilgiri hills), Kondh or Kul (Orissa), and Brohui (Baluchistan).
Durga Puja	A ten-day Bengali festival in October commemorating the ten-day battle and ultimate triumph of the goddess Durga over a demon.
Durga	'Hard to Reach'; one of the primary names of the Devi as consort of Shiva. Powerful with weapons in her multiple hands.
Dvipa	Island, referring to ordinary islands and the ring-shaped islands that encircle the world.

Dwarka	Sacred city and the last capital of Krishna in western India, on the Arabian Sea. One of the four dhams.
Evangelical	Refers to pietistic Christian movements that arose in repsonse to the Enlightenment and also dogmatic divisions within Protestantism; empahsizes the unifying power of conversion as an emotional transformation rather than a rational/dogmatic one.
Fa Hien (fourth-fifth century CE)	Chinese Buddhist monk who travelled in India 401-411 during the reign of Chandra Gupta II in search of Buddhist scriptures. The diary of his travels gives much information about temples, monasteries, and Buddhist legends but little about social or political conditions.
Fiqh	Islamic jurisprudence, or the science of interpreting the Shariat; there are four orthodox schools: Hanafi, Hanbali, Maliki and Shafii. The sources of the Fiqh are the Quran, Hadis, Ijma and Quias.
Ganesha	Elephant-headed god (also known as Ganapati) identified as Shiva's son who is 'Lord of Obstacles' and is worshipped at the beginning of ventures so that hindrances might be removed. Not attested before the fifth century.
Ganga Sagara	Place of pilgrimage where the Ganga meets the sea in the Bay of Bengal.
Ganges (Ganga)	A major river of North India considered especially sacred. Its alluvial plain is among the largest and most densely populated in the world and was the core site of Vedic and classical Indian civilization.
Garbha griha	Inner chamber or 'womb chamber' of a temple, where the image of the deity dwells.
Garbhadhana	'Womb-placing'—in ancient times, a husband approached his wife ceremonially, massaging his

body, chanting certain mantras praying for the birth of a child.

Gauri	The 'white' goddess, name of Parvati.
Gaya	Sacred site in north India famous for shraddha rites for the dead.
Gayatri	Also called Savitri: verse from Rig Veda (3.62.10), which is considered as (sometimes divine) essence of the Veda.
Ghat	Landing place or bank along a river or coast.
Ghazal	A lyrical ode, following a set pattern of rhyme, aa, ba, ca, da, ea, fa, etc. Usually a ghazal is a love poem, but occasionally, it has been utilized for other purposes as well.
Girnar	Mountain sacred to Jains and Hindus in Saurashtra, Gujarat.
Godavari	Sacred river of the Deccan in central India, rising in the Western Ghats and flowing east.
Gokarna	Sacred site, linga of Shiva, along the western coast of India.
Gomukh	'Cow's mouth', where a river takes its rise; the most famous Gomukh is where the Ganga emerges from the lip of a Himalayan glacier.
Gopura	Temple tower or superstructure, situated in south Indian temples above the gateways to the temple complex.
Gospel	Literally, 'good news'; usually refers to the four Gospels of the New Testament, which retell the words and deeds of Jesus of Nazreth; can also refer to other similar ancient writings not included in the Christian scriptures.
Gotra	Line of descent of a mythical seer (*rishi*), which orginally represented a sacrificial community;

members of the same gotra may not enter into marriage according to the Dharmasastra.

Granth Saheb (Guru)	It is the most holy book of the Sikhs. It is written in old Western Hindi, Marathi and in some parts in Persian. It is composed of the writings and sayings of the gurus as well as of other saints and reformers who lived before Guru Nanak.
Gupta	North Indian empire from the fourth to sixth century CE.
Guruvayur	Shrine deidcated to Lord Krishna in Kerala; famous for healing.
Hadis	A tradition of the Prophet, a report about some saying or action of his, which, if recognized to be authentic, is considered to be a fundamental source of law; its authority, however, is subordinate to an injunction contained in the Quran.
Haj	The annual pilgrimage to Mecca on the ninth day of *Dhu-I-Hijja*, the month of the *Haj*. It is compulsory at least once in a lifetime for those who can afford it.
Halal	Permitted, allowed; when referring to food, indicates meat that has been slaughtered in religiously prescribed manner.
Hanuman	Monkey hero; faithful servant of Rama, who helped Rama retrieve Sita from captivity in Lanka, worshipped today in his own right as focus of a vigorous cult.
Harijan	'Child of the god', (Hari = Vishnu) used by Mahatma Gandhi to characterize the casteless.
Hardwar	Sacred city of pilgrimage, located where the Ganga enters the plains of India. Site of one of the four kumbh melas.
Hasidism	A form of Judaism emerging in the eighteenth century, focussed on piety and joy, with strong

roots in Jewish mysticism.

Hathayoga	Strict form of physical asceticism within the philosophy of Yoga.
Hijab	Arabic word for veil or external covering; can consist of headscarf alone or full body covering; also known as chador (in Iran) and burqa (in Afganistan)
Hijrah-hijra and Hegira	The flight of the Prophet from Mecca to Medina, which is the begning of the Hijrah era of the Muslims.
Hinayana	The lesser vehicle, the orthodox form of Buddhism.
Hindustan	Persian name for South Asia, literally 'the land of the Indus (Sindhu) River'.
Hindwi or Hindavi	The language of Hind, applied more particularly to the north dialect written in adapted Arabic script, the forerunner of Urdu.
Hiranyagarbha	Golden Embryo, Golden Egg; the unitary source of all complexity of creation.
Hiuen Tsang (c. 600-664)	Chinese Buddhist pilgrim who travelled to India 630-643 CE to collect Buddhist books, images and artefacts. The diary of his travel provides information about life in India at the time of Harsha.
Ijma	The consensus of the Islamic community as a source of law.
Ijtihas	The endeavour of human reason asnd knowledge to understand the application of a religious injunction to a particular situation, interpretation.
Imam	In Sunni Islam, the prayer leader and the one who delivers the Friday sermon; in Shiah Islam, refers to Muhammad's descendants as legitimate successors, not prophets, but divinely inspired, sinless, infallible, and the final authoritative interpreter of God's will as formulated in Islamic law.
Indra	Vedic warrior god, wielder of the thunderbolt, and

drinker of the intoxicating soma; in later times, a directional guardian (East).

Ishtadevata — 'Chosen deity'; the understanding and image of the divine that each worshipper holds to the heart in his or her devotion.

Ishvara — Lord; refers to the personal Lord; used in compound with other names, it referes to a particular manifestaion of Shiva, such as Vishveshvara, the 'Lord of All'.

Isma'ilis — The followers of Isma'il, believers in his apostolic succession according to the Shi'ah theory of the imamate. They are also called the sect of the seven, because they believe in Isma'il being the seventh imam and his being followed by cycles of seven imams in eternal succession.

Ithna asharis — Believers in twelve imams. They reject the imamate of Isma'il. They form the larger wing of the Shi'ahs.

Jagannath/ Jagannatha — 'Lord of the Universe'; name of Krishna as he dwells in Puri, Orissa. Also, name of seventeenth-century poet, author of the 'Ganga Lahari'.

Jaina — Supporters of the ascetic reform movement of Mahavira, the founder of Jainism.

Jambudvipa — Rose Apple Island; in Indic cosmology, the world we live in, a lotus-shaped island with four petal-contintents, centered at Mount Meru, located in the middle of an expanding universe of surrounding seas and ring-shaped islands.

Jati — Caste.

Jihad — Literally: 'the utmost endeavour', mainly used for taking up arms in a righteous cause, which is sometimes called jihad bi's-saif, 'the utmost endeavour with the sword'.

Jizyah — A poll-tax levied upon able-bodied zimmiz who can

afford to pay the tax after the satisfaction of their needs. Priests, hermits, servants of the state, cripples, women and children are exempt.

Jnana   Wisdom, transforming knowledge

Jyotirlinga   'Linga of light', the manifestation of Shiva as an unspeakably briliant and fathomless column of light.

Ka'bah   The sacred shrine at Mecca.

Kabir (1440-1518)   Bhakti mystic who attempted to synthesize Hinduism and Islam. He renounced rituals but spiritualized yoga and proclaimed this inner yoga to be the only way by which one might know God.

Kailasa   Himalayan peak located in what is today Tibet; destination of Buddhist and Hindu pilgrims; for Hindus, the mountain abode of Lord Shiva.

Kala   Time, death and destiny.

Kali   'Black Goddess', both mother of life and fearsome weapon-bearer; sometimes the shakti of Shiva, sometimes the supreme Mahadevi, unattached to any male deity.

Kalidasa (c.400)   Sanskrit writer of the Gupta period whose famous poem is the *Meghadut* (Cloud Messenger) and whose best known drama is *Sakuntala*.

Kama Sutra   A text on erotics (C. 300-500) attributed to the sage Vatsyayana, designed for the cultivated townsmen and courtesans as well as married couples of the Gupta period.

Kama   God of passion; India's Cupid, who arouses lovers with his flower arrows; one of the four *purusharthas*, the aims of life, here the pursuit of passion or pleasure.

Kamakshi   'Love-Eyed Goddess' whose most famous shrine is Kamakhya, in Assam; also dwells prominently in Kanchi in Tamil Nadu.

Kanchi	One of the seven sacred cities of India, situated in the Tamil south, embracing major Vaishnava and Shaiva temples.
Kanyadan	Virgin-giving or formal gift of the daughter to the bridegroom.
Kanyakumari	'Virgin Goddess' at the tip of southern India, protecting and blessing; her name was popularized in British times as Cape Comorin.
Karim	Benign, one of the names of God.
Karma Bhumi	Literally, the 'land of action'; Bharata, where action can produce results and lead to freedom.
Karma Yoga	One of the main forms of yoga which aims at salvation through deeds. There are many other forms of yoga such as *bhakti yoga*, salvation through faith, *gyan yoga*, through knowledge, *mantra yoga*, through mantras or spells, *hatha yoga*, through physical culture, *raja yoga*, through spiritual culture.
Karma	An act, and its results, which will be manifest in time.
Karttikeya	Deity, 'Son of the Krittikas', also known as Skanda, Murugan, or Kumara, the hero son of Shiva.
Kashi	Popular and ancient name for Banaras, the luminous, the 'City of Light', from *kash* 'to shine.'
Kaveri	Sacred river of south India, rising in the hills of Karnataka and flowing south and east across Tamil Nadu.
Kayastha	A caste-cluster of writers, village record keepers, and government officilas. Known from the Gupta period (fourth-fifth century CE), they served the Mughals and other rulers in various parts of North and Central India.
Kedara, Kedarnath	Shrine and area sacred to Shiva, located in the Himalayas in the state that is now Uttarakhand; one of the northern *char dham*; one of Shiva's *jyotirlingas*.

Kevalin or Kaivalin	Those who have achieved a state of Kaivalya, i.e. realization of their own self.
Khanda (Kanda)	A section of land (as in Kedara Khanda) or of a literary work (as in *Kashi Khanda*, a lengthy section of the *Skanda Purana*).
Khanqah	A hospice where the Sufi Shaikh and his disciples live.
Khariji	A Muslim sect which does not believe in the canonical necessity of the *Khilafat*.
Khasi	An Austro-Asiatic language of the Mon-Khmer group spoken in Assam, not closely allied to the Mon-Khmer languages of Burma, Thailand and Vietnam.
Khojah	An Isma'eli Shi'ah sect that migrated to western India, especially Punjab and Sind, where they have become traders and merchants. The Aga Khan is the leader of their chief branch.
Khuda	God.
Khwaja	A Persian title of respect. In the Sultanate it was used for the officer in each province who kept the revenue accounts.
Kolhapur	Temple city on the bank of the Panchaganga river in Maharashtra, sacred to Mahalakshmi, the Goddess.
Kolkali	A dance form developed by Moplahs in which twelve men with sticks and tiny cymbals attached dance in a circle.
Krishna	A heroic figure of Indian mythology, seen as an incarnation of Vishnu, with Mathura (Muttra) on the Yamuna river, his alleged birthpalce. Krishna's life is the subject of much literature and art in later medieval India (post-ninth and tenth century) including Krishna as child god, as pastoral divine lover, and as hero.
Krittikas	The Pleiades, the six stars who are the mothers of Shiva's son, Karttikeya.

Kshatriya	A ruler of the ruling varna; the second of the four main ranks of traditional Hindu society. The function of Kshatriyas was military protection.
Kshetra	Field, land; pilgrimage place that comprises an entire area.
Kshetrapala	Guardian or protector of a place.
Kubera	The Hindu god of riches and treasure, guardian of the northern quarter, also well known in Buddhism and Jainism; ususally depicted as a dwarf.
Kuf	Adequate (companion for mariage); the doctrine which encourages marriages between groups which are compatible.
Kulin	Brahman 'noble', Brahman subcaste.
Kumbha Mela	Great pilgrimage fair and bathing festival held once every twelve years at Prayaga, today's Allahabad.
Kumbha	Round water pot, sometimes consecrated to represent the Devi.
Kumbhakonam	Temple town along the Kaveri river in Tamil Nadu; site of the great bathing tank and Mahamaham bathing festival.
Kumkum	Red powder used decoratively in personal adornment or in ritual.
Kund	A pool, especially a pool for ritual bathing, either clay-banked or with steps for access to the water.
Kurma	The tortoise avatara of Vishnu; the name of one of the Puranas.
Kurukshetra	Sacred site in north India, capital of the legendary King Kuru; the battlefield of the great war described in the Mahabharata.
Lakshmana	Brother of Rama who accompanied the hero during his forest exile.
Lakshmi	Goddess of beauty and wealth; consort of Vishnu.

Lanka	The island capital of Ravana in the Ramayana; identified today with the island of Sri Lanka.
Lila	Play, both as a human and divine activity.
Lilasthalas	In the landscape of Braj, the 'places of play', the sites of Krishna's playful and loving relations with the villagers and milkmaids.
Linga	Phallic symbol worshipped as representing the presence and power of the deity. Lingas date from the Harappan civilization; they are most commonly connected with Saivite cult practice.
Lingayat	An anti-Brahman Saivite devotional (*bhakti*) sect following the teaching of Basava (twelfth century), whose members frequently wear a Siva *linga* as a sign of their affiliation. Lingayats are concentrated in Mysore, and much of their religious literature is in Kannada.
Loka	World, in a geographical or spatial sense; includes the meanings of both 'space' and 'light', thus, the illumined world, the world that shines forth.
Lokaloka	Literally, 'world-unworld'—an infinitely distant mountain range at the edge of the universe beyond which there is no light at all.
Madapa	The assembly hall in which worshippers gather in a Hindu temple. Orginally, the hall was separate from the sanctum sanctorum; later it was connected by a vestibule.
Madurai (Madura)	An ancient temple city in Tamil Nadu located on the banks of the Vaigai river, once capital of the Pantiya dynasty, famed for its large temple to the goddess Meenakshi.
Mahabharata	One of the two great epics of India, the other being Ramayana. It is the world's longest epic. Its author is said to be the sage Vyasa who composed it in 24,000

verses; now it totals 1,10,000 couplets. The epic is woven around the great battle of the Kurukshetra between the Pandavas and Kurus which is ascribed to the period 850 BCE and 650 BCE.

Mahabodhi Temple	'Temple of the Great Enlightenment'; located at Bodh Gaya; originally early Gupta, restored many times by pious Buddhists.
Mahadeva	'Great Lord'; an epithet describing one of the aspects of Shiva.
Mahant	Head of monastery or *math*.
Mahatmya	The 'glorification' or 'praise' of a deity, a place, a ritual; the eulogistic literature containing such praises.
Mahavira (c.540-468 BC)	'The Great Hero', a title given to Vardhamana, the founder of Jainism. He renounced earthly life, begged for his food, wore no clothing, and through these methods became conqueror of his body and achieved *nirvana*
Mahayana	The greater vehicle—that form of Buddhism which adopted beliefs and practices orignally foreign to it.
Maheshvara	'Great Lord', Shiva.
Makar Sankranti	A new year festival celebrated on the first day of the solar month of *Magh* (between 12 and 14 January), a great mela is held at Prayaga (Allahabad) called *Magh Mela*.
Maliccha	Also *Malishta*. An unclean outsider, used for non-Hindus.
Mama-pheras	A marriage custom when the maternal uncle takes the bride round the bridegroom four times.
Manasa	The lake, sometimes called Manasarovar, at the foot of Mount Kailasa.
Mandakini	One of the high tributaries of the River Ganga, rising

near Kedarnath and joining with the Alakananda at Rudra Prayag.

Mandala	'Circle', spiritual sketch or drawing that serves as an object of meditation.
Manikarnika	One of the primary tirthas of Banaras, the cremation ground.
Manjusri	The bodhisattva of meditation or Supreme Wisdom whose function is to stimulate understanding; portrayed in art with a sword to destroy error and a book to enlighten all men.
Mantra	A sacred formula or utterance, a prayer.
Manu	Presumed author of the influential *Manavadharmasastra*, 'The Law Book of Manu'.
Mara	Destroyer, Evil One; according to Buddhist legend, the tempter and enemy of the Buddha and his religion who, by appealing to Siddhartha Gautama's sensual and material instincts, tried to dissuade him from renouncing the world.
Maruts	A group of Vedic gods who accompanied Indra across the sky in their chariots, singing martial songs, and epitomizing the recklessness of the storm.
Matha (Mutt)	A Hindu monastery; such monasteries began to flourish in the Middle Ages when they functioned as refuges for monks and learning institutions for the young.
Mathura	One of the seven sacred cities of liberation, located in central north India on the Yamuna river; early centre of Buddhism; famous as the birthplace of Krishna.
Matsya	The fish avatara of Vishnu; the name of one of the Puranas.
Maurya Empire	Indian empire (ca. 320-185 BCE)
Maya	Creative power (of a god), magic, trick, illusion,

etc. A key concept based on its earliest meaning, namely—creative power and activity of a god to manifest phenomenal reality. This is 'illusion' when not understood by normal men. Later philosophy, particularly that of Shankara and his followers, used this term to denote the existential ('illusory') status of the phenomenal world.

Mecca	Holy city of the Mulsims; scene of the Prophet Muhammad's first preaching; direction faced in prayer and pilgrimage goal of many Muslims throughout the world.
Medina	City in Arabia where Muhammad took up residence in 622 CE, after he had fled his persecutors in Mecca.
Mela	A fair, especially a religious fair or bathing festival to which people often come from great distances on pilgrimage.
Mimamsa	'Enquiry, investigation'; probably the most conservative school of the six darsanas, an exegesis of the ritual portions of the Vedic literature.
Mirabai (b. 1550)	A Rajput widow who, in spiritual life, became the bride of Krishna and left a legacy of devotional (bhakti) love poetry.
Mitakshara	One of the two main divisions of Hindu law; a commentary on Yajnavalkya written by Vijnanesvara (eleventh century).
Mleccha	Literally 'barbarian'; non-Aryan, or foreigner; any person who does not speak Sanskrit and does not conform to Hindu norms.
Moharram	'That which is forbidden' (or sacred): the first month of the Muslim calendar; also the Muslim festival during the first ten days of that month commemorating the martyrdom of Husain, grandson of Muhammad, observed primarily by Shi'ahs, but also some Sunnis.

Mobed	A Zoroastrian priest.
Moksha	A 'letting go' or a 'release' ; the ultimate goal of the Hindu religious life; release from the cycle of reincarnations and the consequences of causality.
Moplah	A group of Muslims living on the Malabar Coast of India, whose uprising in 1921 seriously damaged national efforts at Hindu-Muslim cooperation.
Mount Meru	The symbolic mountain at the centre of the lotus-shaped world and its surrounding universe.
Mudra	In both visual arts and dance, a hand gesture to convey particular meanings.
Muezzin	One who issues the call to prayer from the top of the minaret.
Muhtasib	An officer of the Muslim governments who prevented the committing of any public nuisance or flagrant and wilful breach of the moral code and law.
Mujahid	One who struggles against infidels on behalf of Islam, derived from the Arabic word 'to exert oneself vigorously against, to fight against.'
Mukti	Liberation, moksha
Muni	Sage, seer, ascetic, first mentioned in the *Rig Veda*, as a class of non-Brahman esoteric holy personages. Later *muni* came to be a general term for a holy man, often suffixed to the name of a revered author of a sacred Sanskrit work.
Murti	Form, likeness; the consecrated image of the deity as a focus for darshan.
Muslim	One who submits or surrenders himself or herself to God and his will; one who follows Islam.
Muwwahhid	A monotheist. The Druz use it for one who has reached the highest stage in spiritual progress and

attained freedom from exoteric as well as esoteric bonds of religion.

Naga Serpent; serpent deity, associated with pools and streams; co-opted by all the great deities in their rise to supremacy.

Nagarjuna (second century CE*)* Buddhist monk who founded the Madhyamika school of philosophy and developed the doctrine of Sunyata ('emptiness') as the school's central concept.

Nakshatra The series of 27 (or 28) constellations comprising the ancient Indain astronomical system and serving as a basis for astrological prediction.

Nalanda Buddhist monastery and centre of learning in Bihar, founded in fifth century CE, offering training in both Buddhist and Vedic knowledge, and continuing till destroyed in 1197 by the Muslim invasions.

Naman Caste mark of Vaishnavites. Three lines, one red perpendicular and two white at an incline meeting at the base and forming a sort of trident.

Namdev (fifteenth century) Maharashtrian *bhakti* saint, supposedly of low caste, who attempted to bring Hindus and Muslims closer together; also a poet who played a part in the development of early Urdu.

Narada Celestial sage, busybody of the sages who instigates many a plot and drama.

Narasimha Man-lion avatara of Vishnu, slays demons who can be killed by 'neither man nor beast'.

Narayan Deity mentioned in Brahmana literature who came to be identified with Vishnu.

Narmada Great river of central India, rising at Amarakantaka and flowing west to the Arabian Sea; river of countless riverside shrines, including Omkareshvara, and circumambulated by pilgrims.

Nashik Site of Simhasta Kumbh Mela on the River Godavari;

	famous of old as hermitage where Rama, Sita and Lakshmana lived during their exile.
Nastika	A category describing non-orthodox Indian philosophical schools. The term—from na-asti meaning 'it is not'—refers to those schools that do not acccept the authority of the Vedic-Upanishadic traditions and hence are not regarded as conveying true philosophic knowledge.
Natya Shastra	An authoritative work on drama, dance and music, the authorship of which is attributed to Bharata; it was probably compiled in the early centuries of the Christian era.
Nayar (Nair)	A caste-cluster in Kerala claiming Kshatriya status with a matrilineal family structure, unique in its absence of an institutionalized husband-father role.
Nirguna	Literally, 'without attributes', referring to Brahman, to which no qualities, attirbutes, or adjectives may be ascribed; contrast to saguna, 'with atrributes', able to be described.
Nirvana	A 'blowing out': in Buddhism it refers to final release from transmigration by extinction of desires and passions and the giving up of the illusion of selfhood. It refers to the state of bliss transcending all categories of existence.
Nishkala	Literally 'without parts', referring to the fractionless, indescribable, transcedent Shiva; contrast to sakala, 'with parts', visible and comprehensible.
Nivritti	Returning to oneness, cessation, repose; opposite of pravritti, spinning forth, evolving.
Niyoga	Similar to system of levirate of ancient Jews legalized by many by which a man could have intercourse with his childless brother's widow or the wife of an important kinsman, in order to raise issue for the

other's family without incurring any sin.

Nyaya	Philosophical system of logic.
Om (Aum)	Mystic monosyllable and sacred explanation, the object of profound religious meditation and reverence throughout Hindu India, taken to symbolize all sound and reality.
Omkareshvara	Shrine of Shiva on an island in the Narmada River; one of *jyotirlingas* of Shiva.
Padma Purana	One of the eighteen *Mahapurana*; contains extensive sections on cosmology, geography, and the lore of pilgrimage places.
Padma	Lotus.
Padmasambhava (eighth century CE*)*	An Indian prince, turned Buddhist monk and missionary, who carried Buddhism to Tibet in 750 CE.
Pali Canon	The collection of Buddhist scriptures consisting of the three major divisions (baskets or *pitakas*) preserved by the Theravada school, according to the Sinhalese tradition committed to writing in Ceylon in first century CE.
Panchakroshi	'Five kroshi', a circular pilgrimage with a radius of about five kroshas, or ten miles. The circular pilgrimage route around Kashi, but also a popular designation for a fivefold pilgrimage.
Panchatantra	'Five treatises', a collection of fables intended mainly for the instruction of kings and ministers in worldly affairs. The fables are prefaced by a king's concern over the ineptitude of his sons and his commissioning of a sage to instruct them.
Panchayat	A generally-recognized authority group within a caste or village or extending over several castes or villages that settles disputes, regulates moral conduct, and establishes standards for dowry, *jajmani* relations etc. Although the term 'panchayat' suggests a council

of five, the actual number of panchayat members varies widely depending on local circumstances and the particular case being reviewed.

Panda   A priest serving in a temple or at a pilgrimage site.

Pandavas   The five brothers, sons of King Pandu, including Yudhishthira, Bhima and Arjuna, whose epic battle with their cousins, the Kauravas, is told in the *Mahabharata*.

Pandharpur   Prominent pilgrimage city of Lord Vithoba, a form of Krishna, on the Bhima river in Maharashtra.

Panini (end of fourth century CE)   One of the world's greatest grammarians, whose *Astadhyayi*, analysing and standardizing the Sanskrit language in 4,000 succint rules, has provided a model for grammarians ever since.

Panth   'Path': a sect, custom, or religious order.

Parashurama   Rama with the Axe, an avatara of Vishnu, his father a Brahmin, his mother a Kshatriya; renowned for many exploits in the epics and Puranas; forced the sea to retreat from the Konkan coast of India, now called Parashurama Kshetra.

Parinirvana   'Final blowing-out': the death and entry into final bliss of a being who in his lifetime has attained perfection (*nirvana*). The term is used specifically to describe the death of the Buddha.

Parthiva linga   An earthen *linga*, the simplest pinch of clay into which the presence of Shiva is invoked.

Parvati (Uma)   Wife of Shiva, 'Daughter of the Mountain', so named because she is the daughter of Himalaya. Parvati tried to win the love of the ascetic Shiva, succeeding only after she became an ascetic. Their son, the war god Skand, rid the world of the demon Taraka.

Pasupata   Saiva ascetic group.

Pasupati   'Lord of Beasts'; an epithet of Shiva signifying that he is the patron god of reproduction in animal life. In sculpture this is represented by a four-armed man in a posture of blessing, while from one of its hands a small deer springs.

Pasupatinath

Form of the god Shiva worshipped in Kathmandu, Nepal.

Patanjali (second century BCE)

Grammarian, author of the *Mahabhasya*, who commented on both Panini and Katyayana in order to criticize and expand their grammars.

Pentecostal

Refers to churches that emphasize possession by the Holy Spirit and speaking in tongues.

Pinda

Rice ball, shaped ritually to constitute part of a new, subtle, spiritual body represented in death rites.

Pir

The spiritual leader of a Sufi order; more genrally an Islamic saint.

Pitarah(pl.)

'Forefathers'.

Pitha

A sacred place of pilgirmage.

Pongal

The festival of Pongal is celebrated in South India on the advent of the new year and coincides with Makar Sankranti of north India i.e. first day of the solar month of *Magh* (between 12 and 14 January)

Prabhasa

Sacred site and *jyotirlinga* of Shiva on the coast of Saurashtra in Gujarat; also called Somnath.

Pradakshina

Circumambulation; honouring by walking around, keeping the object of honour to one's right.

Prajapati

'Lord of Creatures'; chief god of Vedic mythology, regarded as the primeval person and protector of life, who was sacrificed and dismembered in the world's creation.

Prakrit

Collective term for middle Indian languages or dialects.

Prakriti

'Nature', in the philosophy of the Samkhya consists

of primal material of three qualities (*guna*) from which the world develops.

Pralaya Universal dissolution after one of the last aeons of time called a *kalpa*, or a day of Brahma.

Prana Breath, both the spiritual breath of a person and the breath of a deity established in an image.

Prasad Divine grace; in worship, the food offered to the deity and returned, consecrated.

Pravritti Flowing forth, active manifestation, arising; complement to nivritti, returning, cessation.

Prayag/ Prayaga '*Place of sacrifice*', a tirtha at the confluence of the Ganga, Yamuna, and mythical Sarasvati rivers; duplicated widely in sacred geography, most prominent Prayaga is today's Allahabad.

Prayas-Chitta 'Penance', ceremony of purification performed when a person does a thing regarded as taboo according to scriptures.

Preta 'Spirit', i.e. of a dead person. Certain rites are performed to help the *preta* or spirit to become a *pitri* or ancestor.

Prithvi Earth, living and dynamic; Prithvi Sukta is the Vedic hymn to the Earth.

Protestant ethic Term coined by sociologist Max Weber, who noted that the Calvinist branch of the Reformation fostered a belief in working hard and living simply for the glory of God, and as proof that one was among those destined to be saved; such an attitude, Weber said, contributed to the accumulation of wealth needed for investment and fueled the Industrial Revolution and the flourishing of capitalist societies.

Protestant The churches, beginning at the time of Martin Luther, that reject mediation of the church through apostolic succession as necessary for salvation in favour of direct personal relationship with God in Christ.

Puja	Worship, ordinarily including the presentation of honour offerings (*upacharas*) to the deity.
Pujari	One who conducts worship in a Hindu temple.
Punya	Goodness, a good or meritorious act.
Purana	'Ancient Story'; the 18 main Puranas are the sacred texts of popular Hinduism. Compendia of legends and religious instructions, they contain much ancient material but in their present form they date back to earlier than fourth century CE.
Purdah	Seclusion of women from men who are not relatives, segregation of the sexes.
Puri Jagannath	A festival celebrated at Puri, Orissa in June/July, when the image of the god Jagannath, his brother, and his sister are paraded through the streets on a huge temple chariot.
Purnima	Full-moon day of the Hindu lunar calendar.
Pururavas	Hero of an ancient Indian legend extending back to the Rig Veda (X, 95) and the *Satapatha Brahmana*, and retold by Kalidasa.
Purus(h)	'Person', in early Indian mythology it signified the Primal Man from which all other men sprang. In philosophical discourse it came to describe the essential soul (*purusa*) which is at rest as opposed to the existential world which evolves (*prakriti*).
Purusa	In the *Rig Veda* the primeval man from whom the world emerges; in the philosophy of the Samkhya, spirit and inner core of essence of Man.
Purusasukta	Creation myth in the *Rig Veda* (10.90), in which the emergence of the world through the sacrifice of the primal man Purusa is described.
Purushartha	Aim of human life, of which there are traditionally

four: *kama* (pleasure), *artha* (wealth and power), *dharma* (righteous action), and *moksha* (liberation).

Pushakara 'Lotus Pool'; site sacred to Brahma in present-day Rajasthan.

Pushan A god frequently referred to in the Vedas, worshipped by the Aryans; a nourisher of all created beings, shown as carrying an ox-goad and riding in a cart drawn by goats.

Pushti Maarg 'Path of Grace', a sect of devotion to Krishna.

Qazi A judge.

Qiyas One of the sources of the *fiqh*, the principles of applying hadis to new situations by the use of analogy.

Quran Holy book of the Muslims who believe it to be the very word of God; a revealed book sent down in Arabic through the Angel Gabriel to His Messenger the Prophet Muhammad, a person of about 20 years from about 610 CE; the original key in Heaven as a well-guarded tablet. The record of Muhammad's inspired utterances, found not only in the memories of men but according to later traditions, written on shoulder blades, palm leaves and stones collected after his death under the third Caliph Usman (644-655 CE) and found in the authorized version of 114 suras or chapters.

Rabbinic A rabbi is a teacher; the name came to designate the Judaism of the *dual Torah* created by the Pharisees, which came to be normative in the premodern period.

Radha Divine love and consort of Krishna, whose longing for union with her lord exemplifies the bhakti ideal of the worshipper longing for union with God.

Rahim Merciful, one of the names of God.

Rakshasa One of the categories of mostly ferocious night-haunting beings referred to as demons, at enmity with the gods, disrupters of sacrifice.

Rama Lila	'Rama's sport'; a dramatic festival occurring in villages and cities of North India during the latter part of September or early October, portraying events from the Ramayana.
Rama	Hero of the Ramayana, virtuous king of Ayodhya, who underwent voluntary exile to enable his father to keep his promise. He is regarded by Indians as the the epitome of justice and virtue and is identified as the seventh incarnation of Vishnu.
Ramacharitmanas	Hindi Ramayana, 'Holy Lake of the Deeds of Rama', composed in the sixteenth century by Tulsidas in Varanasi.
Ramadan	Month of fasting, ninth month of the Muslim calendar.
Ramakrishna Paramahansa, Sri (1836-1886)	A Bengali saint and devotee of the goddess Kali, who through bhakti and austerities experienced union with various forms of God including non-Hindu forms. Swami Vivekananda, his most famous disciple, founded the Ramakrishna Mission Movement.
Ramanuja	Eleventh-century south Indian thinker who gave a philosophical foundation to the Vaishnava devotional movement known as Shrivaishnavism.
Ramayana	The Hindu epic celebrating the legend and deeds of Rama; Valmiki's Sanskrit epic or one of the many vernacular epics.
Rameswaram	Sacred site on the coast of Tamil Nadu where Rama is said to have worshipped Shiva and built a bridge to Lanka to retrieve Sita from her imprisonment by Ravana: *jyotirlinga* of Shiva.
Ramjanmabhumi	Site honoured as the birthpalce of Rama in Ayodhya.

Raslila	High point of the cycle of Krishna lilas, enacting the circle dance in which Krishna multiplies himself to dance at night with the gopis.
Ratha Yatra	Chariot pilgrimage in which the divine image is taken from the temple sanctum for procession in the streets; especially famous in Puri, when Krishna Jagannatha is pulled in huge chariots.
Ratri	The goddess of night to whom a hymn is addressed in the *Rig Veda*.
Ravana	The demon king and villain of the Ramayana epic, who abducted Sita and carried her to his kingdom in Sri Lanka. In the end of the epic, Ravana is destroyed by Rama.
Rig Veda	The first and most authoritative of the four Vedas which is ascribed to the period 1500 to 2000 BCE, holy books of the Hindus, is composed of hymns and psalms of praise to the gods, recited by the sages, which was orally passed from generation to generation till finally it had a fixed text in 300 BCE.
Rishi	Inspired seers whose wisdom and insight are represented in the *Rig Veda*.
Rudra	A Vedic god who according to legend lived in the mountains, was an excellent bowman, and evoked fear among men who wished to avoid his arrows of disaster. After Vedic times he became less significant, but many of his aspects were assumed by Shiva.
Rudraksha	Literally, the 'Eye of Shiva': the large, bumpy, brown berries or seeds used for rosaries.
Sacraments	Ritual actions, such as baptism and Holy Communion, said to impart the grace of God to Christians, usually through the mediation of ordained clergy.
Sadhu	A Sanskrit term meaning 'good', 'virtuous',

commonly used to refer to a saint or holy man especially one who has renounced the world.

Sadr-u's-sudur   The highest religious dignitary of the Muslims under Muslim governance in the subcontinent. He was the head of the department of religious affairs.

Sagara   Ancient king of the Ikshvaku sun dynasty whose 60,000 sons were burned by the fury of an angry ascetic; his descendant brought Ganga from heaven to earth to give life to the dead sons.

Sagotra   Of same gotra.

Saguna   'With qualities'—referring to a divine reality that is describable, with attributes and adjectives; contrasts with *nirguna*.

Saivasiddhanta   Spiritualistic trend of Saivism.

Saivite   A devotee of god Shiva, the cult of the Shiva worshippers dating from before the Christian era and representing aspects of popular religion from Kashmir to South India. In the latter region one of the most prominent sects of the Saivites, the Saiva Siddhanta, developed c. eleventh century.

Saiyid   A descendant of the Prophet.

Sakala   'With parts'—referring to an understanding of Shiva that is describable, with faces and parts; contrasts with *nishkala*.

Saktaism   The cults of goddess worshippers. In Hinduism they centre around the wife of Shiva; in Buddhism, the cult centres around tantric groups that employ sexual symbolism and sexual practices as means of salvation.

Sakti   'Energy or potency', usually ascribed to a god's wife—more specifically to the consort of Shiva—who represents the energy and activity of a god. In early medieval India her cult was popular.

Sakyamuni   A name designating Gautama the Buddha; Sakya was the tribe or clan over which Suddodhana, Gautama's father, ruled. Muni means 'sage', hence Sakyamuni means the 'sage of the 'Sakyas'.

Salat | Official prayer or worship performed five times each day.

Sama Veda | Book of chants drawn largely from the hymns of the *Rig Veda* and employed by a special group of priests, the *udgatr*.

Samaveda | 'The wisdom (existing) in melody', Vedic Samhita, with instructions for the correct singing of the Veda hymns at sacrifical acts.

Samdya | Brahmanic morning and evening ritual

Samhita | A 'putting together', i.e., a compilation; or collection; specifically, the four collections of verses consisting of the respective Vedas.

Samkhya | Philosophical system: The recognition of the difference of individual consciousness and deep core of essence brings salvation.

Samsara | The cycle of transmigration in which the soul of any living thing continually dies and is reborn. Salvation in Hinduism involves release (*moksa*) from the cycle of transmigration.

Samskaras | Sanskrit term commonly translated as sacrament is applied to the rituals observed during any of the transitory phases in the life of a Hindu.

Sanchi | Village located in Madhya Pradesh, site of a famous Buddhist stupa dating from the third century BCE.

Sangam | Confluence of rivers.

Sangha | The order or brotherhood of Buddhist monks. Entrance into the order was achieved by shaving the head, donning the ascetic's robe, and accepting the precepts. Despite no central governing authority, the monastic rules of the *Vinaya Pitaka* kept a certain degree of uniformity within the Sangha.

Sankalpa	Vow of intent taken at the outset of any ritual activity.
Sankara (788-820 CE)	A Brahman worshipper of Shiva, a philosopher, and founder of the *Advaita Vedanta* school. He advocated a strict monism that allowed no second principle alongside the Absolute, Brahman.
Sanskrit	Classical Indian language, standardized by the grammatician Panini (fifth century BCE).
Santoor	A musical instrument.
Sanyasin (Sanaysai)	The fourth *asrama* or stage of life in which a man completely renounces his ties with the world, becomes a homeless wanderer, and practises asceticism.
Saptapadi	Seven steps. Refers to Hindu custom of taking seven steps before the fire by the bride and groom together. Each step represents a particular blessing, namely food, strength, wealth, happiness, progeny, cattle, devotion.
Saraswati	Goddess of learning and arts; sacred river of ancient India, now disappeared, said to be present in many confluences of two rivers as an invisble third.
Sastra	Treatise, instruction, code; a text containing materials of political, legal, and moral nature, sometimes an expansion and versification of an earlier *Sutra*.
Sati	Consort of Shiva who committed suicide because of her father Daksha's insult to Shiva, reborn as Parvati.
Satpathabhahmna	'The Brahmana of the hundred paths', the most comprehensive, but not the oldest Brahmana.
Sayyid (Syed)	A chief; also a name used by those who claim descent from Husain, the son of Muhammad's daughter, Fatima.
Shahadah	The Muslim proclamation of faith: 'I bear witness

that there is no god but al-Lah and that Muhammad is his Messenger.'

Shaikh	'Old' man, a term used for a Sufi who guided disciples; also used to denote a caste or class among Indian Muslims.
Shariat (Sharia)	The law of Islam, governing all the rules that govern life.
Shastra	Teachings: sacred treatise or body of learning, such as the *Dharmashastra*, the 'Teachings About Dharma.'
Shi or Shiah	Follower(s), partisan (s); refers to those who followed the leadership of Ali, the nephew and son-in-law of Muhammad, as Muhammad's successor, whose who believe that leadership of the Muslim community should belong to Muhammad's descendants.
Shikara	Spire of a temple, literally the 'peak'; a mountain peak.
Shiva	'The Auspicious'; many -powered deity, both creator and destroyer, who, along with Vishnu and Devi, is widely worshiped as the Supreme.
Shivratri	'Night of Shiva', every month, the fourteenth of the waning fortnight; the year's greatest Mahashivaratri is in either the winter month of Magha or Phalguna.
Shraddha	Rites for the dead performed after cremation to nourish the deceased for passage to the world of the ancestors.
Shri	'Good Fortune', the name of a goddess, the consort of Vishnu, along with Bhu; an honorific title.
Shringara	The decoration and adornment of a divine image, whether a *linga* or an image of one of the other deities.
Shrirangam Temple	Great temple of Vishnu as Ranganatha on an island in the Kaveri river in the city of Tiruchirappalli.
Shudra	The fourth of the four castes.

Shukla	The waxing fortnight (*paksha*) of the lunar month.
Siapa (Punjabi)	Beating of breasts as a sign of mourning.
Sikhs	Followers of the doctrine of Guru Nanak, Islamic-influenced reform movement.
Silsilah	Literally 'chain', 'continuation', used for a brotherhood of Sufis following the same techniques of spiritual development.
Sindhu	The Sanskrit name of the Indus river.
Sindoor	Powder made from red lead, used for anointing the image of deities and the foreheads of worshippers.
Sita	Daughter of King Janaka, faithful wife of Rama, kidnapped by Ravana and recovered by Rama with the aid of Hanuman.
Sitala Devi	Sitala, 'Cool', goddess of small-pox propitiated in eastern, western and central India.
Skanda Purana	The most extensive of the eighteen major Puranas, its seven parts organized around the major *tirthas* of India.
Smrti	'The remembered', the handed-down Veda.
Soma	Divine intoxicating nectar pressed, pounded, and strained from plants in Vedic ritual; identified with *amrita*, the nectar of immortality.
Somanatha/ Somnath	Shrine of Shiva, a *jyotirlinga*, on the coast of Saurashtra in Gujarat; also known as Prabhasa in Sanskrit literature.
Sraddha	Ancestor ritual.
Srisailam	Shaiva shrine, one of the *jyotirlingas*, on the banks of the Krishna river in northern Andhra Pradesh.
Srishti	Creation, the act of creation; literally, the 'pouring forth', as a spider puts forth a web from its body.
Sruti	'The heard', the revealed Veda.

Stupa	A Buddhist monument, shaped like a dome, where the earthly relics of the Buddha are honoured.
Sufism	The doctrines, principles, and practices of Islamic mystics (Sufis) stressing the immanence rather than the transcendence of God. The name is derived from the Arabic word for 'wool' characterizing the garments these mystics wore in protest against many of the worldly ways of their fellow men. The Sufis were outstanding Muslim missionaries in India beginning c. twelfth century.
Suhrawardi	One of the orders of Sufi mystics, concentrated largely in the region of Sind.
Sunnah	The traditions of belief and action established by the Prophet considered to embody the interpretation of the revelation contained in the Quran.
Sunnah; Sunni	The al-sunnah: term used to denote the majority group of Muslims whose Islam is based upon the Koran, the hadith and the sunnah (q.v.) and upon the Sharia (q.v.) rather than upon the devotion to the Imams (q.v.) as expressed by the Shiah (q.v.)
Sunni	'One of the path'; one of the two major sects of Islam, distinguished from the Shias in that the Sunnis recognise the first four *Khalifas* (Caliphs) as the rightful successors of Muhammad.
Sutra	'Leading thread', as Vedanga in the widest sense is counted among the Vedic literature, a rule book (e.g., for philisophy, ritual, grammar).
Svarupa	God's 'own form'—not an image created by human hands, but a natural self-manifestation of the divine.
Svayambhu	Self-manifest, describes certain lingas and images that are said to be uncreated, to have appeared of their own accord.
Svetaketu	Son of the saint Uddalaha, authority on Vedic ritual;

author of a treatise on *Kama Sutra* mentioned in the epic Mahabharata.

Synagogue	A community centered on the study of Torah and prayer to God; the building used to house these activities also came to be known as synagogues.
Tali or Mangalasutra	A little golden or gold-coloured ornament on a gold chain known as 'tali' tied around the bride's neck, a relic of an ancient Devadasi rite.
Talmud	The oral Torah, recorded in the *Mishnah,* and the commentary on the *Mishnah* called the *Gemara.* There are two Talmuds: the Bavli (Talmus of Babylonis) and the Yerushalmi (the Jerusalem Talmud); the former is considered the more comprehensive and authoritative.
Tantra	An esoteric religious movement that emerged after the Gupta period, emphasizing the union of opposites, especially symbolized by male and female.
Tapas	Heat; especially the heat generated by ascetic practice, believed to be creative, like the brooding heat of a mother hen.
Tarpana	Regular ritual offerings for the deceased; literally 'satisfaction', for the rites give satisfaction to the departed.
Ta'ziyah	A model of the tomb of the martyred Husain, grandson of the Prophet Muhammad, usually made of wood and paper carried in Muharram processions in India.
Tazkira	Literally 'narration', often used for accounts of Sufis.
Tejas	Lustrous brillance, the power of the gods.
Tilak, B.G.	1856-1920, nationalist leader of the Indian National Congress and advocate of swaraj—self-rule; aroused resistance to British rule in his native Maharashtra through the use of Hindu issues and symbols.

Tirathankaras	'Ford finder' or ford makers, the title of Jain patriarchs of the highest order because they show men the passage through the dark waters of life. There are supposed to be 24 tirathankaras.
Tirtha	Ford, crossing place, both literally and symbolically; a place of pilgrimage, bathing place.
Tirthayatra	The journey (yatra) to a sacred place; pilgrimage.
Tirupati	Pilgrim town and hilltop temple of Shri Venkateshwara in what is now Andhra Pradesh; one of India's most popular pilgrimage sites.
Tithe	According to Hindu system of reckoning a lunar year has 354 to 360 days, based on lunar months. A lunar day is called *tithi* or *tithe*.
Torah (Hebrew)	The Law of Moses as outlined in the first five books of the Bible: Genisis, Exodus, Leviticus, Numbers and Deuteronomy, which are also collectively known as the Torah.
Trikaya doctrine	Doctrine of the three bodies of the Buddha.
Trinity	God as Father, Son and Holy Spirit; meant to suggest that the transcendent God can be immanent in the world without losing his transcendence—when God acts in the world (as son or spirit), God does not cease to be father and Creator of the universe; therefore God is not many gods but one God in three persons.
Trivandrum/ Thiruvananthapuram	Modern and thriving city in Kerala whose name, Abode of the Infinite Lord, derives from its most ancient and famous temple, Padmanabhaswamy, where Lord Vishnu reclines on Ananta, the Endless.
Triveni	Literally, the 'triple braid', referring to the confluence of three rivers, flowing together, as at Prayaga.
Tryambaka	Three-Eyed Shiva; name of the *jyotirlinga* in the hills of the Western Ghats near Nashik.

Tukaram (1598-1649)	A Shudra, bhakti poet-saint of Maharashtra who used Islamic as well as Hindu symbolism.
Tulsi	Sacred basil plant (*Ocimum tenuiflorum*) offered in worship, used ceremonially in countless ways; a goddess consort of Krishna.
Tulsidas (1532-1623)	Author of the popular Avadhi (Hindi dialect) poetic version of the Ramayana, the *Ramacharitamanasa*, and several other works dealing with the Rama legend.
Ulama (Ulema)	'Ulama' is the plural of '*alim*', 'one who knows' a learned man, applied more commonly to a doctor of Muslim law and theology.
Upanayana	Initiation of the Twice-Born, thread ceremony.
Upanishad	A 'Sitting Near', referring to a student sitting near his teacher. The Upanishads are a series of 108 treatises, the approximately 15 oldest and most important of which were composed. c.600–300 BCE. In them are first presented such central Hindu doctrines as transmigration and the unity of Brahman and Atman.
Vaidyanath	Temple town and *jyotirlinga* of Shiva in Deogarh, now in the state of Jharkhand; popularly called Baidyanath.
Vaishnava	Pertaining to the cults of Vishnu; a worshipper of Vishnu.
Vaishno Devi	Popular mountaintop temple to the Goddess, located near Katra in Jammu and Kashmir.
Vaishya	Third of the four castes, traditionally merchants and farmers.
Valmiki	The first poet and legendary sage to whom the epic Ramayana is ascribed.
Vamamargi	A follower of the left-hand path, applied to those followers of Tantric Hinduism who indulge in sexual orgies as the highest form of worship.

Vana	Forest; woods where ascetics and sages have their hermitages.
Varanasi	Name of Banaras, the city on the Ganga between the Varana and the Asi Rivers.
Varna	'Colour', professional class; mythical concept, with which Indian soceity is divided into priests, warriors, merchants and servants.
Varuna	A deity of Aryans; Prince of Oceans commanding white horses; ultimately received the worship of fishermen.
Vayu	Wind; as deity, the guardian of the northwest.
Veda	Wisdom, knowing. The sacred literature considered to be 'heard' or 'revealed' (*shruti*).
Vedanga	'Limb of the Veda', six complementary sciences of the Veda in the narrow sense; astronomy (*jyotisa*), phonetics (*siksa*), metrics (*chandas*), grammar (*vyakarana*), etymology (*nirukta*), and ritualistics (*kalpa*)
Vedanta	'End of the Vedas', referring to the Upanishads, that represent the culmination of the Vedic scriptures. More specifically one of the six *darsanas* of Indian philosphy evolving c. seventh century and elaborating philosophical speculations begun in the Upanishads.
Venkateshwara	Deity, considered to be a form of Vishnu, resident at the famous pilgrimage temple of Tirupati.
Vidhyachal	The hill shrine of Vindhyavasini Devi near Mirzapur in Uttar Pradesh.
Vikramasila	Buddhist monastery and centre of learning in Bihar; one of the foremost purveyors of *Vajrayana* Buddhism to Tibet in the eleventh century.
Visarjana	Sending forth; either the committal of ashes to the river after death rites or bidding farewell to

the temporary presence of the dviine in an image, following worship.

Visvadeva	A comprehensive term applied to a group of minor gods.
Visvamitra	One of the greatest rishis of the Hindu mythology; guru of Rama, in the epic Ramayana; also figures in the Mahabharata.
Vrata	A vow; religious obeservances done in fulfilment of a vow.
Wahhabi	A sect of Muslim puritan revivalists, founded in Arabia in the eighteenth century by Muhammad bin Abdul Wahhab. The Wahhabis emphasized the unity of Allah, the right of the individual to interpret the Quran and the *Hadith* and rejected the four orthodox law schools. The movement first came into India c. 1804 in Bengal.
Yajna	Sanskrit term commonly translated as sacrifice; one of the main pillars of the Vedic religious system.
Yajurveda	'Knowledge of the ritual sayings', handed down in two versions (black and white Yajurveda), Vedic Samhita with instructions for the sacrifical ritual.
Yaksha, Yakshi	Divinity of ancient India, associated with trees, pools and vegetative abundance.
Yamuna	Sacred river of north Inida, rising at Yamunotri, skirting Delhi, Vrindavan, Mathura. Agra and joining the Ganga at Prayaga.
Yantra	A 'device' for harnessing the mind in meditation or worship. A diagram, usually of geometric interlocking triangles and circles.
Yatra	'(Holy) journey', pilgrimage, procession.
Yoga	'A yoking'; one of the six *darsanas* that emphasized psychic training 'yoking' the soul to the divine as the chief means of salvation. The basic text of the

Yoga Darsana is the Yoga Sutra of Patanjali. Any act of discipline—either mental or physical—whereby the soul of man is 'yoked' to the divine and is freed from earthly confinements.

Yogini   Emblem of female creativity; female generative organ; the 'seat' in which a *linga* is established.

Yudhishthira   Eldest of the five Pandava brothers, son of Kunti, fathered by Dharma, and thus the righteous one of the brothers.

Yuga   The 'ages' of the world, four in number: *krita, treta, dvapara,* and *kali*; the first being the perfect age of the beginnings, the last being this age of strife—our age.

Zakat   Almsgiving, one of the Five Pillars of Islam: 2.5 per cent tithe on one's net worth to help the poor is required of all Muslims.

Zimmi   A non-Muslim living in the protection of Islam, a non-Muslim resident of a Muslim state whose authority he recognizes.

Selected Further Reading

Appadurai, A., *Modernity at Large: Cultural Dimensions of Globalization*, Vol. 1, Minneapolis: University of Minnesota Press, 1996.

Advani, L.K., *My Country My Life*, New Delhi: Rupa, 2007.

Barthes, Roland, *Mythologies*, Translated by Annette Lavers, New York: Hill and Wang, 1972.

Basham, A.L., *The Wonder That Was India*, Reprint, New Delhi: Rupa, 1954.

Bijapurkar, R., *We Are Like That Only: Understanding the Logic of Consumer India*, New Delhi: Penguin/Portfolio. 2007.

Biyani, Kishore, *It Happened in India*, New Delhi: Rupa, 2007.

Bose, N.K., *The Structure of Hindu Society*, New Delhi: Orient Longman, 1975.

Chopra, P.N., ed., *Religions and Communities of India*, New Delhi: Vision Books, 1998.

Das, Gurcharan, *India Unbound*, New Delhi: Penguin/Viking, 2000.

Dawkins, Richard, *The God Delusion*, London: Black Swan, 2006.

de Mooij, Marieke, *Consumer Behaviour and Culture*, California: Sage Publications, 2004.

Dehija, Vivek, and Rupa Subramanya, *Indianomix: Making Sense of Modern India*, New Delhi: Vantage Books, 2012.

Doniger, Wendy, *The Hindus: An Alternative History*, New Delhi: Penguin, 2009.

Doniger, Wendy, and B.K. Smith, trans., *The Laws of Manu*, New Delhi: Penguin, 1991.

Dube, S.C., *Indian Society*, New Delhi: National Book Trust, 1990.

Durkheim, E., *The Elementary Forms Religious Life*, Translated by J.W. Swain, New York: The Free Press, 1915.

Eck, Diana L., *India: A Sacred Geography*, New York: Harmony Books, 2012.

Engel, J.F., R.D. Blackwell, and P.W. Miniard, *Consumer Behaviour*, Seventh Edition, Florida: The Dryden Press, 1993.

Esposito, J.L., D.J. Fasching, T. Lewis, *Religion and Globalization: World Religions in Historical Perspective*, New York: Oxford University Press, 2008.

Goffman, Erving, *Gender Advertisements*, Boston: Harvard University Press, 1979.

Haldane, J., *An Intelligent Person's Guide to Religion*, London: Duckworth, 2003.

Huntington, P.S., *The Clash of Civilizations and the Remaking of World Order*, New York: Simon & Schuster, 1996.

Kakar, S., and K. Kakar, *The Indians: Portrait of a People*, New Delhi: Penguin, 2007.

Kautilya, *The Arthashastra*, ed. L.N. Rangarajan, New Delhi: Penguin, 1992.

Khilnani, S., *The Idea of India*, New Delhi: Penguin, 1997.

Kotkin, J., *Tribes: How Race, Religion and Identity Determine Success in the New Global Economy*, New York: Random House, 1993.

Madan, T.N., *Religion in India*, ed. T.N. Madan, Oxford in India Readings, New Delhi: Oxford University Press, 1991.

Müller, Max, *India: What Can It Teach Us?*, Reprint, New Delhi: Penguin, 2000.

Michaels, A., *Hinduism: Past and Present*, Translated by Barbara Harshaw, New Delhi: Orient Longman, 1998.

Murthy, N.R., *A Better India A Better World*, New Delhi: Penguin/ Allen Lane, 2009.

Nanda, M., *The God Market: How Globalization Is Making India More Hindu*, Noida: Random House, 2009.

Nehru, J., *The Discovery of India*, New Delhi: Penguin Books, 2008.

Nilekani, N., *Imaging India: Ideas for the New Century*, New Delhi: Penguin, 2008.

Parameswaran, M.G., *Ride the Change: A Perspective in the Changing Indian Consumer, Markets and Marketing*, New Delhi: Tata McGraw Hill, 2009.

Radhakrishnan, S., *Religion, Science and Culture*, New Delhi: Orient Paperbacks, 1968.

Rajagopal, A., *Politics after Television: Hindu Nationalism and the Reshaping of the Public in India*, New York: Cambridge University Press, 2001.

Sathyamurthy, T.V., *Region, Religion, Caste, Gender and Culture in Contemporary India*, New Delhi: Oxford University Press, 1996.

Sen, A., *The Argumentative Indian: Writings on Indian Culture, History and Identity*, London: Penguin, 2005.

Thapar, R., *A History of India,* Vol. 1, New Delhi: Penguin, 1996.

Twitchell, James B., *Shopping for God,* New York: Simon & Schuster, 2009.

Varma, P.K., *The Great Indian Middle Class,* New Delhi: Penguin/ Viking, 1998.

Walker, Benjamin, *Hindu World: An Encyclopedic Survey of Hinduism,* New Delhi: Rupa, 2005.

Weber, M., *The Protestant Ethic and the Spirit of Capitalism,* Translated by P. Baehr and G. Wells, London: Penguin, 2002.

Index

Aastha, 94
Adler & Roth, 108
Advani, L.K., 68
advertising, 31, 36, 100, 159, 168; cinema, 62–63; objection to, 116, 160–63; radio, 101; religious music, 153; religious symbolism in, 11, 123–28, 193; television, 62, 163; women in, 12–16; in women's magazines, 180
Advertising Standards Council of India (ASCI), 162–63
ahimsa, 7, 84, 179
air fresheners, 99
Airtel Kumbh tariff plans, 71
Ajmer dargah, 67, 70
Akbar, 151
Akshardham temple, Delhi, 69
Akshaya Trithiya, 5, 41–42, 46, 59
Amar Chitra Katha, 97, 192
Ananda Vikatan, 169
Andeleeb, Syed Saad, 138

animal sacrifice, 51
Ariely, Dan, 177
Armstrong, Louis, 149
Aryans, 25, 51, 76, 83, 106, 149
Ashoka, 7, 66, 70, 166
astrological predictions (astrology), 53–54, 59
Ataturk, Mustafa Kemal, 130
Atharva Veda, 85, 150
Aurangzeb, 152
auspicious and inauspicious buildings, 48–51; circumstances, 29; periods, 8, 32–37, 42, 47, 53–54, 59; wedding dates, 20, 59
Ayurveda, 94, 104, 140, 141

Bachchan, Amitabh, 75, 90, 126
Badrinath, 67, 71
Bagawathar, Chembai Vaidyanatha, 152
Baisakhi, 5, 38
Bajaj, 22, 124, 125

Bal Ganesh, 95
Balaji Telefilms, 98
Bangaram Island Resort, 123–24
Bangladesh, 129–30
Banker, Ashok, 96
Basava, 151
Bashir, Javed, 154
Basilica of Our Lady of the Mount, Mumbai, 70
Batra, Anurag, 94
Beasley, Hamilton, 187
beauty industry and Indian weddings, 22–23
belief in God, 49–50
Benedict XVI, Pope, 51, 173
Bennis, Warren, 187
Bernbach, Bill, 159
Bhagavad Gita, 76, 96, 141
Bhakti movement, 8, 141–42, 151
Big Bazaar, 34, 46–47, 132
Bijoor, Harish, 45
bindi and mangalsutra in Indian advertising, 8, 9–18, 162, 193
Biswas, Basudev, 136
Biyani, Kishore, 46
Black Friday in the US, 38
Blaze Films, 62
Bollywood, 18, 22, 23, 42, 75, 90, 95, 119, 155; religious stereotypes, 159–60
brand archaeology, 30–32
brands and wedding market, 22
Brihadaranya Upanishad, 179
Buddha, 7, 100
Buddhism, 7, 51, 84, 106, 141, 172; Theravada, 143
Buddhist sites in India, 70
Bulleh Shah, 149
Burqa Avenger, 135
burqa, 129–35

Cama, Shireen, 147–48
Carlson Hotels Worldwide, 69
Carnatic music, 152, 154, 156
Casino Group, Kochi, 123
Cassian, 20
Castrol, 148
Cathcart, Thomas, 178
Cayla, Julien, 11
Chaitanya, 151
Chakraborty, S.K., 184
Chakravarty, Subhas, 129
Chandogya Upanishad, 85
Chandrika, 15
Chennai Carnatic music season, 36
Chhota Bheem, 95, 155
Chinnamoulana Sahib, Sheikh, 152
Chinnaponnu, 154
Chishti, Khwaja Moinuddin, 70
Chishti, Sheikh Salim, 70
Christian(s), 6, 46, 121, 130, 139, 142, 158–59, 160, 161, 163, 177, 180, 186; calendar, 19–20, 37; church architecture, 58; consumers, 54, 78, 115, 193; idolatry, 107; Protestant, 2, 70; religious music, 148–49; religiosity, 143; television and

radio channels, 94; vegetarian/non-vegetarian food, 88, 121; women, 131

Christianity, 8, 148, 159, 161

Christmas, 5, 37–38, 46, 126

Churchill, Winston, 67

cinema advertising, 62–63

classical dance forms, 151

Coca-Cola, 122, 154

Coke Studio, 154–55

comics, 97

Confucianism, 178

consumer(s), consumer's, 24, 26, 31–32, 35, 37, 38, 45, 47, 58, 100–1, 109, 145, 147, 177; behaviour, 1–6, 129, 193; Christian, 54, 115; conservative, 14, 52; ethical beliefs, 177; Muslim, 8, 54, 83, 113–19, 132; perspective, 56; religious orientation, 86–87, 97, 128, 178, 192–93; religious segmentation, 120–22; religious tourism, 72; tradition and modernity, 51; women, 15

Culien, Patrick, 185

cultural and religious differences, 189–90, 193

cultural and religious diversity, 45–46

Cycle Brand, 101

Dalai Lama, 70

Datar, Srikant, 185

Dead Man Walking, 149

decision theory, 50

Deepika, 95

Deshmukh, Aniruddha, 19

destination wedding, 23

Devon ke Dev...Mahadev, 92, 93, 153, 155

Dewarists, The, 155

Dharamsala, 70

Dilwara temples, Mount Abu, 70

Diwali, 5, 37, 43, 44, 46, 125

Dodge Ram, 124–25, 126

Dominic, Jose, 123–24

Domino's, 117

Doniger, Wendy, 66

Doordarshan, 62. *see also* television

DraftFCB Ulka (Ulka Advertising), 9

Dravidians, 51

Durga Puja, 5

Durkheim, Emile, 137, 144

Dwarka, 66, 67

Dwyer, Rachel, 119

Eid, 5, 35, 45

end of season sale, 35

Event and Experience Marketing Association of India (EEMA), 21–22

event management companies, 22

Fabindia, 18, 102

Facebook, 40, 41

Fa Hien, 84

Fair and Lovely, 153

Faith@Work, 186

fasting, 20, 44, 66, 86–87, 113, 194

Femina, 13

Fernandes, Mincy, 40

festivals and consumption
    behaviour, 5–6

fish market, 82–83

food: habits, 87–89; market, 82–
    83; and religion, and Muslim
    consumer, 83–89

Fortune Hotel, 69

Fox Traveller, 155

Francis, Pope, 51–52

Freud, Sigmund, 2

Gaga, Lady, 133–34

Galaxy Surfactants, 190

Gandhi, M.K., 76, 96, 105, 107

Gandre, Pushpa, 164

Ganesan, Sivaji, 75

Ganesh Chaturti, 5, 41, 44, 128

Ganesh, K., 173

Ganesh, Meena, 173

Ganga Dasahara, 44

Garvin, David, 185

gender stereotyping and
    advertising, 14

generation gap, 74–75

Gitanjali, 42, 108

God (TV channel), 94

Godrej Storwel, 22

Golden Temple, Amritsar, 70

Goonjan Mal, 173

Grant Medical College, 181

Gregorian calendar, 19

GRT Thanga Maligai, 20

Gupta, R.K., 152

Guruvayurappan, 96

Haj, 71, 113, 172

Haji Ali Dargah, Mumbai, 70

halal food market, 117–18, 121

Hamara Bajaj, 125

Hangal, A.K., 160

Hanuman, 95

Harley-Davidson, 51–52

Harvard Business School, 72, 185

Harvey, Paul, 124

Hassan, Dr Hussein Hamid, 114

Himalaya, 140

Hindu(s): calendar, 20, 32–
    34, 37–38, 46; Code Bill,
    21; concepts and business
    strategy, 97; festivals, 43–44;
    scriptures, 66–67; weddings,
    24–26; vegetarians and non-
    vegetarians, 83–85

Hinduism, 7–8, 68, 93, 101, 107,
    118, 141, 161, 178, 187, 191,
    192

Hindustan Unilever, 127

Hindustani classical music, 151–
    52

Hitler, 53

Hofstede, Geert, 189

Holi, 44

holy rivers, 66

homa, 51

home, divine touch, 55–60

Hongkong Bank, 164–65
hotel industry and religious tourism, 69
Hungama, 153
Huntington, Samuel, 185
Husain, M.F., 168
Hussain, Zakir, 152
Hyundai, 125

ICICI Bank's International Business Group (IBG), 164–65
idol worship, 106–7
Immortals of Meluha, The, by Amish Tripathi, 96–97
incense stick market in India, 100–01
Indian diaspora, 103
Indian mythologies, 93
Indian Ocean Band, 154
Indian Society of Advertisers and Advertising Agencies Association of India, 162
IndiGo, 117, 153
individualism–collectivism, 189
information technology (IT), 171–75; services industry, 86
Islam, 8, 10, 76–77, 101, 107, 111–13; finance and banking, 114–16; five key pillars, 113; halal food market, 116–18
Islamic pilgrimage sites, 70
Iyer, P.A., 103–4

J.J. Hospital, 181
Jain, S.P., 188

Jainism, 7, 70, 84, 141
Jama Masjid, Delhi, 70
Jaslok Hospital, 136–38
jaziya, 113
Jews, 7, 159

Kabir, 151
Kahn, Otto, 187–88
Kakkar, Prahalad, 9
Kakkar, Priya, 9
Kale, Anjali, 169
Kalnirnay phenomenon, 35–36, 167
Kamakshi temple, Madurai, 118
Kamban, 151
Kant, Amitabh, 124
Kant, Emanuel, 178
Kapoor, Anil, 147–48
Kapoor, Ekta, 98
Karunanidhi, M., 43
Karva Chauth, 5, 42–43, 125
Kautilya's *Arthashastra*, 59
Keaton, Buster, 159
KFC, 117
Khan, M.Y., 116
Khatau Sarees, 18
Kingfisher Airlines, 114
kirtan tradition, 151
Klein, Daniel, 178
Krishna Key, The, by Ashwin Sanghi, 97
Kumbh Mela, 71, 72, 185–86

Levy, Henry S., 159
liberalization of the Indian

economy, 3

Life OK, 92

Lifebuoy, 71

Light Roofings Ltd, 111

Liv 52, 140

Lladro, Spirit of India, 107, 109, 110

Lodestar UM, 154

Lord Venkateshwara Watch, 109

Lotus Temple, Delhi, 70

Madkaikar, Ravi, 136, 138

Madura Coats, 108

Maggi, 87

Mahabharat (TV serial), 3, 91

Mahabharata, 3, 7, 42, 83–84, 85, 93, 95, 96, 151, 178, 183

Mahavira, 7

Makara Sankranthi, 44

Malabar Jewellers, 22

Manorama group of publications, 168

Manu, *Manusmriti* (*Laws of Manu*), 7, 25, 76, 78, 79, 81

MARG, 106

marriage market, 19–29

Marx, Groucho, 187

Marx, Karl, 2, 40

masculinity–femininity, 189

Matunga Ayappa Samaj temple, 103

McDonald's, 85–86, 117

McLaughlin, John, 152–53

meditation, 106, 141–44, 177, 186

Meerabai, 151

Megachurch phenomenon in the US, 3

Muhammad, Prophet, 8

Mohapatra, Pradipta, 30, 32

Mont Blanc, 105–6

Moody's Investor Services, 114

More Dreams Per Car, 158–59

MTV, 154–55

Muhammad Shah, 152

Mukhya Mantri Teerth Darshan Yojana, 69

Mundkur, Bal, 164

Munneshwaram, Sri Lanka, 73

Muslim(s), 8, 112–20; in Bollywood films, 119; burqa, new market for, 129–35; global population, 113; in India, 113, 118–21, 161–62; marginalization, 120; polygamy, 119–20; religious sites, 70; weddings, 20; women, 10–11, 119–20, 130–34

mythological characters in advertising, 126

Nadir Shah, 152

Nair, Sameer, 90, 91

Nanak, Guru, 8

Narada, 150

Navratri, 39–41, 44

NDTV, 91

NDTV Imagine, 91, 92

Nehru, Jawaharlal, 21, 52–53

Nerolac, 55, 126

Nestlé, 117

New Year Sale phenomenon, 30–32, 37, 38
Nietzsche, Friedrich, 2
Nusrat Fateh Ali Khan, 149

Ogilvy, 113
Om Namah Shivay, 92
onlineprasad.com, 172
Organic India, 140

Pakistan Coke Studio, 154
Pakistan TV, 127, 135
panchanga, 32, 35–36
Pannikar, K.M., 53, 54
Parikrama Band, 154
Parsis, 8, 126, 158
Parveen, Abida, 154
Pascal's Wager, 49–51, 53
Pattanaik, Devdutt, 13, 34, 97
Periyar, E.V. Ramaswamy, 107
pilgrimage, 59, 61–73, 77, 113, 155, 172, 195. *see also* religious tourism
Pillai, Indu, 81
Pinto, Monia, 10
Poddar, Subodh, 147
Pongal, 5
Ponna, 151
pornography, 114
power distance, 189
Praveen, Jensy, 40
Premji, Azim, 183
professionalism and efficiency, 16
Protestant Reformation, 38
Protestant Work Ethic, 2–3

puja ritual, 5, 44, 47, 48–54, 99–104; concept of, 51; market, 102–3
Puranas and epics, 7, 93, 192

Rafi, M.M., 111–12
Rahman, A.R., 83, 156
Raina, Mohit, 92
Rajagopalachari, C., 96
Raksha Bandhan, 43
Ram Charan, 186
Ram Lila, 151
Ramadan, 20, 87, 112, 113, 190, 194
Ramakrishna Mission, 180
Ramanasramam temple, 70
Ramnavami, 44
Ramani, R.V., 180–81
Ramayana Trail, 73
Ramayan (TV serial), 3, 91
Ramayana, 7, 84, 91, 93, 96, 106, 150–61
Ramcharitmanas, 151
Rameswaram, 66, 67
Ras Lila, 151
rasi theory, 48–50
Ravi Varma, Raja, 167, 169
Ravishankar, Sri Sri, 186
Raymond, 19
Raza, S.H., 168, 169
Real Image Media Technologies, 61, 63
religion(s): based films, 95; and calendar art, 167–68; and caste and vegetarians/

non-vegetarians orientation, 83–86; and consumer behaviour, 1–6, 129, 193; and economic growth, 2; and health, 136–45; implications in HR management, 188; implications in marketing, 188; origins in India, 6–8; and tourism industry, 5

religiosity, 1–2; and subjective well-being, 137

religious: affiliation and type of product advertised, 160; amusement parks, 72; art, 164–70; beliefs and practices, 2, 5–6, 59, 127; diversity of India, 161; festivals, effect on sales, 45–47; groups as cultural stereotypes, 125–26; media market, 94–96; music, 74–75; and advertising, 146–56;— fusion, 153–55; mythologies, 91–93, 171; stereotypes, 158–63; symbolism, 11–12; television market (religious channels), 94–96, 97–98, 109–10, 151, 165, 169; tourism, 5, 63, 65–66

religiousness, role in ethical behaviour, 177–83

Revital, 71

Rig Veda, 7, 150

Rodeo Drive, 109

Roy, Jamini, 168

Rudra Life, 102

Rudra Shakti, 102

Rudrabali sacrifice, 76

Rumi, 149, 186

Sabarimala temple, 5, 65, 66, 71

Sagar, Ramanand, 91, 95

Salaam Halal Insurance, 115

Salgaonkar, Jayant, 35–36

Sama Veda, 150

Sanghi, Ashwin, 97

Sankara Eye Care Institution, 180–81

Sankara Eye Foundation (SEF), 179–80

Sankara Netralaya, Chennai, 181

Santoor, 9–10

Saravana Stores, 46–47

Sarfarosh, 119

sari and women consumer, 35, 39–40; and Indian advertising, 9, 12–16; Navratri colour coordinated, 40; origin of word, 16; transformations, 17–18; in weddings, 29

Sarkozy, Nicolas, 130

Satapathy, Ganapathi, 170

satellite television, 62, 79

scientific thinking, 50

seafood, consumption in India, 86

sex determination tests, 77

sex ratio among Hindus and Muslims, 77, 120

Shakti (musical group), 152, 153

Shankar, L., 152

Shankar, Pandit Ravi, 149, 152
Shankara, 67, 68
Shaw, George Bernard, 178
Shilpi, 169
Shirdi, 66, 69, 70, 96, 173
Siddha, 140
Sikhism, 8, 141
Shivratri, 44, 87
Skype, 103
Sopariwala, Dorab, 106, 118
Sound Trek, 155
Sound Trippin, 155
spirituality: and business, 184–91; and charity, 181, 184–91; and good health, relation, 144
Sri Lanka's tourism ministry, 73
Srinivasan, R., 73
Srivastava, R.K., 115
St Thomas Cathedral, Chennai, 70
St Xavier's shrine, Goa, 70
Star Bazaar, 87
Star One, 92
Star Plus, 90
Strings, 154
suicide rates and religion and religiosity, 137
Sukhbodananda, Swami, 186
Superbowl ads, 124
superstitions, 19, 49
Surdas, 151
swastika, 53

Tagore, Rabindranath, 196
Tanishq, 16, 42, 125

Tata Consultancy Services (TCS), 171
Tata Docomo, 15, 74, 153
Tata Indica, 22
Tata Swach, 71
Tata, J.N., 183
television, 3, 62, 83, 90–93, 124–25, 154, 193; advertising, 9–15, 35, 62, 127, 158, 161, 164; increasing penetration, 79; rating points (TRPs), 62; religion and mythology-based serials and channels, 94–97, 155, 191; satellite, 62, 79
Thanksgiving, 38
theme wedding, 29
Thirukkural, 177
Thiruvalluvar, 2
Thomas the Apostle, 8
Thukaram, 151
Thyagaraja, 151
Tilak, Bal Ganghadar, 41
Times Music, 153
timing, importance, 31
Tirupathi temple, 5, 63, 65, 67, 69, 71, 72, 98, 153, 173
Titan, 125, 153
tradition and modernity, 51
Tripathi, Amish, 92, 96–97, 153
Tulsidas, 151
Twitchell, James B., 3

Ulka, 164
Unani medicine, 140
uncertainty avoidance, 190

Upanishads, 7, 85, 106
urbanization, 69
Uttarakhand disaster, 71–72

Vaishno Devi temple, 5, 65, 69, 71, 172
Valentine's Day, 5, 42, 109, 128
Vastu and Indian homes, 5, 56, 58–60
Vasudev, Jaggi, 186
Vedas, 24, 76, 93
Veedol lubricants, 125
vegetarian and non-vegetarian, 82–89
Vimanika Comics, 97
Vinayakram, Vikku, 152
Vipassana meditation, 143–44, 186
Viswanathan, Hema, 132
Vivek & Co, 31–32, 35, 37
Vivekananda, Swami, 67, 68, 96, 107, 142
Voltas Mega Laundrette, 147–48
Voltas, 146–48

Walker, Benjamin, 16, 66–67, 140
Walmart, 99
Warhol, Andy, 168
washing machine market, 146–47
Weber, Max, 2, 187, 194

wedding, 19–29; auspicious period, 19–20; and beauty industry, 22; destination wedding, 23; horoscope matching, 23–24; planning, 22, 24; registry, 27–28; religiosity, 21; types in Hinduism, 24–25
Wilder, Marshall P., 187–88
Wipro, 9, 117, 190
Wipro Unza, 117, 190
women: access to education, 79, 80; role in Indian society, 75–81; portrayal in advertising, American, 13–14; Indian, 9–18; prayers, 74–81
WomanMood I and II, 78–79
WorldSpace, 155–56

Yajur Veda, 150
Yesudas, 152
yoga, 7, 141–44
Yoga Sutra, 141
YouTube, 125, 127, 154

zakat (purification of wealth), 112
Zampango Comics, 97
Zeb & Haniya, 154
Zee Jagran, 94
Zee TV, 90
Zoroastrianism, 7, 8, 178